THE HISTORY OF
THE LITERARY AND PHILOSOPHICAL SOCIETY
OF NEWCASTLE UPON TYNE
1896-1989

ROBERT SPENCE WATSON
Painted by H. Macbeth Raeburn from the original by Sir George Reid

The History of the Literary and Philosophical Society of Newcastle upon Tyne

VOLUME II
1896-1989

CHARLES PARISH

With contributions by J. A. V. Chapple, S. T. L. Harbottle, Peter C. G. Isaac and John Philipson

Vires acquirit eundo

The Literary and Philosophical Society
of Newcastle upon Tyne
1990

© 1990 The Literary and Philosophical Society
of Newcastle upon Tyne, Newcastle upon Tyne, NE1 1SE

ISBN   0 9514922 0 9

Designed by Henry D. Davy and printed in
Baskerville type by Printers (Coast) Limited,
158 Whitley Road, Whitley Bay, Tyne & Wear, NE26 2LY

To
John Sisson

Contents

	Page
Introduction	1

Chapter
1. The Society and its library, I	7
2. The Society and its library, II	34
3. The Society's building and Bolbec Hall	56
4. University Extension Courses	61
5. Miscellaneous Lectures	72
6. Robert Spence Watson Lectures	104
7. Biographical essays	
I. Unofficial lives: Elizabeth Gaskell and the Turner family, by J. A. V. Chapple	106
II. Captain George Dixon, circumnavigator and honorary member, by Charles Parish	121
III. William Bulmer (1757-1830), fine printer and honorary member, by Peter C. G. Isaac	137
IV. W. K. Loftus: an archaeologist from Newcastle, by S. T. L. Harbottle	164

Appendices
1. The Sebroke crozier and the nineteenth century *Newcastle Museum,* by John Philipson	197
2. Officers of the Society, 1897-1989	217
Index	221

NOTE: The biographical essays were given originally as lectures to the Society. John Philipson's paper on the Sebroke crozier was given as a lecture to the Society of Antiquaries of Newcastle upon Tyne.

Illustrations

		Facing Page
1.	Frontispiece: Robert Spence Watson	
2.	Exterior of the Society's building	8
3.	Sir James Knott Room	9
4.	Main Library (1988)	56
5.	Main Library (c.1830)	57
6.	Lecture Theatre (1860-1966)	72
7.	Loftus Room	73
		Page
8.	Marmaduke Tunstall	196
9.	George Allan	196

NOTE: Illustrations Nos. 1-4 and 7 are from photographs taken by James C. Lane. No. 5 is reproduced by permission of Sotheby's.

The Contributors

J. A. V. Chapple is Professor of English in the University of Hull. He is the author of *Science and literature in the nineteenth century*, 1986 and, assisted by J. G. Sharps, of *Elizabeth Gaskell: a portrait in letters*, 1980. With Arthur Pollard, he edited the standard edition of *The letters of Mrs. Gaskell*, 1966.

S. T. L. Harbottle, MA, was Honorary Secretary of the Literary and Philosophical Society of Newcastle upon Tyne, 1957-1968, Vice-President, 1969-1978 and President 1979-1986.

Peter C. G. Isaac, FSA, is Emeritus Professor of Civil and Public Health Engineering, University of Newcastle upon Tyne. He was Sandars Reader in Bibliography, University of Cambridge, 1983-1984 and is a Vice-President of the Bibliographical Society.

Charles Parish, FLA, was Librarian of the Literary and Philosophical Society of Newcastle upon Tyne, 1963-1987.

John Philipson, MA, FSA, is Editor of *Archaeologia Aeliana*. He was Vice-President of the Literary and Philosophical Society of Newcastle upon Tyne, 1960-1968 and President, 1969-1978.

Acknowledgements

I am indebted to the other contributors and, for help and advice, Henry D. Davy, Norman McCord, Margaret Norwell and John Philipson.

I thank the Society of Antiquaries of Newcastle upon Tyne for permission to reprint S. T. L. Harbottle's paper on W. K. Loftus and John Philipson's on the Sebroke crozier.

Bibliographical Note

The primary sources for Chapters 1-6 are the Annual Reports, Minutes and Catalogues of the Literary and Philosophical Society of Newcastle upon Tyne. Secondary sources for these chapters are noted in the body of the text. Sources for the biographical essays in Chapter 7 and the essay at Appendix 1 are given at the end of each essay.

Introduction

The history of the Literary and Philosophical Society of Newcastle upon Tyne for its first century of existence was written by Robert Spence Watson, lawyer, Liberal politician and educationist.[1] It is a noble book, written 'in the irregular and infrequent leisure of a busy professional life,' animated by the author's personality and directed by his conviction of the importance of the Society's contribution to the cause which he held most dear and of which he wrote: 'From the address delivered by William Turner when the Society was founded in 1793 to the most recent brochure issued by the Committee more than a century afterwards, the furthering of education in all, but especially in the highest, branches ... was, is, and should ever be its chief *raison d'être.*'

Robert Spence Watson died on 2nd March 1911. In an obituary notice in the Society's report for that year it is recorded that 'he became a member of the Society in 1853 at the age of sixteen. His father, Joseph Watson, was its Honorary Secretary from 1852 until 1860. Two years later Spence Watson was appointed to the office and held it until 1890 when he was elected Vice-President. In 1900 he succeeded Lord Armstrong as President. Between 1868 and 1898 he delivered eighty lectures to the Society, chiefly on English language and literature. Under his guidance the whole weight and influence of the Society were thrown into the cause of education. No man more thoroughly realised the spirit of the noble tradition founded and nurtured by the Society of service, not to its members only, but to the community at large.' Among the many services he rendered for and through the Society were his advocacy for a college of further education in Newcastle, and his vital contribution to the establishment there of University Extension Lectures.

A contribution by the Society to the programme arranged

---

[1] Watson, Robert Spence. *The history of the Literary and Philosophical Society of Newcastle upon Tyne (1793-1896)*, 1897.

by the University of Newcastle upon Tyne to celebrate the centenary of the foundation in 1871 of its precursor, the College of Physical Science, was a lecture by Sydney Middlebrook which was delivered in the Society's lecture room on 30th April 1971.[1] In the course of his lecture Mr. Middlebrook spoke of Robert Spence Watson as 'a man of outstanding character, warm and vivid in personality, rich in friends, fertile in ideas, undeviating in principle, with an exceptional gift for leadership. In his private life his two chief passions were angling and mountaineering; in his public life, politics and education. It is impossible to exaggerate his services to education, not only as successively Secretary, Vice-President and President of the Lit. and Phil. but as a devoted supporter (with his wife Elizabeth) of the Ragged and Industrial School in City Road, as a member of the School Board for 23 years, as the life-long President of the Tyneside Sunday Lecture Society, and the founder, in conjunction with the Girls' Public Day School Trust of a high school for girls in Gateshead which later developed into the present Central Newcastle High School, and as Chairman of the Books and House Committee of the Newcastle Central Library from its opening in 1880 until his death.' At an earlier point in the lecture Mr. Middlebrook mentioned that Spence Watson was a member of the Council of the College of Physical Science from 1871 until his death, that in 1873 the governing body of the college invited him to continue the class in English language and literature which he had taken for the previous four years but thenceforward as a member of the college staff, and that in 1910 he received the crowning honour of being elected President of Armstrong College as the College of Physical Science was then named. The University of St Andrew conferred on him the honorary degree of LL.D., the University of Durham that of D.C.L. Campbell-Bannerman secured for him a place in the Honours List as a Privy Councillor for 'long and great public service.' After his death Michael Sadler, Vice-

[1] Middlebrook, Sydney. *The advancement of knowledge in Newcastle upon Tyne: the Literary and Philosophical Society as an educational pioneer*. Newcastle upon Tyne, The Literary and Philosophical Society, 1974.

Chancellor of Leeds University, said that his highest title to distinction was 'as one of the founders of our present educational system.'

In his will Spence Watson bequeathed to the Lit. and Phil. the sum of £200. In 1912 an appeal was made to members of the Society for a sum to defray the cost of a portrait of him and, at the same time, subscriptions were invited to endow a lectureship in English language and literature to be called 'The Robert Spence Watson Lecture.'[1] It was recommended that the legacy should be added to the amount subscribed and that the interest from the amount remaining after defraying the cost of the portrait be used for the expense of the lecture. The fund was called 'The Robert Spence Watson Memorial Fund.' The portrait was painted by H. Macbeth Raeburn from the original by Sir George Reid. It was unveiled on 24th September 1912 by Thomas Burt, M.P. A reproduction forms the frontispiece to the present work.

In 1917, the Robert Spence Watson Lecture was delivered by Gilbert Murray to an audience of 745. His subject was *Literature as revelation* and it was subsequently printed by the Society.[2] He prefaced his lecture with a tribute to Robert Spence Watson for whom "I have had during many years a high admiration . . . The first time I met Dr. Spence Watson and heard him speak was at a great meeting in the St James's Hall, London, held to congratulate the Irish leader, Parnell, on the collapse of the criminal charges made against him by the *Times* newspaper . . . The whole situation was intensely dramatic — as well as extremely instructive. The meeting, addressed by Parnell himself and by two famous Newcastle men, Dr. Spence Watson and Mr. John Morley, was one of the most thrilling I have ever attended . . . There are some people to whom politics seem a kind of magnificent game, a game of much skill and not much scruple. There are some again who regard political life as a kind of arena in which different parties and different classes and different trading corporations struggle and intrigue for their respective interests. But to those two men I have mentioned politics

---

[1] A list of these lectures forms Chapter 6.
[2] Murray, Gilbert. *Literature as revelation.* 1917.

formed neither a pleasant game nor an exciting intrigue, far less an indirect way of pursuing your own interest. To them politics came as a revelation and a duty. They saw, or believed they saw, one or two fundamental truths on which the whole life and *morale* of the nation depended; and, these truths once seen, it became an unquestioned duty, through fair weather or foul, through good report or evil report, to pursue them and live for them. I always felt with Dr. Spence Watson that his political principles had much of the quality of a religion. They threw light all round them upon the non-political parts of life; and though he was a vigorous fighter, I believe that like most religious his strong principles rather increased than lessened his general human charity.'

The history of the Literary and Philosophical Society of Newcastle upon Tyne from its beginning to the present day may be divided into three parts. The first is the story of the Society as a learned society conducting and encouraging research by means of its lectures, its laboratory apparatus, its museum and its growing library. The second part shows much of the work it initiated being gradually taken over by institutions with specialised interests which had their roots within the Society. During this period the Society materially assisted the setting up of the Society of Antiquaries of Newcastle upon Tyne, the Natural History Society of Northumberland, Durham and Newcastle upon Tyne, the North of England Institute of Mining and Mechanical Engineers, and the College of Physical Science which evolved into the University of Newcastle upon Tyne, while itself becoming a major centre for further education by its work through and for the University Extension Movement and by means of its miscellaneous lectures. In the third part, although the directly educational work of the Society continued through its lectures and concerts and its association with University Extension classes, its library plays a dominant rôle. Spence Watson deals admirably with the first part of this history as he does with a good deal of the second. The present work follows from where he brought his to a conclusion except that because the space he gave to the library was relatively small I have sought to correct the imbalance by outlining its story from the beginning. The biographical essays in Chapter 7 also supplement rather than continue his work. They were all given, in recent years, as lectures to the Society. All contribute to its history and throw light upon some of the people associated with it. The paper on *The Sebroke crozier* at Appendix 1 has been included because it gives the clearest account yet written on the relationship between the Society, the Natural History Society and the Society of Antiquaries of Newcastle upon Tyne.

CHAPTER ONE

The Society and its Library
I

The library was acknowledged, in the middle years of the 19th century, to be the most effective of the Society's activities in keeping its membership together. By the end of the century, its original objects long achieved, the Society had as its principal concern the maintenance of a general library. Thirty years later, at a time of general economic depression, when every item of expenditure was being anxiously examined, its Committee affirmed its belief that it would be contrary to the best interests of the Society if any policy were adopted that would be likely to affect adversely the efficiency of the Society's activities and that of the library in particular. And fifty years later still it is clear that the survival of the Society in its present form is because of its library and that it is also because of its library that the Society can look forward with confidence to the future.

At the very beginning of the Society's existence its founders did not contemplate the establishment of a general library. Viewing the new society as one for debate and discussion they thought of a library as a necessary ancillary: a special library appropriate to a learned society. At the first general meeting in February 1793 the question of a library was left for future deliberation. Nevertheless, one of the rules approved by this meeting gave members the right to recommend, and general meetings the right to direct, the purchase of books. It may be assumed that the books were to be generally such works as would relate directly to the expressed objects of the Society. Works dealing with those subjects which were prohibited matters of discussion at its meetings: religious and political questions of the day, and the practical branches of law and physic, were to be excluded. In December 1793 the Rev. Edward Moises, headmaster of the Grammar School, proposed the appointment of a Committee for the purpose of establishing a general library of the Society and in the same month the proposal was accepted, subject to the exclusions mentioned above. The care taken to avoid political and religious discussions within the Society is readily understood when the political and religious controversies of the time are considered. It is certain that its founders had very much in mind the example of the Birmingham Library, a proprietary institution of which Joseph Priestley had been secretary, which, a few years before, had been torn by the quarrel between Establishment and Dissent.

Edward Moises was led to the making of his proposal by the lack, in Newcastle, of a proprietary library. This was unusual. These libraries, the true precursors of the public libraries which were gradually set up after the passing of the Public Libraries Act in 1870, were established in many places during the last quarter of the 18th century and the early years of the 19th century, especially in the manufacturing towns of the Midlands and the North. The term 'proprietary' as applied to them is used to distinguish them from the rate-supported libraries of a later date. At first, and for many years, proprietary libraries were frequently referred to as public libraries because they were open to all those, regardless of class or creed, who could afford the entrance fees and annual subscriptions. Payment of an entrance fee gave a member a share in the undertaking, this share becoming an item of personal property which could be sold or bequeathed. The newly formed Newcastle society rejected the proprietary principle, one of the reasons for doing so being that it foresaw that a large interest might come, in course of time, to be vested in illiterate persons, infants or absentees. To prevent this it was proposed that the Society be given a right of pre-emption, but this was considered dangerous because a number of members might combine in selling out and cause financial difficulties for the Society. At length it was agreed that the library and other property of the Society should always be considered as the undivided property of the general body for the time being,

The Society's Building ▷

and that every member should pay an annual subscription only and should be understood to receive a sufficient compensation for this subscription in the information derived from the Society's meetings and the use of its books and other property. This decision was liberal and enlightened and was, possibly, unique when it was taken. In some cases where the proprietary principle had been adopted and where, as was usual, there were limits imposed on the amount of the annual subscription that could be charged, entrance fees, not bound by these limits, rose sharply during inflationary periods to as much, sometimes, as twenty-five guineas, and this effectively restricted the membership of these institutions to the well-to-do. This, in later years, was held against the proprietary institutions which were accused, somewhat unfairly, of becoming, to use the cant phrase, 'haunts of privilege', while claiming to serve everyone.

The expressed objects of the Society were first enumerated in a paper by the Rev. William Turner, Unitarian minister of the Hanover Square Chapel, entitled *Speculations on the propriety of attempting the establishment of a literary society in Newcastle*. This paper was read, at a meeting called for the purpose, in the New Assembly Rooms in Westgate Street on 24th January 1793. In his introduction William Turner referred to the Royal Society and to the provincial society that might be compared with it — that of the Manchester Literary and Philosophical Society. He saw as a possibility the establishment of similar provincial societies becoming general, and gave his reasons for looking upon Newcastle as a favourable seat for such an institution. The principal ones were:
1. The two great natural productions of the area: coal and lead.
2. The importance of investigating new mineral treasures, the means of agriculture, and the possibilities of inland navigation.

◊ Sir James Knott Room

3. The need for research in the mathematical sciences.
4. The desirability of a centre for 'literary intelligence'.
5. The need for research into the wealth of antiquities in the region.
6. The opportunities for painting and description afforded by the beautiful scenery of the district.

The principal objects of the new society, which had its true beginning in Turner's paper, and which accepted and approved his suggestions, were mainly scientific and were to be directed especially to the application of science and new scientific discoveries to the growing industry and trade of the North East.

Although the intention to form a general library was expressed within a year of the foundation of the Society most of the books it first acquired, often as gifts (which were solicited), were, in conformity with its principal objects, scientific in character. This is revealed in its first catalogue printed as part of the annual report of the Society in 1796. It lists over 500 works grouped by size as folios, quartos, octavos and duodecimos, with a separate section for maps. A supplement was published, also as part of the annual report, in the following year. In 1798 a complete catalogue was produced as a separate pamphlet which also contained the Society's rules and a list of its members. In 1799 another supplement was printed with the annual report and this became the regular practice. In 1801 another complete catalogue, still arranged by size, was again issued separately. It ran to 17 octavo pages. Yet another separate catalogue, a complete one of about 4,000 books, was printed in 1807 and prefixed by an historical sketch of the Society. The entries were still grouped by size of book and this form of arrangement was continued until 1811. In that year the first attempt at a catalogue arranged by subject was made. It was the work of William Turner. In it the entries were divided into broad subject groups and within each broad group the arrangement was alphabetical by author. There was a general index. It was a great improvement upon its predecessors and shows that in thirteen years the Society had assembled a library of which it could be proud. A short analysis is given below.

Under each subject group are given the names of some of the authors there represented. The number of pages devoted to each group is also shown.

Class I
THEOLOGY, NATURAL AND REVEALED. 2p
Berkeley, Butler, Priestley, Paley.

Class II
CIVIL HISTORY, BIOGRAPHY, ANTIQUITIES, etc. 12p.
Biographia Britannica, Blair, Boswell, Brand, Burnet, Clarendon, Gibbon, Holinshed, Hooke, Hume, Johnson, Maurice, Orme, Robertson.

Class III
VOYAGES AND TRAVELS, DESCRIPTION OF COUNTRIES, etc. 13p
Anson, Barrow, Bruce, Camden, Cook, Dalloway, Forster, Pennant, Young.

Class IV
GENERAL AND BRITISH POLITICS, POLITICAL ECONOMY, etc. 8p.
Bentham, Blackstone, Howard, Malthus, Parr, Price, Selden, Sinclair, Adam Smith.

Class V
PHILOSOPHY OF THE HUMAN MIND, ETHICS, EDUCATION, etc. 4p.
Beattie, Blair, Browne, Burton, Edgeworth, Ferguson, Godwin, Hartley, Locke, Shaftesbury, Voltaire, Wollstonecraft.

Class VI
MATHEMATICS, NATURAL PHILOSOPHY, MECHANIC ARTS, etc. 8p.
Adams, Atwood, Bailey, Bruce, Chapman, Euler, Fenwick, Gray, Horsley, Hutton, Newton, Playfair, Smeaton, Wallis.

Class VII
NATURAL HISTORY, CHEMISTRY, CHEMICAL ARTS, MEDICINE, etc. 14p.
Andrews, Beddoes, Berkenhout, Bewick, Boerhaave, Bolton, Boyle, Brisson, Buffon, Clanny, Curtis, Dalton, Erasmus Darwin, Davy, Donovan, Fothergill, Franklin, Garnett, Hull, Kirwan, Lavoisier, Lettsom, Linnaeus, Montagu, Parkinson, Ray, Sibthorp, Sowerby, Gilbert White, Withering.

Class VIII
AGRICULTURE, GARDENING, etc. 4p.
Bailey, Culley, Evelyn, Fenwick, Forsyth, Loudon, Marshall, Miller, Young.

Class IX
FINE ARTS, ARCHITECTURE, PLATES OF ANTIQUITIES, etc. 4p.
Avison, Barry, Burney, Cellini, Flatman, Fuseli, Gilpin, Hogarth, Opie, Repton, Reynolds.

Class X
CLASSICS, ORIGINAL AND TRANSLATED, etc. 4p.

Class XI
WORKS IN MODERN LANGUAGES. 1p.
Collected works, mainly in French, by Buffon, Fontenelle, Rousseau.

Class XII
DICTIONARIES, GRAMMARS, CATALOGUES, etc. 2p.
Ainsworth, Dawson, *Encyclopedia Britannica*, Grynaeus, Jamieson, Johnson, Lemprière, Lye, Murray, Walker, Catalogues of libraries: Bamborough, Liverpool Athenaeum, Royal Institution.

Class XIII
ENGLISH POETRY, etc. 9p.
Akenside, Barbauld, Beattie, Burns, Byron, Campbell, Chatterton, Chaucer, Coleridge, Collins, Cowper, Crabbe, Donne, Drayton, Drummond, Dryden, Dyer, Gay, Goldsmith, Gray, Johnson, Jonson, Lamb, Landor, Massinger, Milton, Percy, Pope, Prior, Ramsay, Ritson, Scott, Shakespeare, Southey, Spenser, Swift, Thomson, Wordsworth.

Class XIV
BELLES LETTRES, CRITICISM, etc. 3p.
Akin, Bentley, Blair, Burke, Capel, Malone, Warton.

Class XV
COLLECTED WORKS, MISCELLANEOUS WRITERS. 6p.
Bacon, Browne, Burke, Erasmus, *Harleian Miscellany*, Johnson, Montagu, Ouseley.

REVIEWS AND MAGAZINES
Analytical Review, Anti-Jacobin Review, Critical Review, Edinburgh Review, Annual Register, Gentleman's Magazine, Monthly Magazine, Monthly

Review, *Philosophical Magazine, Repertory of Arts and Manufactures, Annals of Botany, Annales de Chimie, Farmer's Magazine, Spectator, Quarterly Review.*

TRACTS
[collections] on Mathematics, Natural Philosophy, Archaeology, Criticism, Chemistry, Mineralogy, Medicine, Mechanics, Marine Engineering, Politics, Topography, Botany, Agriculture.

TRANSACTIONS OF LEARNED SOCIETIES
Royal Society, Mémoires de l'Institut National des Sciences et Arts, Memoirs of the Literary and Philosophical Society of Manchester, Medical Society.

MAPS, PLATES etc.
Armstrong, Arrowsmith, Cary, Ortelius, Sonnini, Tuke. Sections of the strata in coal and lead mining districts.

From this broadly classified catalogue the priorities of the Society in selecting its books can be traced, as can, also, the widening of the scope of the library. In quantity of entries natural philosophy, mathematics, the mechanic arts, natural history, chemistry, pure and applied, and medicine still hold the lead, but they are closely followed by voyages, travels and description of countries, and by history, antiquities and biography. English poetry, the classics and belles lettres are well represented as are the fine arts and architecture. Lesser groups, in decreasing numbers, are political economy, agriculture and horticulture and theology. There are no novels. The old system of arrangement by size was reverted to for the annual supplements until 1819 when a new catalogue on the plan of 1811 was compiled. It contained 132 octavo pages and was provided with an author index. In succeeding years the lists of additions which formed part of each annual report were arranged by subject classes to correspond with the 1819 catalogue.

In 1825 the Society moved into its new building. Its library then contained about 8,000 volumes and an examination of it in its new Library Room exposed deficiencies. The committee reported that the library was lacking in the standard works of learning and science which 'are necessary to make this a library of reference, as well as of mere reading.' It was found, also, that many of the more popular books had become soiled and worn and must be replaced.

It was feared that even without the expense that this would entail there would be difficulty in providing the £230 a year considered necessary for the purchase of new books and £90 required each year for the purchase of works in continuation, transactions of other learned societies, reviews, philosophical journals, and magazines. It was noted, too, that it had become desirable to buy additional copies of popular works to 'accommodate members, in any adequate way, with new and interesting books'. As Spence Watson wrote in describing the difficulties encountered in finding money to meet the often conflicting demands of members and to continue to build the library: '... there were difficulties ... such as are, I suppose, incident to all institutions of this kind. Resolutions were passed occasionally that the Reference Department of the library should be more carefully attended to, or, in other words, that in the purchase of books the Committee should aim at obtaining those which are too costly for private purchase, and those which, though not perhaps immediately popular, remain for all time of actual service to the student, and give character to a collection.'

In 1827, the library then containing about 9,000 volumes, work began on a new edition of the catalogue and this appeared in 1829. It was compiled by Thomas Hodgson, one of the proprietors and editor of the *Newcastle Chronicle,* who had first become a member of the Society in 1805 and continued to play a prominent part in its management until his death in 1850. In his history of the Society Spence Watson tells us that Hodgson was a classical scholar, an antiquarian and a printer of note who contributed to the town's Typographical Society. He gave the *Chronicle* 'the position of the leading political organ between York and Edinburgh'. His catalogue preserved the familiar arrangement under broad subject classes but care was taken to extend its usefulness by exhibiting, in greater detail than before, the subject content of the books. Classified supplements were published annually until 1834 when a consolidated supplement, arranged alphabetically, was issued. This was in addition to the annual supplements of accessions which were classified.

In its report for 1842 the Committee gave much space to the library. It recorded the addition of many expensive and valuable works including a high proportion of scientific books especially in chemistry, engineering and geology 'which were useful and suitable in the studies of many persons resident in this neighbourhood of chemical manufactures, mechanical arts and coal and lead mines'. Also recorded were notable additions to History and Biography and especially to Ecclesiastical History, hitherto a weak section. Also noted are important additions to British topography and a recommendation was added that a yearly sum be set aside for the purpose of gradually completing the collection of county histories. There were also, it was recorded, additions of important works of voyages and travels. Mention was made of the acquisition, by purchase, deposit and gift, of parliamentary papers, the debates of the two Houses of Parliament and Statutes at Large. It was noted that few publications of merit had appeared within the previous year in the fields of moral philosophy and education but that these few had been obtained. On the other hand there had been many important works published on natural history and many of these had been acquired. Additions were also made of recent books on agriculture and horticulture, and the fine arts. With the exception of Duval's *Aristotle* no addition to Classics had been made during the year because that section was already a strong one. Numerous purchases had been made 'in the lighter department of literature in order to meet a demand for the publications of the day among the great majority who take out books'. The Committee invited its successors to consider ways of meeting the demand and 'at the same time carry out the grand object of the Society in the formation of a library and procuring as complete a collection as possible of standard works. It should, doubtless, be the object of a Committee rather to lead the tastes of the Society than to pander to a corrupt desire for trashy works; and, therefore, due care should be taken that the books purchased in this department should be the best of their kind. At the same time, it should be remembered that very many of the members, being engaged in arduous professions, will not feel inclined, after the labours of the day are closed, to read other than the lighter works; and hence the great demand which exists for magazines and books of a light nature.' In this connection it was recommended that two or three copies of the best magazines, e.g. the *Edinburgh* and *Quarterly* reviews should be bought. It was remarked that 'every day's experience shows that it is by those persons who subscribe for the use of the books the institution is principally supported'. This report of 1842 is of special interest because it shows the serious attention given by the Committee to the problems of book selection and the legitimate demands of members. That it failed to find ways in which the problems it set might be solved can hardly be held against it; with limited resources many of the problems were then insoluble. However, successive Committees addressed themselves to the task. The librarian reported constant discontent arising from the great difficulty experienced by members in getting new books and suggested the purchase of several copies of the more popular works, as well as the magazines and reviews. By 1846 a large supply of magazines and reviews was being bought as well as many of the more popular books. The result was an increased membership. A few years later it was decided to borrow, instead of continuing to buy, the more popular books and an arrangement was made with Mudie's under which, in return for an annual subscription, the firm undertook to keep the Society supplied with a large number of the newest books and to exchange them for others on a regular basis. This hiring scheme, from which the library's 'H' section of the present day takes its title, continued until 1894 when it was again decided to buy, and afterwards to re-sell to members, many of the more popular works. It is fair to say that, in the space of a few years after 1842, the chief problems connected with the library had been largely solved. A reduction of the annual subscription[1] in 1856 resulted in a

[1] Robert Stephenson had offered to discharge half the Society's debt providing the other half was raised from elsewhere and the annual subscription was reduced to one guinea. The offer was accepted and the conditions met.

large increase in the membership and a consequent increase in the demand for books. The complaints, however, became fewer and it appeared that the arrangement with Mudie was meeting the requirements, and the increased income from subscriptions made it possible to pay for this and also to give proper attention to the more serious aspects of the work of the library.

There was a long gap after 1829 before another complete edition of the catalogue was compiled. It appeared in 1848 and contained entries for about 25,000 volumes. Much thought had been given to its production and although it was decided to adhere to the old principle of division into broad subject groups, the sub-divisions were made more numerous and an alphabetical index both of authors and subjects was added. An addendum was a classified list of books which had been presented to the Society by W. G. Armstrong whose father, Alderman Armstrong, had desired that the Society should be invited to select from his library such scientific works as it did not already possess. Armstrong gave so liberal an interpretation to his father's wish that 1,284 works of great value were added to the library. The books were mainly, but not all, scientific works and included a splendid collection of works on mathematics which, it was claimed, put the Society in possession of a more complete mathematical department than any other provincial institution. Two supplements to the catalogue were printed, the first, in 1858, contained entries for about 6,000 works and the second, in 1869, entries for an additional 3,000 works. Lists of annual additions, each arranged in one alphabet, were published down to 1884.

The North of England Institute of Mining and Mechanical Engineers, the Mining Institute as it was usually called had its beginnings within the Society but, since 1852, had become an independent institution in premises adjoining those of the Society. Relations between the two bodies had always been cordial and, in 1870, it was proposed that the link between them should be made even closer under an arrangement which involved:
(a) The transference of the scientific works in the Society's

library to the Institute's Wood Memorial Hall.
(b) The construction of a bridge between the two buildings to provide free communication and make easier the joint use of both sets of rooms.

It was proposed, further, that the Institute should engage to spend not less than £50 a year upon the extension of its collection, providing the Literary and Philosophical Society continued to spend not less than that sum on the annual purchase of scientific books. The combined scientific library was to be under the charge of the Society's librarian but the books were to remain the property of the respective societies. This scheme was implemented in 1873 and one of the immediate advantages to the Society was that it helped to relieve the pressure on space that its growing library had been making during the preceding dozen years. A later advantage to both bodies was that it greatly helped in the provision of accommodation for the College of Physical Science which began its life in the Institute's and the Society's rooms. The arrangement with the Mining Institute, which lasted until 1882, when it was modified to permit the Mining Institute to use all its space for its own books, helped to ease pressure on shelf space in the Society's library, but it did not solve the problem. This was done, at least for the then foreseeable future, by an arrangement between the Society and the North Eastern Railway Company, made in 1885, under which the Society gave up to the Company land on the west of the Society's building in return for land to the south upon which a fresh wing (the present Reading Room)[1] was added to the Society's premises.

When the extension to the library had been completed in 1889 the Committee gave its attention to the question of the arrangement of the books and their cataloguing. It had been decided in 1887 to use the Dewey Decimal Classification. As a first step it was decided to make a complete card catalogue which would ultimately form the copy for the printed catalogue. The work was to be done with the help of a number of members, and the method was to cut the old printed catalogue into single entries and mount them on

[1] Now named The Sir James Knott Room.

cards. This ended in the failure that might have been foreseen, and possibly was. It was then decided to engage four assistants to work under the superintendence of the sub-librarian, Henry Richardson, and Mr. Frederick Emley, Honorary Secretary, who had first suggested the use of the Dewey Scheme. By June 1891 the work had progressed so far that it became possible to rearrange the whole of the library on the shelves according to the Dewey Class numbers and the catalogue cards were filed in two sequences: one, in the order of the classification, and the other, a copy of the first, in alphabetical order of author. The card catalogue was completed by the end of 1891 except for revision.

Early in the same year it had been decided to strike out that portion of the Society's laws which prohibited the purchase or hire of books on controversial divinity, of novels, and of works on the practical departments of law and physic, leaving the determination of the books that should be hired or purchased entirely in the hands of the Committee. It had taken a hundred years to achieve this position. In the Society's early days there were very good reasons for its refusal to admit certain classes of books and these have been set out earlier. Sometimes, opposition to the purchase of particular books was voiced by the membership or by the public at large. As early as 1796 a protest was made against Hume's *Essays*, Cudworth's *Intellectual system* and Paley's *Evidences of Christianity* and the books were removed from the shelves. What may be described as an uproar was occasioned in 1829, over the addition to the library of Byron's *Don Juan*. As Spence Watson observed: 'One curious feature of these discussions was the introduction of letters written to individual members by gentlemen living at a distance and of more or less literary distinction, and another was the great part which the press of the district took in the fray. The book had to be withdrawn, but from the observations made in the annual report for the year, the Committee evidently felt aggrieved at the way in which its selection had been attacked, and "the peace and comfort" of the Society had been disturbed.' Novels were for long a problem. Those which appeared in the magazines taken by the library were, of course, admitted, but not when they were published as separate works. In 1832 an attempt was made to persuade the Committee to order the *Waverley* novels but it failed because the Committee took the view that it was not the plan of the Society to admit novels into the library. Nevertheless, some got in, although in small quantity. *Waverley* only of Scott's novels, for example, and even that had been presented. As a result of the decision of 1891 library editions were purchased of the works of Dickens, George Eliot, Fielding, Scott, Smollett and Thackeray. In addition many cheap editions of popular novels were bought and many more hired from Mudie.

The centenary of the foundation of the Society was celebrated by a conversazione which was held in the rooms of the Society and the Mining Institute on 7th February 1893. On the following morning a fire broke out upon the Society's premises and did great damage to the building and its contents. The library suffered, many volumes having been destroyed, either by fire or by water, and many more damaged. Immediate, and energetic, steps were taken to repair the damage and within two years all the rooms were completely restored. A list of the books destroyed was made, and, with the exception of biographies, subsequently printed. In the annual report printed in 1895 it was reported that nearly half the lost books had been replaced, the remainder, with few exceptions, being out of date or duplicate copies, were considered not to be worth re-purchase. 16,000 slightly damaged books were put aside for re-binding and repair and of these, 11,000 had already been dealt with. It was reported, also, that 3,400 books had been bought in addition to those replaced. It was considered that by the end of 1895 the library would be 'in a more satisfactory condition than it had ever been before.' The claim was a just one. The Society had been fortunate in losing comparatively little, and in possessing the means and the will to make it good. It benefited, too, in a number of ways. The disaster brought valuable gifts from many parts of the country, there was a satisfactory settlement of the claim for insurance compensation, and the publicity attending it resulted in a large increase in membership and a stirring of interest and activity within the membership of which one result was the formation of what were called sectional societies.

The sectional societies were small groups within the Society of members with special interests. They were formed in 1895 and were: Economic, Debating, Chess, Photographic, and Shakespeare societies. The programme of the Economic Society for 1895-6 began with an address on *The economic aspect of Merrie England* and continued with papers on foreign trade, international bimetallism, land compared with other property, the causes of the present low range of prices, the eight hours day, municipal finance, and the national income. It caused discussion within the Society when objections were raised that the probable introduction into its discussions of contemporary political problems would contravene the Society's Laws. Early in 1896 the Committee accepted a resolution to sever its connection with the Economic Society. At the ensuing annual meeting a contrary resolution that the connection should continue was carried. In consequence the President, Lord Armstrong, resigned his office. This led to the convening of a special meeting in July at which a resolution to cease the connection was carried as was a further one to ask Lord Armstrong to withdraw his resignation. This he did. The result was the cessation of the Economic Society as a sectional society but its resolution into an independent society — with the good wishes of the parent society, the Lit. & Phil. It must be added that the sectional societies, vigorous for a few years, became inactive and, one by one, ceased to function. An exception seems to have been the Economic Society which re-appeared in 1930 in a reconstituted form and with a change of name to the Newcastle Economic Circle as a radio discussion group under the auspices of the Society. This seems to have come about without opposition.

It was fortunate that the new card catalogue of the library was undamaged by the fire and in 1896 work upon its revision was resumed. Assistance and advice were required and Melvil Dewey was asked if he could recommend a competent assistant to carry through completion and printing.

Dewey seems to have made no recommendation but, incredibly, gave as his opinion that two months' work would suffice. Further advice was sought and R.A. Peddie of the St. Bride Foundation, was engaged to work upon the catalogue with Henry Richardson the Society's librarian and his assistant T. H. Marr. Peddie was engaged in August 1896 and worked until the end of the following year when his services were dispensed with. In the end it was left to Richardson and Marr to complete the revision and prepare the copy.[1] The catalogue, the Society's last in printed form, was published in 1903 and included entries for all works added to the library up to the end of September 1901. The total number of books in the library at that time was about 60,000. The catalogue has a main subject section plus another subject section for works relating to Northumberland, Durham and Berwick-upon-Tweed. A single alphabetically arranged author catalogue expanded to form a name catalogue, i.e. a catalogue consisting of entries under authors plus subject entries for biographical and critical material, covers both sections. No subject index was compiled. Instead the relative subject index of the Dewey Decimal Classification scheme was reprinted and appended to the catalogue. An appendix contains a list of works about the Society, a list of lectures, addresses and papers read before its members of which the Society held manuscript or printed copies, and a list of syllabuses of University Extension lectures given on the Society's premises. It was printed on linotype by Andrew Reid and Co. of Newcastle upon Tyne. It demonstrated that the library was important in far more than a local sense. It was the index, expertly compiled, to what was primarily a working library which had been assembled to meet not only the varied needs of a diverse membership but also to provide reference facilities for the public at large. Collection and preservation had never been the principal considerations in the building of the library but they were always important secondary ones and the catalogue revealed the Society's

[1] The card catalogue which had provided the copy for the printed catalogue was, and is, used in the library, entries for all later additions being incorporated.

possession of many rare and valuable items. There were about 500 books and pamphlets printed before 1701, many early locally-printed works, a large collection of rare tracts,[1] a comprehensive range of county histories, early and late, good collections of State Papers and Public Records, early books of voyages and travels, important early works on science and technology, good sections on history, literature and biography, and a wide range of periodicals and reviews. The 1903 catalogue was indeed a triumph, note-worthy at the time of its appearance and useful as a bibliographical tool ever since. Peddie, who contributed to it, performed another valuable service when he compiled a list of books printed in Northumberland and Durham, together with an index to illustrations of Newcastle appearing in books, magazines and illustrated papers, and presented them to the Society of Antiquaries of Newcastle upon Tyne. The list of locally printed books became the principal source for the list of books printed in Newcastle, 1639-1800, that forms part of Richard Welford's *Early Newcastle typography, 1639-1800,* first published in *Archaeologia Aeliana,* 3rd series, vol.iii, and issued as an overprint in 1907. The entries in this list are arranged in chronological order and give the initials of the libraries or private collections in which the books and pamphlets described could be found. For about one hundred of these the Society is given as a location and in almost all cases the items are still in its possession.

Recovery after the fire of 1893 had been rapid and the condition of the Society, as the century drew to a close, could be contemplated with satisfaction. The Society, with its library, had improved its standing, and acknowledgement of its status was made in 1897 when the American delegation to the Second International Library Conference included in its programme a northern tour and was entertained at a conversazione in the Society's rooms. Its librarian, Henry

---

[1] This collection of pamphlets and other ephemera is in 600 volumes. Much of the material is of the late eighteenth and the nineteenth centuries, its subjects the issues and concerns of the times, e.g. slavery, parliamentary reform, agriculture, commerce and trade, inland navigation and the beginnings of the railway system.

Richardson, was a delegate to this conference. Within the Society there were other causes for satisfaction. There were more members than ever before, an addition to its amenities, a Ladies' Room, became available in 1899, and the Society's lectures were being well attended; even, sometimes, too well, for some members having failed to gain admission, it was decided to admit only members to those lectures expected to attract very large audiences, to reduce the number of course tickets available for sale to the public, and also to increase their price. As expected this had the effect of inducing more people to join the Society.

On the other hand the Society lost, in 1900, two members who had brought distinction to it: Lord Armstrong and Dr. Dennis Embleton. Armstrong, who had been the Society's President since 1860, first became a member in 1836 and had taken an active interest in its affairs for over fifty years. In 1844 he gave two lectures on hydro-electricity. In 1845 he gave three more lectures: the first on *The spheroidal condition of liquids . . .*, the second on *The employment of a column of water for propelling machinery*, and the third on *Steam and the characteristics of voltaic and frictional electricity*. In 1846 he took a leading part in the Society's first conversazione and, in the same year, gave a lecture on *The principles and operation of the electric telegraph*. In 1874 he gave four lectures on his visit to Egypt in 1872 and, fifty-one years after his first lecture to the Society, he gave an experimental lecture *The novel effects of the electric discharge*. In 1859 he paid for the construction of a new lecture theatre in the Society's building and gave £700 towards the cost of the new library wing, the Reading Room, in 1889.

Dennis Embleton, physician, naturalist and antiquary, was born in Newcastle in 1810. He and his brother Thomas were brought up by their uncle, George Hill of Kenton, who was a colliery viewer. The brothers were sent to Witton-le-Wear School. Thomas was trained by his uncle as a mining engineer. Dennis was apprenticed in 1827 to Thomas Leighton, surgeon in Newcastle and went on to further his studies in London hospitals. In 1838 he was appointed Lecturer in Anatomy and Physiology to the Newcastle School of Medicine and, in 1852, Reader in Medicine at the

University of Durham. In 1857 he became a Fellow of the Royal College of Physicians. In 1870 the Newcastle School of Medicine became more closely connected with the University of Durham and Embleton was appointed first Professor of Medicine. He also held the positions of physician to the Newcastle Infirmary and physician to the Newcastle Dispensary. He joined the Society in 1828 and, in later years, took a leading part in its affairs. He became a Vice-President in 1878. The first lectures he gave, in 1844, were on *Animal mechanics*. Among his later contributions were two lectures on *The respiration of animals and plants* (1848), one on *The extinct gigantic birds of New Zealand* (1851), two upon *The dwarf races of mankind* (1878) two upon *The ancient inhabitants of Britain* (1880), and two upon *A visit to Madeira* (1882).[1]

The new President, elected in 1901, was Robert Spence Watson. The report on the first year of his presidency notes that the number of members (2,377), of books circulated (122,525) and of the sum spent on the purchase of new books (£1,081) were all the highest attained during any one year of the Society's existence. Interest in the miscellaneous lectures had continued to grow so that over the year there had been an average attendance of 527. Finally, the whole of the subject catalogue was ready for the printer. For this, and for much other work of a responsible nature, acknowledgement was made to the Society's librarian, Henry Richardson to whom was given a substantial increase in salary. Without doubt he had earned it. He had a staff of four and his library was open from 10 a.m. until 10 p.m.

In 1904 the Society lost another distinguished member by the death of Sir Isaac Lowthian Bell, metallurgist, chemist and pioneer in industrial enterprise, whose membership extended from 1837, a period of sixty-eight years. He was a member of the firm which became known as Messrs. Losh, Wilson and Bell, of the Walker Ironworks on Tyneside. He married Margaret, second daughter of Hugh Lee Pattinson, F.R.S., a Vice President of the Society from 1857-1859, and celebrated as the inventor of the process for extracting silver

[1] An obituary notice of Dr. Embleton by F.W. Dendy is in *Archaeologia Aeliana*, Vol XXIII. 1902.

from lead. In 1850, in partnership with his father-in-law, Lowthian Bell started chemical works at Washington. His firms became, in his lifetime, a gigantic concern employing in mines, collieries, iron and chemical works some 6,000 workpeople. He was twice mayor of Newcastle, in 1854-1855 and 1862-1863, F.R.S. in 1875, and honoured with a baronetcy in 1885. He was an active promoter and supporter of Armstrong College. The *D.N.B.* records: 'Bell's scientific attainments rank very high. For the last fifty years of his life he had few superiors in general knowledge of chemical metallurgy and he was an unrivalled authority on the blast furnace and the scientific processes of its operation. Between 1869 and 1894 he embodied in papers in the Iron and Steel Institute's *Journal* the results of exhaustive experimental researches.' He contributed, also, to the *Transactions* of the North of England Institute of Mining and Mechanical Engineers. The foregoing particulars are given here, not only for their interest in themselves, but also to show the way in which outlets were being provided by this time by specialist institutions for the dissemination of research information which, less than fifty years earlier, might have been communicated to the Literary and Philosophical Society.[1]

The re-arrangement in accordance with Dewey Decimal Classification and the compilation of a card catalogue based upon it gave the library a form which, in all essentials, has remained unchanged to the present day. But there has been continuous growth and revision. Growth has been regular, with the result that the library of 60,000 books of 1901 has become the library of 130,000 of the present time. Revision has also been a regular and constant exercise. For example, in 1895, a programme was begun which involved the checking of the standard works in the library against those listed in Sonnenschein's *Best Books* and the consequent preparation of desiderata for submission to experts. By 1905 this particular exercise was, as the report for that year claims,

[1] Lowthian Bell's grand-daughter was Gertrude Margaret Lowthian Bell (1868-1926), scholar, historian and archaeologist, who travelled much in the Middle East and was Political Officer in Baghdad during World War I. She lectured to the Society in 1907 and 1908.

receiving recognition in 'a gratifying way', the circulation of books in all classes having advanced and the total circulation having increased by more than 14%.

The experts whose advice was sought during this and other revision exercises were almost certainly members of the Society or members of the staff of Armstrong College which meant, particularly at this time, the same thing. The Society has been fortunate in this respect and has been well served by its honorary officers, by its committees, and by the many members who have been willing to place special knowledge at its service. Spence Watson, in his *History*, pays deserved tribute to those who gave so freely to the Society and it is pleasant to record that similar tribute may, and should, be paid to those who have continued this disinterested service right up to the present time. Many of them had long and uninterrupted periods on the Society's Committee and there can be no doubt that the Society thereby gained immeasurably. Nevertheless, the view has sometimes been expressed, as a criticism, that the Committee is a self-perpetuating body. A correspondent to the *Newcastle Chronicle* on 19th January 1905 had this to communicate: 'The Annual General Meeting of the Literary and Philosophical Society of Newcastle upon Tyne . . . takes place according to rule at seven o'clock on the first Tuesday in February . . . when the Committee, consisting of a president, four vice-presidents, a treasurer, two secretaries, and twelve others, will be elected. The whole of the committee retire annually, but the officers, as distinguished from the twelve usually designated as committee, are all eligible for re-election; and one does not know what dire calamity might happen if the members were to make a change, or even nominate some other person than those already serving. . . Of the Committee, "Those four[1] of the twelve who, during their year of office shall have attended the committee's meetings the least frequently, shall be ineligible for the ensuing year." But having been punished for their inattention, they may be nominated again in the following year; and, judging by the long custom of the past, they will be

---

[1] Now (1989) two.

elected to supply the places of the four going out who, in their turn, will have to wait their year in outer darkness before again being returned to office; and so on *ad infinitum*'.

From its earliest days the Society benefited from generous gifts from its members. Spence Watson gives proper acknowledgement for those received during the period covered by his *History* and it should be noted now that later generations have been no less generous. In 1895 Joseph Crawhall, the younger, presented an autograph letter from Thomas Bewick written to his wife from Wycliffe where he was making drawings for his *History of British birds* from the museum which was afterwards purchased by the Society. Crawhall was executor of the will of Miss Isabella Bewick. He died in 1896 and, in 1908, his sister, Miss Mary E. Crawhall, presented a number of books by him 'of such rarity and interest' that, as the report for that year stated, 'it is intended to place them in a separate case. Mr. Joseph Crawhall, or members of his family have been intimately connected with the Society for about a century . . . The remarkable picture of Newcastle worthies . . . is by Joseph Crawhall [the elder 1793-1853] and was likewise presented to the Society [by Miss Crawhall] to replace a copy of four of the figures which was lost after the fire.[1] This copy has recently been recovered; it was found in the parlour of an inn in Newcastle, having been purchased some years ago by the landlord, who restored it to the Society without charge as soon as its ownership was proved.' The four "worthies" are Nathaniel Clayton, H. Cramlington, Alderman Foster and Sir Thomas Burdon. It is entitled *Reminiscences, No. 1*.

In the report for 1913 there is evidence of the Society's flourishing state. Membership had passed the 3,000 mark, interest in its lectures had been keen, with an average attendance at the miscellaneous lectures of 585, and good attendances at the Cambridge University Extension lectures. In addition there had been four special lectures[2] and afternoon lectures for young people had been given during the

[1] See Spence Watson p.109.
[2] See p.76.

Christmas holidays. In the section dealing with the library it was noted that in the 21 years since the prohibition on the admission of fiction was removed the membership had nearly trebled and the circulation of books had increased fourfold. The connection was obvious. The increase in subscription income was important and in obtaining it the provision of fiction had played an important part. In the following year the fiction was organised into a separate section with its own catalogue and an assistant was appointed to devote her chief attention to the section and to advise members on its use. It was also decided to make separate sections for children's books and for music, each with its own catalogue and with a special classification for music. The formation of the last of these sections, its later development into the music library of the present day, and the introduction into the Society's programmes of performances of music is outlined below.

The Society already possessed many books on music, as distinct from scores, and these books and, of course, later additions, were grouped with the growing collection of scores to form a music library. In the formation and arrangement of this section the Society was fortunate in having as its advisers W.H., later Sir Henry Hadow and W. G. Whittaker. Sir Henry Hadow, scholar, educationist, composer, critic and historian of music, was a brilliant lecturer in classics, music and literature who, between 1902 and 1923, gave eighteen lectures to the Society. In 1909 he became Principal of Armstrong College and held the post until 1919. From 1916 to 1918 he was Vice-Chancellor of the University of Durham and, from 1919 to 1930, Vice-Chancellor of the University of Sheffield. From 1920 until 1934 he played a prominent part in national education in his capacity as Chairman of the Consultative Committee of the Board of Education. One of the reports issued by this Committee, *The education of the adolescent* (1927) became known as the *Hadow Report*. He was an early Chairman of the Society's music sub-committee and a generous donor to its music library. William Gillies Whittaker, music scholar, conductor and composer, was born in Newcastle upon Tyne in 1876. He studied science at Armstrong College and, after turning to music, joined its staff in 1898. He devoted himself particularly to choral conducting. He founded the Newcastle Bach Choir in 1915, and took the Choir to London in 1922 for a three-day festival, and to Germany in 1927. In May 1924 the Choir gave the first complete modern performance of Byrd's *Great Service* in Newcastle Cathedral and repeated it, later that year, at St. Margaret's, Westminster and at Oxford. In 1929 he became Gardiner Professor of Music at Glasgow University and Principal of the Royal Scottish Academy of Music. Between 1917 and 1922 he lectured to the Society on four occasions. He was also lecturer for the Cambridge University Extension Course for the autumn term of 1922. His subject for this course was *The appreciation of music* and there was an average attendance at his lectures of 394, at his classes, 120, and 36 students sat for the final examination. He was co-opted to the Society's music sub-committee in 1917.

Two others who should also be mentioned are Ernest Markham Lee, author, composer, lecturer and examiner in music and Sir Richard Runciman Terry. Markham Lee also helped build the music library with advice on suitable acquisitions. He gave two University Extension Courses in the Newcastle centre: one in 1919 and another in 1929. Sir Richard Terry was a generous donor to the newly-formed music library. Born in 1865, he was the elder son of Thomas Terry, schoolmaster of Newcastle, by his wife, the daughter of Walter Runciman of Dunbar, and sister of Walter, later Lord Runciman. The career that gave him international fame began in 1896 when he became Director of Music at Downside where his talent for choir training enabled him to present the liturgical music by sixteenth-century Catholic composers that he made his lifelong study, bringing to light by his research hitherto unknown masters of the Tudor polyphonic school culminating in William Byrd. In 1901 he became Director of the new choir of Westminster Cathedral where he remained for twenty-three years. He lectured to the Society on three occasions: in 1907, when his subject was *Forgotten English Composers, including Tallis, Byrd, Morley and Tomkins*. His audience numbered 690. The other lectures were given in 1917 and 1921.

More than seven hundred scores were added in 1914 with the object of forming a collection that would contain the complete works of the great composers and a representative selection from others, with special attention to British and, in particular, north-country composers. In 1917 the Purcell Society publications were bought and also sets of the Breitkopf and Härtel editions of Bach, Mozart and Schubert. A selection of modern music, British, French and Russian was purchased from a list prepared by W. G. Whittaker with assistance from W. H. Hadow and E. Markham Lee. In 1909 scores by Avison, Shield, Thomas Wright, Abraham Mackintosh and Thomas Ions were added to the collection of works by northern composers. The following year was notable for the number of gifts, including 187 scores and books on music from J. B. Clark and additional Avison scores, the gift of Thomas Henderson and C. F. Thorp. On this foundation and by means of regular additions, including *Musica Britannica* and the Bärenreiter editions of Bach, Berlioz, Handel, Mozart and Schütz, the present music library was built.

In 1942 a gramophone record lending library was begun which, at the present time (1989) contains about 9,000 recordings with an associated collection of miniature scores.

Lectures on music and lecture-recitals featured regularly in the Society's programmes. Many of the lecturers came back time after time and were greeted by large audiences. This was particularly true of Arnold Dolmetsch, Cecil Sharp and H. Walford Davies who, between them, lectured on seventeen occasions between 1898 and 1919. In the latter year 850 people managed, somehow, to get into the lecture theatre to hear Mrs. Kennedy Fraser on *Songs of the Hebrides*. Even then it seems that many were unable to gain admission for she returned to repeat the recital in the following year to an equally numerous audience. Music also featured in the Cambridge University Extension courses up to their ending in 1935. When similar courses, arranged in association with the Extra-Mural Department of King's College were resumed in 1948, the first was on *Landmarks in musical history*, by Arthur Milner. Dr. Milner returned, each succeeding year until 1956. He was followed, from 1958 to 1964, by David Barlow who was succeeded, but not until 1968, by Christopher Wood who has conducted courses each year from then until the present time (1989).

From 1972 until 1975 the Society contributed to the Newcastle Festivals of these years by making its lecture room available, free of charge. It was used, principally, for lunchtime concerts.

In 1979, Noel Broome, musician, teacher of music and a member of the Society, arranged a series of lunchtime concerts, mainly of chamber music, which have continued, each year, from then until the present (1989). No fees have been paid to the players at these concerts and no charge has been made for admission, either to members or to the public. The concerts have always been of high quality. They have contributed substantially to the musical life of Newcastle and to the reputation of the Society.

The association of the Society with Armstrong College, always close, and particularly so in the use of the Society's library, became even closer in 1915 when the College, having been made into a military hospital, was in need of accommodation for itself. Several rooms in the Society's buildings were given up for college classes without charge except for lighting and heating. Moreover, the Society granted the use of its library to all Armstrong College students attending those classes, together with the use of the Ladies' Room, the Record Room and the Smoking Room as Common Rooms.

The report for 1918 records 'with deep thankfulness, the signing of the Armistice . . . During the four and a quarter years of the war the usual lecture courses have been continued and have afforded a welcome relief to members from the stress of war conditions. By the free use of the Society's rooms for national, educational and military purposes, by the distribution of books and magazines amongst the soldiers and sailors, and by the provision of a motor ambulance, the Committee has done what it could . . . It is gratifying that notwithstanding war conditions the Society has continued to flourish and is now stronger than at any previous period of its history.'

By 1919 the membership had grown to over 5,000, the highest figure reached either before or since. The librarian, Henry Richardson, had a staff of eleven, the total income was £5,650 of which subscriptions supplied £4,644. In that year £2,472 was spent on books and £1,349 on salaries. The net cost to the Society of its lecture programme for 1919 was £292.

The Photographic Survey of Northumberland and Durham, the Roman Wall and the Scottish Border, first proposed in 1922 was begun in 1923. Some three thousand photographs, drawings and engravings had been acquired, many of them presented in 1924 by the executors of the late Mr. Robert Blair supplemented by material from the Newcastle Society of Antiquaries. The classification adopted for this collection was based upon that of the Surrey Photographic Record Society. By the end of 1925 all the material received had been catalogued and classified. This special collection was sold in 1933 to the Newcastle Public Library for a nominal charge subject to an assurance that it would be maintained and continued. The assurance thus asked for and gladly given has been honoured in the most handsome way.

CHAPTER TWO

The Society and its Library
II

By 1922 the librarian, Henry Richardson was approaching the end of his career. To assist him a sub-librarian was appointed in the person of F. Wolff who had had experience in the Bodleian, but Wolff resigned for health reasons in the following year. He was succeeded in 1924 by E. Austin Hinton who became librarian on Richardson's resignation in 1925. The burden which Richardson carried was a heavy one and when, in 1924, he expressed a desire to be relieved of some of his duties, an arrangement was made for him to work during mornings only until September 1925 which was the date fixed for his retirement. He had given thirty-five years service as sub-librarian from 1890 and librarian from 1892 and was granted a retiring allowance of £250 a year. The Committee placed upon record its appreciation of the great service which he had rendered to the Society: 'His personal devotion to its interest has been unfailing . . . Special attention is drawn to his work in replacing the library after the fire of 1893; but the monument to his achievement will always be the library catalogue published in 1903.' His is an important figure in the Society's history, especially in that of its library. He was the last of its non-professional librarians who were engaged primarily to perform and supervise purely routine duties while much of the other work was undertaken by the honorary officers. Richardson, however, by his competence and his integrity, achieved a more important position in the management of the Society than any of his predecessors.

Spence Watson has no entry under 'Librarian' in the index to his *History* and the successive occupants of the post are not included in the lists of officers which form one of its appendices. But there are occasional mentions in the text of the librarian and, more rarely, of the sub-librarian. The early librarians were recruited from local booksellers of whom, during the eighteenth century, there were several in Newcastle who also conducted lending libraries from their shops. The most celebrated were Barber, Charnley and Bell. By 1746 Joseph Barber was established at the head of the Flesh Market on the High Bridge, moving later to Amen Corner where he offered a choice of 1,250 volumes of standard literature to his subscribers. William Charnley followed Barber to the Flesh Market in 1757 and had 2,000 volumes to lend. John Bell the elder had his shop in Union Street. These shops were literary clubs patronised by the élite and their proprietors were men of mark. Charnley and Bell became the first librarians of the newly formed Literary and Philosophical Society to which they also supplied books. They obliged until 1798 when, the demands of trade proving pressing, they gave way to Robert Spence who was succeeded in turn by John Marshall. Marshall was a printer who held strongly radical views. He was dismissed in 1817 for having printed and published a pamphlet entitled *A political litany* thereby offending, while holding a post within the Society, against its rule of aloofness from religious and political questions of the day. A later holder of the post was John Thornhill who was also curator of the Society's museum and became a member of the committee of the Natural History Society.[1] He assisted George Wailes who was a member of the Literary and Philosophical Society's committee to compile the catalogue of 1848. Thornhill, who served the Society in a dual capacity for thirty years, retired in 1863 and was followed as librarian by William Lyall who took a major part in the production of supplements to the 1848 catalogue and whose intimate knowledge of the stock of the library was invaluable to its users. His first sub-librarian was Joseph Skipsey, the pitman poet, who requires more than a brief mention. His appointment, made in 1863,

---

[1] The Natural History Society of Northumberland, Durham and Newcastle upon Tyne was founded from within the Literary and Philosophical Society in 1829. For many years the two societies worked side by side until, in 1884, the Natural History Society moved to a new home, the Hancock Museum. A fuller account of the relationship between the Literary and Philosophical Society, the Natural History Society and the Society of Antiquaries of Newcastle upon Tyne is given in Appendix 1.

was the result of a kindness: the recommendation of a friend, probably Spence Watson. Skipsey was born in 1832 and began work in the pits when he was seven years of age, regularly spending sixteen hours of each working day in the dark. He educated himself. In 1859 he printed a collection of his lyrics which, as he wrote in the preface to his *A book of lyrics, including songs, ballads and chants* (1881), 'earned him the respect of several eminent persons in the North of England.' He escaped from the pits, although he was obliged, more than once, to return there in later years, when he became a sub-storekeeper at the Gateshead Iron Works. That was in 1859, the year of publication of his first book. Four years later he was appointed sub-librarian of the Literary and Philosophical Society. His tenure of the post was short and was ended by him, as he explained in the preface already referred to, because he found it impossible to support his family on the wage paid to him. Spence Watson, in his *Life of Joseph Skipsey* (1909), gave a different explanation which was that Skipsey proved unsuitable for the post because he spent his time in taking advantage of what must have been seen by him as a heaven-sent opportunity for spending his days reading in a well-lit library. Spence Watson expands, somewhat jocularly, on the proper function of a librarian, or rather, a sub-librarian, which was, he suggested, to know the outsides of books and where they were to be found but not, not anyway in the library's time, to become further acquainted with them. Whatever the true reason for his resignation it meant for Skipsey a return to the pit — a development which, in all probability was greatly regretted by everyone concerned, although the librarian may have taken a narrower view. Skipsey certainly retained the high esteem in which he was held within the Society. He was admitted to honorary membership in 1883. This remarkable man had opened to him, at different times, three more ways of escape before, in the closing years of his life, he entered the haven provided by the support of his family and a small state pension awarded at the instance of Edward Burne-Jones. The first of these, in 1882, was as caretaker of a Board School in Newcastle, the second, in 1888, as a porter at Armstrong College. The third opened for him when his friends, many of them eminent in the literary and artistic world, found for him a post for which they considered him well suited and in which they hoped he might be happy. It was that of Curator of the Shakespeare Birthplace. Skipsey soon tired of his rôle. Spence Watson, who visited him at Stratford, tells us that Skipsey had come to feel that if he were to make it his life's work he would end by doubting the very existence of Shakespeare.[1] Skipsey resigned his post and came home to the North. The story of Skipsey at Stratford-on-Avon was told to Henry James in 1901 by Lady Trevelyan and it provided the germ from which grew his story *The Birthplace* published in 1903, the year of Skipsey's death.[2]

Lyall's sub-librarian from 1890 was Henry Richardson. He, as I have already mentioned, became librarian in 1892. His last sub-librarian, E. Austin Hinton, was appointed in 1924 and became librarian in 1925. He held this post until 1932 when he was appointed City Librarian of Coventry. His term marked, in a most emphatic way, the coming of professionalism to the Society's staff and its effect on the library. It shows also, that it lifted much of the burden of work from the honorary officers. The greater part of the report for 1926, as also for the immediately succeeding years, is devoted to the library, making it clear that it was acknowledged as being the most important of the activities of the Society and defining 'the traditional and most desirable purpose of the Society: the encouragement of serious reading and study.' A reading of Spence Watson's *History* may give the impression that the Society's directly educational work was dominant; in fact the needs of the library were never neglected but from Hinton onwards there is no doubt as to the emphasis and how much was due to him. During his term of office he was responsible for many notable improvements in practical administration, introducing to the Society methods then common in public libraries of which many were highly desirable. One, however, was less so. It was the

---

[1] Watson, Robert Spence. *Joseph Skipsey: his life and work.* 1909.
[2] *The notebooks of Henry James;* ed. by F. O. Matthiessen and Kenneth B. Murdock. 1947.

installation of turnstiles to govern the entrance and exit of members and so, it was thought, to make more difficult the illegal removal of books. Accepted in public libraries these devices caused resentment among the membership and they were, later, discarded. Hinton's work was done in the shadow of industrial depression and in the face of competition from the increasing and improving facilities for the occupation of leisure provided by public libraries, radio and the cinema. The Society's membership declined from 3,757 in 1925 to 2,168 in 1932 and average attendances at lectures for the same period from 352 to 170. There was anxiety over the financial situation of the Society. Constant efforts were made to increase the membership and, thereby, the income, one of which was the issue of a quarterly bulletin to contain lists of additions, reading lists and other material relating to the library. This bulletin first appeared in 1928 and its publication continued until 1944 when the wartime paper shortage put an end to it. It was replaced by a duplicated list of accessions. Another was the issue, also in 1928, of a new prospectus which included information on the co-operative arrangements made with Armstrong College, the North of England Institute of Engineers and Shipbuilders and the Society of Antiquaries of Newcastle upon Tyne under which members of the Society were permitted access to the libraries of those institutions. Another was an appeal to members to help in recruitment and yet another was an advertising campaign which extended to the display of notices in the municipal tramcars.

But the two achievements for which Hinton is chiefly remembered were, firstly, his work to extend professional training to all members of his staff. Very soon after his appointment it had been decided to take, as pupils in the library, girls leaving school who wished to be trained as librarians. In 1927 the Committee reported on the success of the experiment. The girls so taken were designated as 'pupil-assistants'. They did not form part of the regular staff and did not receive a salary although a small weekly sum was paid to them for pocket money. They received practical training and, together with regular members of the staff, were coached for the examinations of the Library Association. There were many successes: some of the pupils obtained posts on the permanent staff, others posts elsewhere and the Society gained a reputation as being a good place in which to train. The second achievement was the part that he played in the establishment of the Northern Regional Library System. In 1929, at the request of the Carnegie United Kingdom Trustees, the Society agreed to lend books from its library to any recognised library in the counties of Northumberland, Cumberland and Durham and also to become an outlier library of the Central Library for Students which, later, became the National Central Library and, later still, the Lending Division of the British Library. The Carnegie Trustees marked their appreciation by making a grant of one thousand pounds, to be spread over three years and to be used for the purchase of books for the Society's library. Towards the end of the same year a conference was held in Bolbec Hall under the auspices of the Carnegie Trustees, with the object of outlining proposals for a regional scheme of co-operation between the libraries of the three northern counties. The scheme was adopted in 1930 with the addition of Westmorland and Middlesbrough and an executive committee was appointed with the intention of making a start on 1st January 1931. The Society's committee offered to provide a regional bureau and central office and its librarian was elected Honorary Secretary and Treasurer. This regional scheme, which received a grant from the Carnegie Trustees to cover the cost of working during its first three years, after which it would be financed by subscriptions from participating libraries, was the first of its kind to be organised. By the end of 1931 the system was in full working order: 1,792 applications for loans had been received, 145 books had been borrowed for members of the Society and the Society itself had lent 614 from its own stock to libraries within the northern area of the scheme plus 230 which were lent to the National Central Library.

That the Society was able to play such an important part in the inauguration and development of the voluntary scheme for inter-lending between libraries which was a principal object at that time of the Carnegie United Kingdom Trust and which rapidly extended to the rest of the country, was a mark of recognition of the importance of its library and a measure of the close personal interest shown by Hinton with the backing of his Committee. The arrangements outlined above continued until 1963 when the space the Society was able to provide having become inadequate, the Northern Regional Library System was moved to the Central Public Library, where Hinton, the man who had done so much to establish it, was by then City Librarian. In appreciation of the Society's past services its librarian was made an *ex officio* member of the system's executive committee and, later, the Society itself was made an honorary member of the system.

The years between 1925 and the beginning of the Second World War were those in which the Society's library was staffed by a series of young librarians, rising in their profession, who all brought new energy, and new ideas, into its service. When Hinton became librarian in 1925 T. H. Marr, who had been a member of the staff since 1893, was appointed sub-librarian, a post which he held until his death in 1930 when M. C. Pottinger, a professionally qualified librarian, took his place. Pottinger assisted Hinton in staff training and continued it when he himself became librarian in 1932. Between then and 1939 there were, one after the other, three professional sub-librarians: J. D. Reynolds who, in 1934, was appointed Borough Librarian of Blyth, S. J. Marks who became Principal Assistant in Dumfriesshire Libraries in 1936, and W. Middleton Martin who joined the staff of the National Central Library in 1939. Pottinger held the post of librarian until 1946, when he resigned on his appointment as Librarian of the Scottish Central Library for Students. He had been absent on service with the Royal Navy from 1940 until 1945.

The war imposed a pause in which services were maintained on a makeshift basis and during which the Society was greatly indebted to its honorary officers and members of its Committee for supervisory work. Many of the older officers and members of Committee had died or resigned. Frederick Emley, Honorary Secretary since 1895, resigned after forty years' service on the committee; Sir Charles Parsons, President since 1916 who had been a member of the Society since 1893, died in 1931, and Alfred Holmes, a member since 1870 and Honorary Secretary since 1893 died in 1933. Sir Charles Parsons was succeeded as President by G. M. Trevelyan, who held office until 1939 when he was succeeded by C. H. Hunter Blair, Alfred Holmes by T. M. Harbottle whose fellow Honorary Secretary, from 1935, was R. H. Fallaw who held office until 1957, the year of his death. Fallaw, an architect, joined the Society in 1919 and became a member of its Committee in 1934. He rendered great service by his expert supervision of the fabric, both of the Society's building and of Bolbec Hall.

During Pottinger's absence on war service Miss G. Brown, a senior assistant in the library, acted as librarian. She was given much help by B. S. Page, Librarian of King's College and a member of the Society's Committee, who gave honorary supervision to the library during the period 1940-1945, and was Chairman of the Music and Gramophone sub-committee until he left to take up the appointment of Brotherton Librarian of the University of Leeds in 1947.

The membership during the 1930s remained steady at around the 2,000 mark but declined during the first two years of the war. This fall was partly accounted for by evacuation from the city and the absence on military service of many of the younger members. By 1941 membership began again to increase, reaching a figure of over 3,000 in 1944 and continuing to rise thereafter to a second peak (the first was reached in 1919 when it was over 5,000) of 3,690 in 1947.

The new librarian who succeeded Pottinger in 1946 was Frank Rutherford who came from the Durham County Library. He and the Committee were encouraged by the continued rise in membership to make plans for post-war reconstruction and re-arrangement. These included the provision of additional shelving for the main library and an extensive re-arrangement of the books which had as its object the bringing of the more recent additions into places of greater prominence and, by so doing, increasing the attractiveness of the library. The plans also involved the conversion of part of the basement in Bolbec Hall into a book store. All this was accomplished by 1949. In addition the lecture programme, including the University Extension lectures, had been resumed.

The next project, on which work began in 1950, was planned as a complete overhaul of the library. A panel drawn from the Committee was appointed to revise the science section. Its brief was to examine the section with a view to the withdrawal of obsolete books and those of 'purely historical interest', the latter to be offered for sale with a preference for local libraries as purchasers. The panel was also given the task of advising on the purchase for the library of new books on science suitable for the educated general reader in order to bring and keep this section of the library abreast of current thought. Other panels were planned to perform similar services for other parts of the library. The brief to the Science Revision Panel put the seal of policy upon what had been a gradual process of change from a library particularly strong in pure and applied science to one that was truly general in character. It was present in the minds of the panel that specialist libraries and specialist departments of public libraries were then providing a service that the Society, in its early years, had supplied to the best of its ability. The policy was a reasoned one and it has continued, so that it may now be said that the books of science bought for the library are generally only those also of interest to the lay reader. It should be made clear, however, that this policy has permitted the purchase of many expensive works of which Needham's *Science and civilisation in China* and Singer's *History of technology* furnish examples. The work of the Science Revision Panel was largely completed by 1951. A number of books, including some bound volumes of specialist scientific periodicals, not required by other libraries in the area, were sold to booksellers. The books of 'purely historical interest' so disposed of were relatively few in number because it was recognised that a strength of the library lay in its possession of older material required by historians of science and which libraries of later foundation did not possess. It must be added that, during later years, there have been a number of occasions on which regret has been felt that particular books had been sold. An Arts Subjects Panel was formed in 1951 and began work on the Philosophy, Psychology, and Religion sections. The emphasis was upon addition rather than rejection as it continued to be when, during the following years, the other sections of the library were overhauled.

Membership, still over 3,000 in 1950, began to decline in the following year and the fall continued until, by the end of the decade it had sunk to about 1,700. The loss of income from subscriptions and increasing costs almost everywhere caused concern which was reflected in the report for 1958 in which year, in order to maintain expenditure, especially on books, it was deemed necessary to draw on invested capital, despite the constant exercise of economy and continued efforts to recruit new members. In 1959 the last of the Society's investments (except those invested in Bolbec Hall) were sold. It was clear that unless regular income could be increased the Society would be in continued difficulty. There were two possible solutions: increasing subscriptions or selling certain assets. The second was preferred and it was proposed to sell the Assyrian reliefs which had been presented by W. K. Loftus in 1855.[1] The view was taken that, immensely distinguished though they were, the reliefs did not make an essential contribution to the main function of the Society: its provision of a library, and the Trustees were authorised to sell them for the best price obtainable; but it was not until 1961 that the reliefs were sold for a net figure of over £35,000.[2] Some pressing repairs and renovations were carried out but the greater part of the sale price was invested in securities and the finances were thus placed upon a surer footing. It was recognised, however, that what had been secured was a breathing space only because costs continued to rise and a new threat had been posed by the provisions of the Rating and Valuation Act of 1961 which ended the

[1] See p.164-195.
[2] The Society had expressed the wish that the reliefs should be sold to an English buyer and they probably were; but by 1966, they were in the Los Angeles County Museum of Art.

exemption from the payment of rates which the Society had enjoyed under the Scientific Societies Act of 1843. Full payment of rates would have imposed an intolerable burden on the Society but happily this catastrophe was partly averted by the registration of the Society as an educational charity and when the blow fell in 1964 the liability was reduced by half.

In 1961 Dr. C. H. Hunter Blair resigned the office of President but remained on the Committee as a Vice-President. He was succeeded as President by T. M. Harbottle whose death, before the end of his first year of office, was a severe loss to the Society. He became a member in 1921, was elected to the Committee in 1930 and served as Honorary Secretary from 1933 until 1957, and as Vice-President between 1958 and 1961. He was followed as President by Col. A. D. S. Rogers.

In 1963 Frank Rutherford resigned from his posts as librarian to the Society and Honorary Secretary and Treasurer of the Northern Regional Library System on his appointment as librarian of the Institute of Education in the University of Durham. He was succeeded as librarian by the present writer who came from the Birmingham Library, a library which resembled that of the Society in many ways but differed from it in having been a proprietary institution. Some part of its history was touched on earlier.[1]

During the years from 1963 to the present there have been many changes and developments of which an account must be given. The principal ones were: the refreshment service, self-organising groups within the Society (which may be compared with the sectional societies of 1895),[2] the lecture theatre reconstruction, binding and conservation, developments in co-operation, the establishment of additional special collections, the poetry competitions, and the development appeal of 1984.

The serving of light refreshments in the library began in an experimental way in 1964 with the object of providing an additional amenity for members who would be charged no

[1] p.8.
[2] p.21.

more than would cover costs. The service quickly became popular and although it has never done more than pay its way, and has often failed to do that, it has become one of the indispensable amenities provided within the library.

In 1965 an increase in subscription rates provoked a number of comments and suggestions of which the essence was that although the increases were accepted as inevitable it was hoped that improvements and additions would be made to the social amenities provided by the Society. As a result the hours during which the refreshment service was available were extended and improvements made to the furnishing and decoration of the Society's rooms. In addition meetings of members were arranged, each taking the form of a short talk on books and libraries followed by discussion, and self-organising groups were set up for members and their friends who shared common interests. Three of these groups, Local History, Play-reading, and Music enjoyed considerable success and continued for a number of years but all, ultimately, ceased to function, partly because of the departure of a few moving spirits, and also because, from 1967 onwards, it became possible to provide accommodation for specialist societies who were seeking a meeting place. One example of this was the absorption of the Music Group by the Newcastle Gramophone Society. Of the other groups, Play-reading continued until 1971 when diminishing attendances forced its closure, but the Local History Group continued for longer. It had as an important objective the encouragement of its members to engage in research, and some idea of the kind and quality of the work done can be obtained from an examination of its programmes for the years 1971-1973. Papers were read on: *The origins of Gosforth, Railway architecture in North East England, Local industrial development, The history of rating, Upper Coquetdale, The golden age of Northumberland, The County Palatine of Durham, The witherite mine at Settlingstones, The gas industry, Prehistoric settlement in Northumberland and the Borders,* and*What the papers said: two centuries of local newspapers.* Visits were paid to Trinity House and to Corbridge church and its immediate surroundings. In 1974 the programme consisted of a course of six lectures, arranged by the University of Newcastle's Department of Adult Education, on *Old Newcastle*, and this was followed in each of the succeeding years until 1983 with further courses arranged in the same way. That brought its activity to an end, at least for the time being, in what was, in effect, a handing over. Details of these university courses are given on pages 69 and 70.

A major reconstruction was begun in 1966. It was the plan of S. T. L. Harbottle who had followed his father as Joint Honorary Secretary in 1957. Concern had been felt for some years at the small use being made of the lecture theatre which occupied a great part of the ground floor of the Society's building. This theatre, which had replaced an earlier one, was designed by John Dobson and the expense of constructing and furnishing it was met by Sir William, later Lord, Armstrong. It was opened in 1860. It was needed then, and for many years afterwards, but the need for a large lecture room had, a hundred years later, long passed. It belonged to the heyday of the public lecture when it was frequently filled to capacity and beyond. For the less frequent and smaller meetings and lectures of the post second world war period it had proved expensive to run and unattractive to use. This may not, by itself, have been sufficient reason to overcome a reluctance to do away with a beautifully designed room which had been the scene of many events of importance in the Society's history, but there were other considerations. Firstly, the need to remove the books stored, in poor conditions, in the basement and on the fifth floor of Bolbec Hall to better and more accessible accommodation, and secondly, the opportunity that would be afforded to increase the space available for letting both in Bolbec Hall and the Society's building, and so provide an alternative investment for the money obtained by the sale of the Assyrian reliefs in 1961. These considerations, together, were compelling and the decision to proceed with the reconstruction was taken. It involved the removal of the existing lecture theatre seating and the construction of a new floor on a level with the entrance hall of the Society's building. Two thirds of the new floor area were reserved for letting as offices[1] while the remaining one third was designed as a members' room which would be so furnished and equipped that it would also provide facilities for meetings of up to one hundred people. The basement below the new floor was used in its entirety as a book store and into it were moved some 40,000 of the older, more valuable and more fragile books together with many 'runs' of periodicals, where they were housed in a secure place specially designed for them and which provided ideal conditions for storage. The work was completed in 1967. The architects were W. B. Edwards and Partners. The new members' room was given the name of the Loftus Room because the reconstruction of which it was part was paid for with the money obtained by the sale of the Assyrian reliefs presented to the Society in 1855 by W. K. Loftus. It was formally opened on 23rd November, 1967 by Sir Humphrey Noble, *Bt*. It was a useful and attractive addition to the amenities provided for the Society's members. It also very quickly came to be regarded as a pleasant place for meetings and this prompted the initiation of a policy to encourage its use in this way. It was consistent with the long tradition of the Society to provide help, encouragement and accommodation for associations and institutions which, although specialised, had aims akin to those of the Society itself, and also it was expected that such use would result in the acquisition of new members. Charges were made but only sufficient to cover administrative costs and the refreshment service was extended to provide an extra facility. At the present time (1989) the Loftus Room is well used: as members' room, for lunchtime concerts, for the Society's lectures, for University Extension and W.E.A. courses, and for the regular evening meetings of at least twelve other societies.

In 1966 the Committee addressed itself to a problem which had awaited solution for many years: that of the conservation of the older and more valuable books in the library. It set out its priorities in these words: 'The Society, since its foundation in the late eighteenth century, has built

---

[1] At the end of a tenant's lease in 1987 this office accommodation was taken back into use by the Society as described on p.54

its library into an important collection that has far more than a local fame . . . Experience has shown, over and over again, that the copy of a book in the Society's library is the only copy in the North East and, often, the only copy in the country outside the great national collections. The committee is of the opinion that although priority must always be given to making the library useful and attractive to the majority of its members by the provision of new books, ways must be found to increase the annual expenditure on the preservation of the older material, for it is in its possession of this material that the special distinction of the Society's library lies.' A beginning was made but, for the next few years, progress was very slow and it became apparent that the ordinary income of the Society was unlikely to permit more than very modest spending on a binding programme. In 1970, therefore, an appeal for assistance was made to leading companies and charitable trusts in the North East, and although the response was less than had been hoped for, it was sufficient to make possible a long overdue start on a planned programme of conservation and for its continuation in succeeding years. In its report for 1977 the Committee was able to report good progress and to acknowledge gratefully the receipt of gifts and grants for its, still open, binding fund. The largest of these grants was from the British Library which responded generously and imaginatively to a direct appeal by granting £10,000 to be spread over three years on condition that none of the books bound or refurbished with the use of this money would subsequently be disposed of without the prior approval of the British Library. In addition the British Library granted a sum of £2,000 annually for three years to assist with staff costs for this additional work. The bulk of the work was done by binding firms but a great deal of the refurbishing and some binding was done on the Society's premises. An approach had been made to the Manpower Services Commission which accepted for its Job Creation Programme the employment of one bookbinder and one learner for one year. With some difficulty a bookbinder, but not a learner, was found by the Employment Services Agency and a workshop was set up in one of the unlet rooms in Bolbec Hall which was furnished with equipment used by the Society many years before and stored for possible future use, supplemented by sundry tools and pieces of equipment bought second hand or borrowed. Advice and practical assistance was given by the University of Newcastle upon Tyne which possessed a library bindery of its own. This 'home' bindery was run for nine months instead of the twelve planned, the binder having found employment with a commercial firm; but in that time much useful work was done and there was also the satisfaction of knowing that this temporary employment had enabled an unemployed binder to continue in his trade. It did not bring the Society's binding programme to an end, but all the work was now put out to commercial binders. In 1980 the British Library extended its grant for one more year with a gift of £4,000 to compensate for the rapid increase in charges for binding which had occurred during the preceeding three years. In the following year it was reported that although a great deal of work remained to be done, the first and most important part of the binding programme drawn up in 1966 had been completed. In 1982 it again became possible to take the Society's bindery into use and to employ a skilled binder who offered her services on a part-time basis. The opportunity was taken to deal with particularly rare books and very useful work was done during the succeeding two years, at the end of which, regrettably, the binder was obliged to withdraw her services. At the same time the work of selecting and sending books to commercial binding firms continued and, with the aid of increased funding after 1984, is being increased.

During 1971 and 1972 arrangements were made with the Polytechnic, the Public Library and the University, all of Newcastle upon Tyne, under which their research students would, in return for a composite subscription paid annually by these institutions, have the right to use the Society's library for the consultation and, in certain circumstances the borrowing, of books and periodicals within relevant fields of study. These arrangements did not cause the Society to abandon its invariable practice of permitting any *bona fide* student to consult material on his subject but had the double merit of specifying those students who could do so as of right and of giving financial help to the Society.

In 1971 the Society, one of the founders of the College of Physical Science in 1871, was invited by the University of Newcastle upon Tyne to take part in the centenary celebration programme. The Society's contributions, in addition to work on the organising committee, were the presentation of an illuminated address to the University and the arrangement of a lecture by Mr Sydney Middlebrook[1] which was delivered in the Society's building before an audience which included the Lord Mayor of the City, senior members of the University, and representatives of the Mining Institute, the Natural History Society of Northumbria, the North East Coast Institution of Engineers and Shipbuilders and the Society of Antiquaries of Newcastle upon Tyne.

The period between the end of the Second World War and the present day has witnessed many changes and great advances in the provision of libraries. In Newcastle upon Tyne the public library service has been greatly extended and improved. So has the University library and there has been an important addition, that of the library of the Newcastle upon Tyne Polytechnic. The Society has been affected by these developments and the view has been taken, occasionally, that the end of its long period of service may be at hand. This, however, is not the view held within the Society, nor is it held in those libraries which are, to some extent, competitors; there, rather, it is thought that the Society's library exists as a partner, providing much material not to be found in libraries of later foundation. This view was made clear when, in 1972 and on the initiative of Keith Harris, then librarian of the Polytechnic, the Newcastle upon Tyne Libraries Joint Working Party was formed. It was devised to bring together in regular meetings the librarians of the Polytechnic, the University, the City, and the Literary and Philosophical Society with the objects of exploring further ways of co-operation, the development and linking of the separate strengths of their libraries, and the exchange

---

[1] See p.2.

of staff experience. This working party, now greatly extended to cover the whole region, is still active.

The early association of the Society with its neighbour, the North of England Institute of Mining and Mechanical Engineers, the Mining Institute as it is commonly called, was described by Spence Watson and its continuation has been touched on in the present work.[1] In 1981 the Society took a prominent part in discussions attending the Institute's plan to maintain its library in its present home in Neville Hall and to secure its future as a building and a library of particular historical and practical importance to the region. Regular meetings between the Society and Institute were held and these continued until 1986 by which time the re-organisation, re-cataloguing and re-classification of the Institute's library of books, periodicals and archives, begun in 1981, was almost completed. The operation was funded by the British Library and was carried out by and under the supervision of Miss Margaret Norwell who, in 1986, was appointed part-time sub-librarian of the Society while remaining part-time librarian of the Institute. This arrangement, which provided professional supervision of the Institute's library, came to an end in September 1986 when the Institute, unable to afford professional staffing, resumed management of its library using clerical assistance from its own office.

The recently established special collections mentioned on page 44 were formed from gifts to the Society. The first was a fine collection of books illustrated by Hugh Thomson which was the gift of Mrs. N. Varty. The second was the extensive collection of books and pamphlets on town planning having particular relevance to the North East which was presented by Mr. R. Rosner. The third, a collection of books on printing and its allied arts, was presented by Mr. John Philipson. The fourth was that part of a substantial private library bequeathed by Mr. T. E. Ellerington which contained modern poetry and books upon it. It is known as the Ellerington Collection and is available for use only in the Society's rooms. The fifth was also a bequest. Mr. A. W.

---

[1] p.17 and 18.

Willis, who died in 1987 and who had been a member of the Society since 1936, a member of its Committee since 1960 and a Vice-President since 1970, was the possessor of another notable private library. He left one thousand of his books, to be selected by the Society, to its library. Among those chosen were many rare books on botany and gardening which, added to the excellent sections on these subjects already in the library, have made those sections even finer.

There are two other collections of which the Society is the custodian but not the owner. One is the Northern Arts Manuscript Collection which contains work by most of the contemporary writers of note in the Northern Arts area. The other is the Morden Tower collection of modern poetry, the published work of contemporary poets who have given readings there. All the material in these two collections appears in the catalogue of the Society's library and may be consulted but not borrowed.

In the paragraph following this one an account will be given of the Development Appeal launched on 19th September 1984. One of its objectives was to make it possible for the Society to promote directly literature in the North East. A move in this direction was made, before the appeal was launched, by the running, under the Society's auspices, of the Basil Bunting Poetry Competition, 1984, which offered prizes for hitherto unpublished poems or collections of poems. The intention was to make this an annual event but in 1985 the *Newcastle Chronicle* organised a poetry competition in association with Bloodaxe Books and Northern Arts to which the Society contributed by making its rooms available for the reading of winning entries, the presentation of prizes and the holding of a poetry workshop for young writers. In these circumstances it was decided that the Society would not hold a competition in 1985 but would hope to join the *Chronicle* and Bloodaxe Books in arranging one for 1986. This was done and for it the Society gave the principal prize of £400 called the Basil Bunting Award and again made its rooms available for readings of entries, the presentation of prizes and a junior poetry workshop. Similar arrangements were made for 1987 but with the addition of a further prize of £250 which had been deposited with the Society for this purpose by the Edward Boyle Trust.[1]

Since its foundation nearly two hundred years ago the Society has made two public appeals for funds. The first, in 1850, after a disappointing start, achieved success with the help of Robert Stephenson. The second was made in 1984. Reviewing, at that time, the recent past, the Committee faced the fact that membership which, immediately after the war, had reached a peak of over three and a half thousand, had declined to about thirteen hundred in the mid seventies and to about twelve hundred by the mid eighties at which point it had steadied. During the period 1977-1983 expenses had continued to rise. In spite of increased rates of subscriptions the position had been reached at which income from these was barely sufficient to pay the salaries bill, while total expenditure had exceeded ordinary income by over £50,000. Fortunately the losses had been made good by gifts and legacies from trusts, firms and individuals; but it was clearly unwise to continue to rely from year to year on the generosity of benefactors, and prudent to consider what steps might be taken to provide more regular income. Massive increases in membership were not to be expected; large increases in subscription rates would be contrary to a consistent policy of the Society from its beginnings and would certainly reduce membership even further.

The 1984 Development Appeal was made with four specific objects and a general one. The specific objects were:

1. to carry out repairs and renewals to the Society's building;
2. to preserve the essential quality of the Society's library by increasing spending on acquisitions, on conservation, and upon microfilm and copying facilities, and to make it possible for the library to continue to develop as a living research library;
3. to make it possible for the Society to assume, without loss to its own services, the management of the unique library of its neighbour, the Mining Institute;

[1] Like arrangements were made for poetry competitions in 1988 and 1989. For both the Edward Boyle Trust provided a prize of £250.

4. to re-endow the Robert Spence Watson Lecture on English literature and language and to provide for its regular printing, and to make it possible for the Society to promote directly literature in the North East.

The figure which the appeal organisers hoped to reach was £350,000. By June 1986 the amount raised and in prospect was £268,000. Since that time the Society has received three substantial legacies, posthumous gifts, as they may be regarded, to the appeal fund. The first two were from former Vice-Presidents, Mrs. G. Hickling, Honorary Secretary of the Natural History Society of Northumbria, who died in 1986, and Mr. A. W. Willis who died in 1987. The third was from Mr. C. P. Crawford who had been a member for over forty years and who died in 1988.

The satisfactory conclusion of the Development Appeal and the legacies mentioned above eased financial anxieties and enabled the Society to move towards the appeal's objectives. By the end of 1986 major building repairs had been completed and increased spending on acquisition and conservation had begun. In addition the Society felt justified in taking back into its own use that part of the ground floor of its own building which, in 1966-1967, had been converted into lettable office accommodation, to satisfy a growing demand for rooms for meetings and conferences. It became possible, for example, to agree to a request by the London College of Music and another from the Associated Board of the Royal Schools of Music to provide accommodation for examinations in music. The association of the Society with these bodies for this purpose began in 1987.

Early in the following year it was proposed that the Society should assist in the arranging of public lectures on the history on science and technology because regular courses of lectures on these subjects were no longer being provided in the city. The proposal was greeted favourably by the Society. It saw an opportunity, and felt an obligation, to so resume an activity which had especially distinguished its own early years. It was decided to plan for an annual course to begin in the autumn of 1988 and that the lectures should form part of the Society's lecture programme. It was also decided that because the lectures were to be open to the public, so also would be the Society's other lectures which, for many years, and with the exception of the biennial Robert Spence Watson Lecture, had been open only to members and their friends.

Robert Spence Watson brought his *History* to a close in 1896 with a confident prediction that another would, a century later, continue his story. This, a little earlier than expected, the present writer has attempted. Looking back over the period of nearly a quarter of a century during which he was happy to be the Society's librarian, there are a number of abiding memories: the constant struggle to make ends meet, the generosity of many individuals and institutions which made it possible, the helpfulness and willing co-operation of colleagues in the other libraries in the region, a congenial staff, and the pleasure of working with honorary officers and members of committee who were both innovative and supportive and who all upheld the ideal of preserving the Society and its great library and maintaining high standards. The general object of the Development Appeal was to strengthen and increase the Society's contribution to the cultural and educational life of the North East and to ensure that this contribution will continue to be made into the twenty-first century and beyond. There are good reasons for confidence that the Society's third historian will be able to report that this was achieved.

CHAPTER THREE

The Society's Building and Bolbec Hall

An account is given in Spence Watson's *History* of the acquisition by the Society of a site in Westgate Road and of the building there of the Society's permanent home.[1] The account is inaccurate in one particular. The land on which the Society's building stands is part of an area once occupied by the town house and grounds of Walter de Bolbec which later became the property of Sir John Nevill of Raby. In 1398 Sir Ralph de Nevill was created Earl of Westmoreland and his town house in Newcastle, heretofore called Bolbec Hall, was re-named Westmoreland House. In 1571 the property was in the tenure of the Bartram family and so remained until about 1731 when it passed to the Orde family. Later the house and grounds were acquired by the families of Stephenson and Gibson and, later still, they were purchased by Silas Angas from whom they were purchased by the Society in 1821. The descent of the property was traced by R. O. Heslop[2] whose notes on the subject were printed in the Society's report for 1907 and thereby corrected what seems to have been a general misapprehension, shared by Spence Watson, that the old house which lay to the west of the Society's building, also called Westmoreland House, which was demolished in 1870 to make space for the Mining

---

[1] Listed, in 1954, as a building of special architectural and historic interest.

[2] Richard Oliver Heslop became a member in 1859, Vice-President in 1911 and President in 1914. His publications include: *A bibliographical list of works illustrative of the dialect of Northumberland*, 1896, *The castle of Newcastle: a short descriptive guide to the Keep, Black Gate and Heron Pit;* 4th. edn. 1906, *Dialect speech in Northumberland:* a lecture delivered to the Society in 1898. He died in 1916 and the Society's report for that year says of him: 'He brought to the consideration of books, and especially of works on local history and antiquities, a fund of special knowledge.'

Main Library (1988) ▷

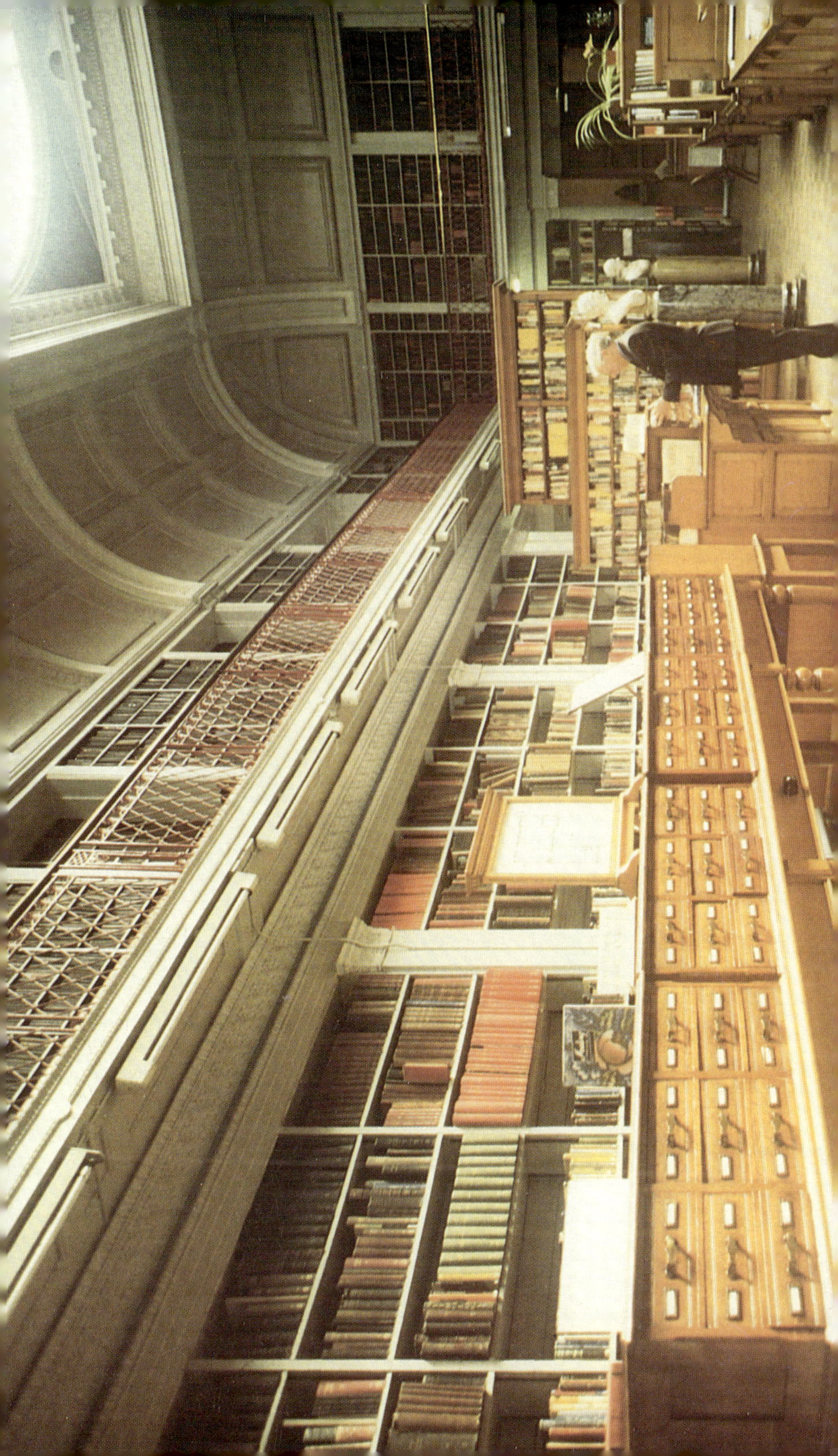

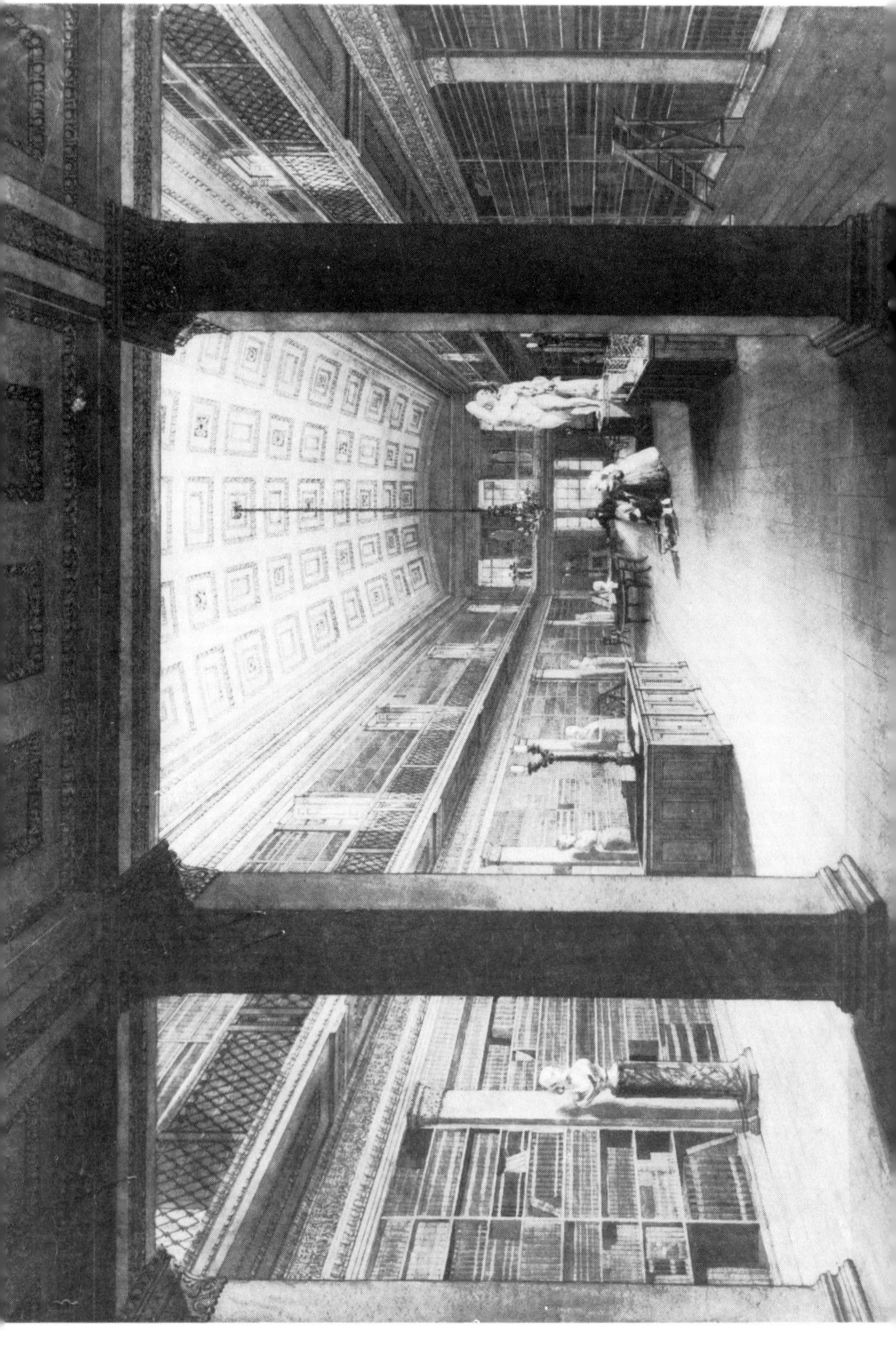

Institute's building, was the Westmoreland House at one time in the possession of the Nevill family. It was in fact a separate property the descent of which was also traced by R.O. Heslop and shown in his notes. The new building for the Mining Institute was called Neville Hall: a misnomer. In 1898 the land to the east of the Society's building, once part of the grounds of Bolbec Hall, was owned partly by the Society, being part of the purchase in 1821 left vacant to provide insulation for the Society's building, and partly by Messrs. Spencer who also owned property upon it and had, also, a right of way over the Society's land. This site was then called Library Place. In the same year Spencer's property, land and buildings, was put up for auction. It was the view of the Society that the acquisition of the site would be an advantage: firstly, because it might, at some time in the future, need more accommodation, and, secondly, because it would give the Society complete control over Library Place. It was decided, because the matter was urgent, to form a syndicate amongst the members with the object of purchase at a price not exceeding £10,000. In June the Secretaries,

◊ Main Library (c.1830)

The Photograph opposite is of a water colour sold at Sotheby's in London in 1987. The Society's bid for it was unsuccessful. In the sale catalogue it was described as a painting of the library of a learned society by an unknown artist. An engraving in *Architectural and picturesque views in Newcastle*, engraved by W. Collard, notes by M. Ross, first published in Newcastle in 1842 establishes that the learned society was the Literary and Philosophical Society of Newcastle upon Tyne. The engraving was from a drawing by Benjamin Green son of John Green the architect of the Society's building. It is possible that the water colour was also by Benjamin Green. He certainly painted one which, as a letter to the Society dated 13 February, 1904 by Mr. P. L. Addison states, was then in the writer's possession. There is a difference between water colour and engraving. The water colour shows in the library a cast of a statue of Milo presented to the Society in 1828 by its sculptor John Graham Lough. An account of the acquisition of the cast, the trouble it caused, and its fate is given in Robert Spence Watson's *History* p. 101-4. In the engraving Milo has been moved to the other side of the room and its former place taken by a statute of James Losh in marble also by Lough which was presented to the Society in 1836 as described by Robert Spence Watson, p.106. This second statue is now in the entrance hall of the Society's building.

acting for the syndicate, reported that they had bought the property for £10,000. There followed much debate: how best to raise the money and free the syndicate? A special general meeting was convened to consider the purchase and, if approved, to take it over and to alter the laws of the Society to enable its trustees to mortgage the Society's property. This done it was decided to borrow the whole of the purchase money on mortgage.

It was not then proposed to occupy any part of the newly acquired property except for one house which was occupied by the Society's porter; but, within a few years, the increasing need for repairs was causing anxiety so that when, in 1906, the Society was approached by the North East Coast Engineering Employers' Association and the North East Coast Institution of Engineers and Shipbuilders with the suggestion that rebuilding might be considered in order to provide premises for themselves, the suggestion was favourably received. A provisional agreement was entered into with the two employers' associations and laid before a special general meeting which approved the project and gave authority to build, to let the premises, and to borrow the necessary money on the security of the Society's freehold property. An architect was appointed in the person of F. W. Rich who had been in charge of restoration work after the fire in 1893. Agreement with the new tenants was completed early in 1907. There arose difficulties over light and boundary with the North Eastern Railway Company, which owned adjacent property but, because the Company also intended to rebuild, agreement was soon reached and included the building of a wall between the two properties at joint expense. The plan of the Society was to put up an office building which would accommodate, initially, the two employers' associations (who had suggested that the new building should be called Bolbec Hall), and which, with other lettings, would form an investment in support of the Society's primary activities. The financial arrangements were settled by a further charge on the property of the Society in favour of the Spencer Trustees who agreed to advance £20,000 in addition to the £10,000 already borrowed for the purchase of the site: £30,000 in all at 3½ per cent per annum on the whole loan, initially for a period of ten years. Principal contracts were entered into with Middlemiss Bros. for masonry, bricklaying and joinery, Dorman Long & Co. for iron construction work and R. Herron for plumbing.

The building was completed in 1909[1] and the tenancies of the employers' associations commenced in May. They occupied the first, second, third and fourth floors. Most of the ground floor was then let to the Yorkshire Insurance Company. The back room on the ground floor and a large room on the fifth floor were taken possession of as an extension to the Society's library. The first of these was named 'Record Room' and the second 'Bolbec Room'. The remaining rooms, four on the fifth floor, were designed as a caretaker's residence but were not so used and remained, for the time being, unlet. Later they provided accommodation for the Society's staff room, a bindery, and offices for the Northern Regional Library Bureau. All four are now let to other tenants. The two rooms used as extensions of the Society's library were vacated, the Bolbec Room in 1967, as described on pages 46-7, and the Record Room in 1970. None of the original tenants remains and the entire building is either let or available for letting.

The interdependence of the accounts of the Society and its principal investment, Bolbec Hall, has had advantages and disadvantages. The 'good' years, which have preponderated, have provided income which has cushioned the membership against rising costs and permitted the keeping of subscriptions at a lower level than would otherwise have been possible. On the other hand there have been set-backs such as the increased interest charge demanded by the Spencer Trustees in 1917, at a time when rentals were fixed, which reduced to an inadequate amount the margin from which to provide a sinking fund. In an attempt to reduce indebtedness contributions were invited from the membership but, in spite of every effort, the outstanding mortgage was still, in 1932, £19,000. At that time interest charges were reduced from $4\frac{3}{4}\%$ to $4\frac{1}{4}\%$ providing that no repayment would be

[1] Listed in 1987 as a building of special architectural and historic interest.

made for five years. What then appeared a good investment to the lender was, inevitably, rather less attractive to the borrower and so a mortgage redemption fund was started. In 1938 half the amount outstanding was repaid, but it was not until 1948 and with the aid of money received from the sale of other investments, that the debt was cleared.

A major difficulty was caused in 1972 by the necessity of substantial capital expenditure, mainly on Bolbec Hall, in order to bring the Society's buildings into line with the requirements of the Offices, Shops and Railway Premises Act and for other repairs and improvements needed, including dealing with an outbreak of dry rot in Bolbec Hall. The total cost was estimated at about £33,000 and it was clear that it would be necessary to raise two thirds of this from new sources. With very great reluctance it was decided to obtain the necessary money by a sale of books.[1] This was done. The repairs and improvements were completed in 1973. They had been supervised by the Society's architects, W. B. Edwards and Partners, and carried out by Middlemiss Bros., the firm which had put the building up in 1907-1909.

Major repairs to the roof of the Society's building were carried out in 1986. They were the first object of the Development Appeal of 1984. The work, supervised by W. B. Edwards and Partners, was done by Stanley Miller Limited. It cost £157,574 to which English Heritage contributed £63,030.

---

[1] Eighty illustrated books of natural history were sold at Sotheby's.

CHAPTER FOUR

University Extension Courses

Robert Spence Watson gives in his *History* an account of the way in which the Society became involved in the University Extension movement and of its association in this movement with the College of Physical Science which led to the affiliation of Newcastle upon Tyne to the University of Cambridge as a University Extension Centre. He noted that from the time that the Society undertook the charge of these lectures in 1882 to the Easter term of 1896 there had been 39 courses of which he gives details. The courses were held on Thursday evenings and each class was followed by a lecture. He calculated that the lectures, to which admission was free to members of the Society, had been attended by more than 90,000 people, that 7,668 had attended the classes, and that 1,023 had taken the final examinations — an average at classes, therefore, of 196, and of those who took the examinations 26.

The courses continued until 1935 when it was decided that the development of similar work by Armstrong College (as the College of Physical Science was then named) had removed the need for their continuance as part of the educational work of the Society. During this later period 70 courses were held which attracted an average attendance of 155 at lectures, 47 at classes and 8 for the examinations. As a general rule one course was given in the Lent term each year and a second in the Michaelmas term. There were departures from the usual pattern on three occasions: one, in 1898 when nine lectures on *Northumbrian history, literature and art* were given, in place of the Lent course, by Thomas Hodgkin, Robert Spence Watson, Richard Oliver Heslop and Richard Welford,[1] the second and

---

[1] The lectures were: *Roman occupation of Northumberland*, by Thomas Hodgkin; *Northumbrian story and song: six lectures*, by Robert Spence Watson; *Dialect speech in Northumberland*, by R. Oliver Heslop; *Newcastle a hundred years ago*, by Richard Welford. They were published together by the Society in 1898. This course was not a University Extension Course and has been excluded from the list which begins on p. 64.

third in 1921 and 1923 when two more courses arranged by the Society and which had been submitted to and approved by the Local Lectures Syndicate at Cambridge, were held in place of the courses arranged by Cambridge. The first of these was again on *Northumbrian history, literature and art*,[1] and the second on the *Natural history of Northumberland and Durham*. Details of these two courses are given in the appended list.

Of the men prominently associated with the University Extension Movement in Newcastle five merit special mention. To the first, Robert Spence Watson, I have paid tribute in the introduction to this work. The second, Alfred Holmes, became a member of the Society in 1870 and its Honorary Secretary from 1893 until his death in 1933. His service to the Movement was recognised by Cambridge University which conferred on him the honorary degree of M.A. A notable feature of the opening of the autumn course in 1917 was the presence of the Vice-Chancellor of Cambridge and the Secretary of the Cambridge Lecture Syndicate to do honour to the Society for its thirty-five years of continuous service to University Extension and, also, to give recognition to Alfred Holmes. The third, Richard Green Moulton, after a long career in University Extension work in this country, became Professor of Literary Theory and Interpretation in the University of Chicago. He lived from 1849 to 1924. Professor A. J. Grant, in an appreciation in the *University Extension Bulletin,* October 1924, wrote: 'With R. G. Moulton there has passed away the greatest figure in the University Extension world ... There were many lecturers but there was only one Moulton. Was there a lecture centre where he had not the record for the largest audience? Fabulous things were reported of his power of attracting.' He was a greatly appreciated lecturer at the Lit. & Phil. Five of his Cambridge University Extension courses given there are

---

[1] One of the lectures was by F. W. Dendy. His subject was *Gilds and their survivals*. It was published by the Society in 1921 together with two others of his given in the Miscellaneous Lectures Series, one in 1909 and the other in 1917, plus an essay by him on Northumberland. Dr. Dendy, lawyer and local historian, was elected a Vice-President of the Society in 1911.

listed in Spence Watson. He was very largely responsible for what his biographer[1] describes as 'a very interesting by-product of University Extension: the Backworth Classical Novel-Reading Union. Backworth is one of a group of mining villages lying between Newcastle and the Northumbrian coast at Monkseaton. When the University Extension movement came along Backworth proved one of the centres which maintained its adherence most consistently.' In 1913 Moulton gave four special lectures (not part of a university course) in the Lit. & Phil., on three plays of Shakespeare at which the average attendance was about 800. In the following year he came again with Biblical studies as his subject and attracted an average audience of about 700. He was invited again in 1915 and his lectures then were on *World literature, The Alcestis* of Euripides and *The Clouds* of Aristophanes. An average of over 500 attended. In the following year his subjects were *Marlowe, The Wandering Jew*, and *Fiction as the experimental side of philosophy* and they were listened to by an average of 400 people. He was engaged to lecture again in 1917 but wartime conditions prevented his travelling from America and his visit was postponed until 1920 when he again chose for his three lectures three plays of Shakespeare which drew an average attendance of 850.

The fourth, Alexander Hamilton Thompson, the distinguished ecclesiastical historian, who lived from 1873 until 1952, was appointed extra-mural tutor by Cambridge in 1897. In 1919 he was appointed to the staff of Armstrong College as lecturer in English, and in 1921 became Reader in Medieval History and Archaeology. In 1922 he moved to Leeds as Reader in Medieval History and, in 1924, he became Professor in the same university. In 1932 he gave the Ford lectures at Oxford and in 1933 he was Birkbeck lecturer at Trinity College, Cambridge. His greatest work of scholarship, *The English clergy and their organisation in the later Middle Ages* appeared in 1947. He was associated with the Lit. & Phil. over a long period, first as Cambridge University Extension lecturer, in which capacity he directed and supervised courses in 1902, 1905, 1906, 1907, 1910, 1915 and 1918.

[1] Moulton, W. Fiddian. *Richard Green Moulton*. London, 1926.

He also took part, after his appointment to Armstrong College, in the course in 1921 on *Northumbrian history, literature and art,* and, in 1923, in the course on *The Natural history of Northumberland and Durham.* He became a member of the Committee of the Society in 1920, and was elected a Vice-President in 1922.

The fifth, Nicholas Temperley, joined the Society in 1866, became a member of the Committee in 1892, and a Vice-President in 1916. He was especially interested in University Extension work, having himself had the distinction of passing many terminal examinations and of receiving the Gilchrist medal awarded to the best student of the year in the Cambridge centres. This was in 1907. His essay was on *Pre-Conquest architecture in Northumberland and Durham.* The course tutor was A. Hamilton Thompson.

In 1948 the Society again became host for University Extension courses but then in association with the Extra-Mural Department of King's College in the University of Durham, formerly Armstrong College. Except for a short interruption caused by the reconstruction of the Society's lecture theatre in 1966-1967 there have been courses each year since. In 1963 King's College became the University of Newcastle upon Tyne.

UNIVERSITY EXTENSION COURSES, 1897–1988

1897
The English citizen — H. S. Mundahl
The great days of Spain — H. J. Boyd Carpenter

1898
Animal and plant life — F. W. Keeble

1899
Modern problems in biology, with a discussion of the present position of Darwinism — F. W. Keeble
Music — H. H. Champion

1900
The redemption of Italy — Bernard Pares
Dante — Philip H. Wicksteed

1901
Italian art — Mrs. R. C. Witt
Photography and its relation to the science of light — J. H. Vincent

1902
Four nineteenth century novelists — A. Hamilton Thompson
Dante's *Purgatorio* — Philip H. Wicksteed

1903
Representative writers of the XIX century — J. C. Powys
The solar system — Theodore E. R. Phillips

1904
The Puritan revolution — W. Moore Ede
The system of the stars — Theodore E. R. Phillips

1905
Beginnings of Gothic architecture in England — A. Hamilton Thompson
The age of Elizabeth — R. F. Hunter

1906
History of Gothic architecture in England — A. Hamilton Thompson
The forces of nature — Douglas Carnegie

1907
Japan — Ernest Foxwell
Medieval castles and dwelling houses in England — A. Hamilton Thompson

1908
Light and sight — Douglas Carnegie
Landmarks of modern history — J. Travis Mills

1909
The Pre-Raphaelite movement: Rossetti and the unity of poetry and art — J. T. Stoughton Holborn
English statesmen of the nineteenth century — J. Travis Mills

1910
English architecture of the Renaissance and in modern times — A. Hamilton Thompson
The world's great explorers — H. Yule Oldham

1911
Men and letters in the eighteenth century — H. H. Williams
Greek art and national life — S. C. Kaines Smith

1912
History of scientific progress from the nineteenth century — G. P. Bailey
Landmarks of modern history — J. Travis Mills

1913
The production and distribution of
  national income — H. M. Hallsworth
The haunts and habits of insects — F. Balfour Browne

1914
Representative men of the nineteenth century — Harold Williams
England & her neighbours in the Far East — Ian C. Hannah

1915
English monasteries of the Middle Ages — A. Hamilton Thompson
Russia and the Russian people — Rothay Reynolds

1916
Two kindred poets: Chaucer & William Morris — Alfred J. Wyatt
Rome and the Middle Ages — J. Travis Mills

1917
Makers of modern music — E. Markham Lee
The Age of Elizabeth — J. H. B. Masterman

1918
Utopias, ancient and modern — W. H. Draper
Modern English novelists — A. Hamilton Thompson

1919
The pianoforte and its literature — E. Markham Lee
Modern art and national life — S. C. Kaines Smith

1920
Some aspects of modern geology — Albert Gilligan
England under the Stuarts — J. H. B. Masterman

1921
Northumbrian history, literature and art

12 lectures as follows: Topography, Godfrey H. Thomson; Prehistoric, A. Hadrian Allcroft; Roman occupation, F. Gerald Simpson; Anglian art and archaeology, W. G. Collingwood; Early ecclesiastical history, C. E. Osborne; Place names, A. Mawer; Historic Northumberland, K.H. Vickers; Religious houses, A. Hamilton Thompson; Military architecture, A. Hamilton Thompson; Art and artists, Walter James; Folk music, W. G. Whittaker; Gilds and their survivals, F.W. Dendy.[1]

English drama in the seventeeth century — Percy L. Babington

1922
Japanese history and civilization — J. Ingram Bryan
The appreciation of music — W. G. Whittaker

---

[1] F. W. Dendy's lecture was published by the Society.

1923
The natural history of Northumberland and Durham
12 lectures as follows: Pioneers and builders, by J. E. Hull; Geology, by David Woolacott; History and geography of the flora and fauna, by A. D. Peacock; Characteristic features of the botanical field, by J. E. Hull; Agricultural conditions and problems, by D. R. Gilchrist; Insect life, by J. W. H. Harrison; Marine biology, by F. W. Flattely; Fisheries, by A. Meek; Bird life, by George Bolam; The wild beasts, by George Bolam; Northumbrian ethnology, by A. Hamilton Thompson; General survey of local biological research, by A. D. Peacock.

Note: This course was designed to follow up the course held in 1921 on local history. Dr. J. W. H. Harrison took charge of details. At the end of the course, a conversazione and a display of literature and specimens illustrating the course was held in Armstrong College.

Ancient Egypt	A. G. K. Hayter

1924
The appreciation of painting and sculpture	S. C. Kaines Smith
Russian life and literature	C. Nabokoff

1925
Opera	P. M. S. Latham
British colonial history	Ian C. Hannah

1926
Some recent developments in modern physics	G. W. Todd
Modern literature	D. R. Hardman

1927
The history of political science from Plato to the present	R. H. Murray
The Romans in Britain	Ian C. Hannah

1928
The Bible as literature	W. H. Draper
Some modern prose writers	A. A. Brockington

1929
The story of British music	E. Markham Lee
Modern drama	L. U. Wilkinson

1930
The contemporary English novel	L. U. Wilkinson

1931
Recent developments in applied physics	E. G. Richardson

1933
Chapters from modern Indian history	J. L. Morison

1934
Exploration in the 20th century — G. H. J. Daysh

1935
The English essayists — L. U. Wilkinson

1948
Landmarks in musical history — Arthur Milner

1949
Shakespeare's contemporaries — Peter Ure
Keyboard music — Arthur Milner

1950
Restoration dramatists — Clifford Leech
Masters of keyboard music — Arthur Milner

1951
Highways in local history — Sydney Middlebrook
Music, past and present — Arthur Milner

1952
Roman Britain — I. A. Richmond
The literature of the piano — Arthur Milner

1953
The development of neo-classical art — Ralph B. Holland
The symphony — Arthur Milner

1954
Chaucer, his art and his age — D. S. Bland
The concerto — Arthur Milner

1955
Modern architecture — J. N. Napper
The sonata — Arthur Milner

1956
The English novel in the 18th century — John Butt
Music today — Arthur Milner

1957
Archaeology in the north of England — Eric Birley
Flamingoes, sooty terns and lungfish — Lord Richard Percy and the Hon. M.W. Ridley

1958
The romantic spirit in music — David Barlow

1959
Aspects of applied psychology — Various lecturers
Piano music, 1790 to the present day — David Barlow

UNIVERSITY EXTENSION COURSES

1960
About the meaning of art	Bruce Allsopp
Masterpieces of keyboard music	David Barlow

1961
Past and present problems in art	A. D. R. Tompkins
Bach and Handel	A. J. B. Hutchings

1962
Newcastle through the ages	Various lecturers
Byways of music	David Barlow

1963
Six centuries of the north of England	Various lecturers
The Christian understanding of God	Various lecturers

1964
Seven educational theorists: Plato, Cicero, Comenius, Milton, Pestalozzi, Rousseau, Newman	W. M. Williams
Byways of music, II	David Barlow

1965
Town planning	Various lecturers
Twentieth century religious thought	J. Mole

1968
Beethoven's sonatas for pianoforte	Christopher Wood

1969
The breakdown of 18th century classical form and music of the 20th century	Christopher Wood

1970
The piano music of Beethoven (excluding the sonatas), Schumann and Fauré	Christopher Wood

1971
The piano music of Brahms	Christopher Wood

1972
Chopin and his successors	Christopher Wood

1973
The pianoforte music of Haydn and Mozart and the harpsichord music of Domenico Scarlatti	Christopher Wood

1974
J. S. Bach and Mendelssohn	Christopher Wood
Old Newcastle	Constance M. Fraser[1]

[1] In association with the Society's Local History Group.

1975
Russian piano music — Christopher Wood
The growth of Newcastle since 1780 — Constance M. Fraser[1]

1976
The development of lieder — Christopher Wood
Aspects of the social history of Tyneside — N. McCord[1]

1977
The development of chamber music — Christopher Wood
Aspects of industrial development in north Northumberland — S. M. Linsley[1]

1978
The development of chamber music — Christopher Wood
Some new findings in the history of Newcastle — Miss R. B. Harbottle[1]

1979
Trends in music, 1879–1979 — Christopher Wood
Life in Roman Britain — Miss L. Allason-Jones[1]

1980
Chamber music of Beethoven, Schumann and other 19th century composers — Christopher Wood
Aspects of Roman life — Miss L. Allason-Jones[1]

1981
French music from Berlioz to the present day — Christopher Wood
Artefacts through the ages — Miss L. Allason-Jones[1]

1982
The music of Scandinavia — Christopher Wood
Science and learning in 19th century Newcastle — W. A. Campbell[1]

1983
Unfashionable composers and some unfamiliar works of recognised masters — Christopher Wood
Printing and the book trade in the North East — P. C. G. Isaac, A. I. Doyle, D. R. Esslemont and W. M. Watson

1984
A triple centenary: J. S. Bach, Handel and Domenico Scarlatti — Christopher Wood

1985
Mahler and Richard Strauss and some of their contemporaries — Christopher Wood

[1] In association with the Society's Local History Group.

1986
French and Italian opera from 1759 to the
  present day   Christopher Wood
1987
The music of Czechoslovakia   Christopher Wood
1988
The chamber music of Beethoven   Christopher Wood

CHAPTER FIVE

Miscellaneous Lectures, Special Lectures, Films and Wireless Discussion Groups, 1896-1989

MISCELLANEOUS LECTURES

Spence Watson provides, in an appendix to his *History,* a list of the miscellaneous lectures delivered to the Society. It ends with seven given in the session 1895-1896. On pages 78-103 the list is continued beginning with the remaining twelve in 1895-1896. Thereafter the division into sessions has been abandoned in favour of division by years.

Miscellaneous lectures, given in the Society's lecture theatre, usually on Monday evenings, were an important part of the Society's activities. Between the years 1897 and 1922 they attracted an average audience for each lecture of about 500, reaching a peak of over 600 in each of the three years after the 1914-1918 war. From 1923 there was a generally progressive decline in attendances which was accounted for by the rival claims of the cinema and radio; and, although lectures were arranged during most of the succeeding years, and still feature in the Society's programmes, the great days of the public lecture as a means of instruction and entertainment have passed.

An examination of the lecture programmes for the years 1898, 1900, 1906, 1916 and 1919, which were not untypical, will show something of their range and quality and will also add some flesh to the bare bones of the list.

In 1898 two lectures by Arnold Dolmetsch, the first on *Old musical instruments,* and the other on *English music of the 16th and 17th centuries* were given to audiences of 603 and 760. In the same year Professor H. Stroud's lecture on *Lord Armstrong's experiments in electrical discharge* was of special interest because

Lecture Theatre 1860-1966 ▷

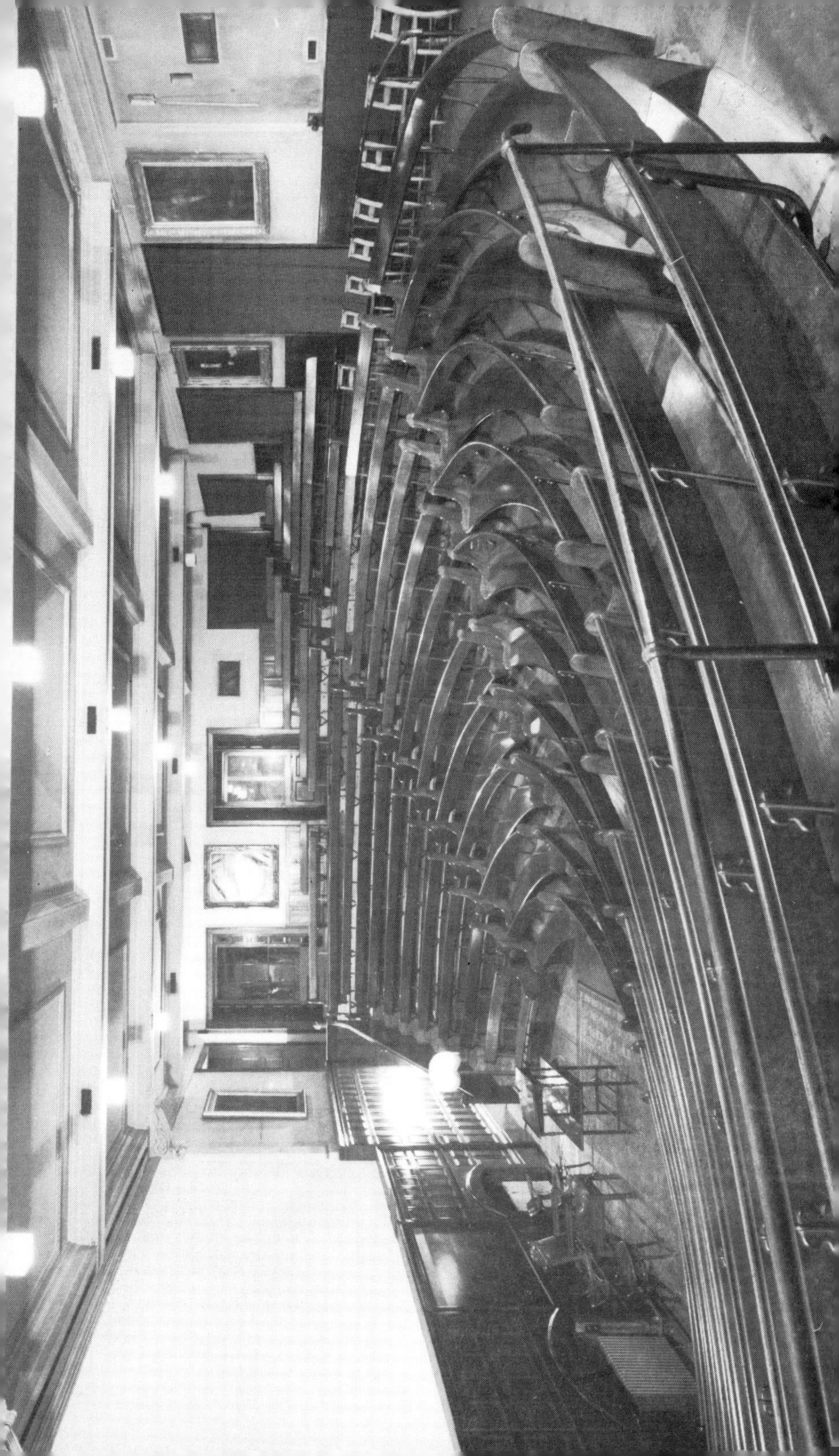

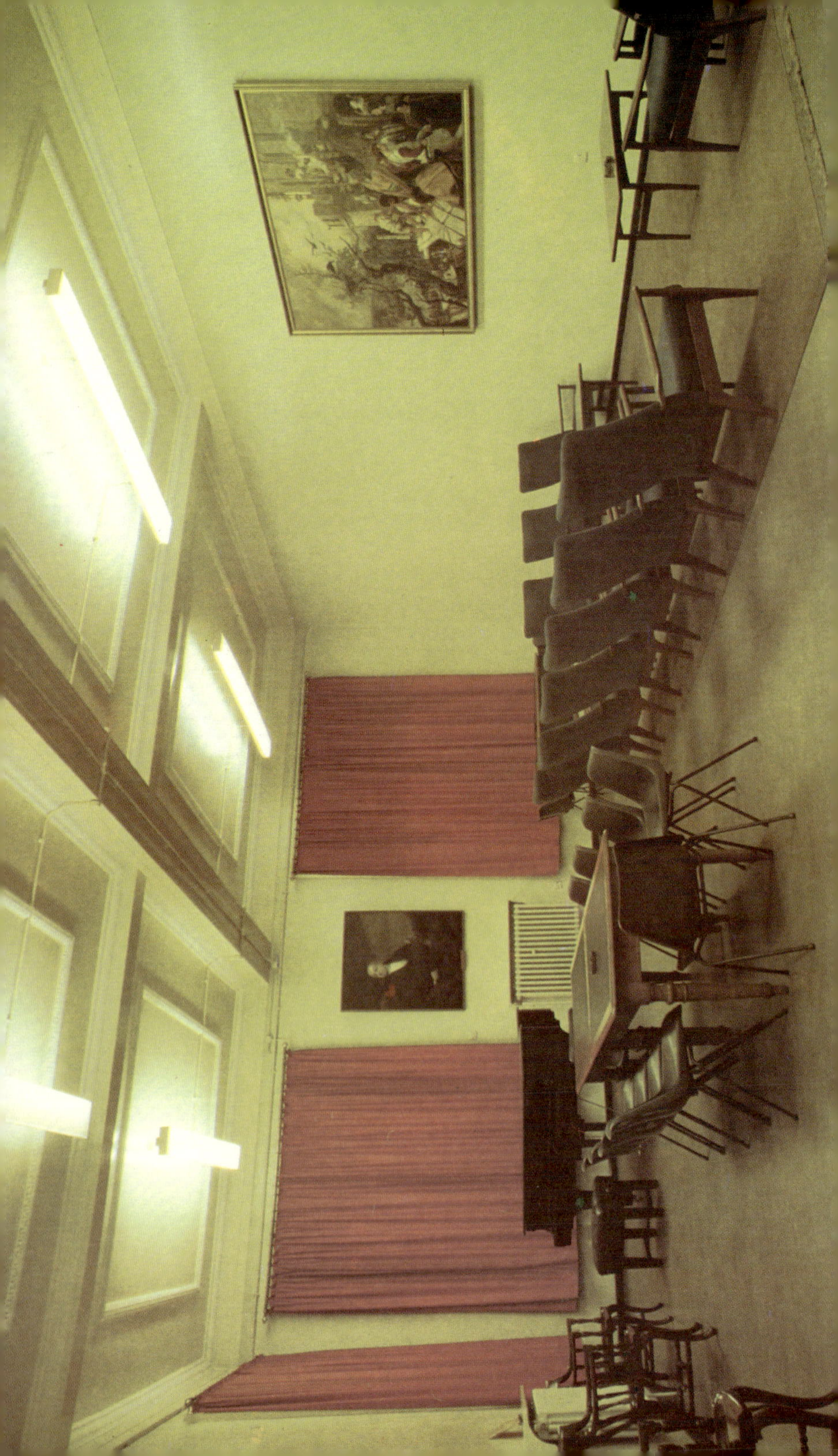

it formed a continuation of Lord Armstrong's *Experimental lecture on the novel effects of electrical discharge* which had been delivered to the Society at its centenary celebration in February 1893. Professor Stroud's lecture was illustrated by the apparatus used by Lord Armstrong in his researches at Cragside and included the famous Wimshurst machine which Lord Armstrong had presented to the College of Physical Science. Also in 1898 J. W. Swan lectured to an audience of 552 on *Modern developments in photography*. Joseph Wilson Swan was a member of the Society from 1851 until his death in 1914. In 1881 he was elected a Vice-President and became President in 1911. He was knighted in 1904. In 1879 he demonstrated to an audience of 700 his incandescent carbon electric lamp.[1] In the following year he lectured on *The progress of electric lighting;* the year after on *The storage of electricty* and, the year after that, again on *Progress in electric lighting.* In 1892 his subject was *Electro-metallurgy*, in 1898, photography, as mentioned above, and, finally, in 1903, he gave two lectures on *Fire and light.*

In 1900 Thomas Hodgkin gave two lectures on *English poets and the redemption of Italy.* The University Extension course in the spring of that year on *The redemption of Italy* and for which the lecturer was Bernard Pares, suggested the subject to him. Thomas Hodgkin, Fellow of University College, London, D.C.L. Oxford and Durham, D. Litt. Dublin, became a member of the Society in 1859, the year in which he settled in Newcastle as one of the founders of the banking firm of Hodgkin, Barnett, Pease and Spence. He died in 1913 in his

[1] In 1979 Dr. R. C. Chirnside, who was, until his retirement, Chief Chemist at the Hirst Research Centre of the General Electric Co. Ltd., and who began his career in chemistry as a pupil in the laboratory of John Pattinson a brother-in-law of Sir Joseph Swan and a distinguished consulting chemist in Newcastle upon Tyne, marked the centenary of Swan's demonstration of his electric lamp by giving a lecture to the Society which was printed as: Chirnside, R.C. *Sir Joseph Wilson Swan, F.R.S., pharmacist, chemist, electrical engineer . . . Lecture to the Literary and Philosophical Society, Newcastle upon Tyne, 14th February, 1979.* Newcastle, The Literary and Philosophical Society, 1979.

◊ Loftus Room

eighty-second year and in the report of the Society for that year it was written of him: 'To the calls of his own profession he added an active participation with the community at large in many phases of its religious, social, intellectual and political life. Yet, with so much expenditure of time and energy in public concerns, he achieved a place in the commonwealth of letters which will be marked by the eight volumes of *Italy and her invaders* and by many other contributions to literature . . . To the work of the Literary and Philosophical Society he brought the qualities of his enthusiastic nature. In 1862 he was elected a member of the Committee, in 1875 he became Honorary Treasurer which office he held for fourteen years. In the year previous to his election as Treasurer he delivered two lecturers to our members on *Claudian, the last of the Roman poets.* These were succeeded by, in 1878, *Aqueleia, the precursor of Venice,* in 1881, *A visit to the Saalburg; or, the Roman Wall in Germany,* in 1898, *The Roman occupation of Northumberland.* In 1900 he gave the two lectures mentioned above, and in 1907, he gave his last lecture to the Society on *The Lord Wardens of the Marches.* He became a Vice-President of the Society in 1891.'[1]

In its report for 1906 the Committee drew attention to growing interest in the miscellaneous lectures, the average attendance having reached 548. As usual there were twenty of these lectures during the year and admission to five of them had been limited to members and associates in response to complaints that there had been occasions in previous years when members had been unable to gain admission because seats had been taken by the public. Members and associates always had free admission to lectures but, at this time, non-members were able to buy course tickets for five shillings or tickets for single lectures for one shilling each. The five 'restricted' lectures were: *To Lhasa and the Valley of the Brahmaputra,* by Major C. H. D. Ryder, R.E., Principal Survey Officer of the Thibet Expedition, *Dramatic*

---

[1] There is a biography: Creighton, Louise. *The life and letters of Thomas Hodgkin.* 1917. Also an obituary notice by F.W. Dendy in *Archaeologia Aeliana,* 3rd series Vol. IX which includes a bibliography. Dr. Hodgkin was a Vice-President of the Society of Antiquaries of Newcastle upon Tyne.

recital, by Ernest Denny, *Jacobitism and Jacobite songs*, by Miss Mary Wilson, *Dramatic recital* by Alexander Watson, and *Dramatic recital* by Miss Ellen Bowick. There was an average attendance for these five of about 750.

Despite the difficulties caused by wartime conditions the average attendance at the miscellaneous lectures in 1916 was 377. The programme was as follows:

Illuminated manuscripts, by John A. H. Herbert, Assistant Keeper of MSS, British Museum; *Medieval figure sculpture*, by E. S. Prior, Professor of Fine Art, University of Cambridge; *The stories of Anton Tchekov*, by W. H. Hadow, Principal of Armstrong College; *The Dogger Bank as a geological study*, by Percy F. Kendall, Professor of Geology, Leeds University; *Virgil's picture of the after-life*, by R. S. Conway, Professor of Latin, Manchester University; *Economics of the War*, by S. J, Chapman, Professor of Political Economy, Manchester University; *The migration of fishes*, by Alex. Meek, Professor of Zoology, Armstrong College; *The tragedy of German history*, by Edmond G. A. Holmes, late Chief Inspector of Elementary Schools; *Lewis Carroll*, by A. C. Benson, Master of Magdalene College, Cambridge; *Unconscious nerves*, by C. S. Sherrington, Waynflete Professor of Physiology, Oxford University; *English Castles and fortified manor houses*, by E. S. Prior, Slade Professor of Fine Art, University of Cambridge; *National England and national Russia*, by Stephen Graham; *Shakespeare as historian*, by F. J. C. Hearnshaw, Professor of Medieval History, University of London; *Industry and commerce after the War*, by S. J. Chapman, Professor of Political Economy, Manchester University; *Music and the War*, by H. Walford Davies, Organist and Director of the Choir at the Temple Church, London; *Napoleon's idea of England*, by H. A. L. Fisher, Vice-Chancellor of Sheffield University; *The mountains of the moon*, by A. R. Hinks, Secretary of the Royal Geographical Society; *Dr. Johnson*, by John C. Bailey; *The Rising of the Earls, 1569*, by the Rev. H. Gee, Master of University College, Durham.

1919 was the year in which the Society's membership of over five thousand was the highest in its history. The miscellaneous lectures in that year are shown below in descending order of popularity, with the largest attendance 850, which was, presumably, the absolute limit afforded by the accommodation because the first three lectures had attendances of precisely that figure. The smallest attendance was 298. They were: *Foch,* by Sir F. B. Maurice; *Folksongs of the Southern Appalachians,* by Cecil Sharp; *Songs of the Hebrides,* by Mrs. Kennedy Fraser; *Modern British folk music settings,* by W. G. Whittaker; *Old English music, dances and musical instruments,* by Arnold Dolmetsch; *My four and a half years as prisoner of war,* by Edgar L. Bainton; *Sir Walter Scott,* by R. S. Rait; *The troubadours,* by Ezra Pound; *The organ of hearing,* by Arthur Keith, Hunterian Professor, Royal College of Surgeons; *Some aspects of social reconstruction after the war,* by Stephen McKenna; *What we owe to Greece,* by T. R. Glover; *Flying and the future of the air,* by W. T. Blake; *The golden eagle and other mountain birds,* by Seton Gordon; *Some people I have known,* by Henry W. Nevinson; *Edmund Burke's social and political philosophy,* by C. E. Osborne; *Illusions of time and space,* by A. S. Eddington; *The rivers of the coal age,* by Percy F. Kendall.

At this time (1919) it was still possible for members of the public to buy session tickets for the miscellaneous lectures and 97 of these were sold; but in 1922 it was decided to exclude non-members because of continued difficulties over seating. In later years a relaxation of this rule permitted members to bring friends and this arrangement continued until 1988 when the Society's miscellaneous lectures were open to the public free of charge.

SPECIAL LECTURES

In addition to its University Extension courses, its miscellaneous lectures and its Robert Spence Watson lectures the Society arranged, from time to time, special lectures. Their purpose was either to mark a special occasion or to give prominence to a particular lecturer. There were four of these special lectures in the spring of 1913. The first, upon Wagner's *Ring,* was given by Nicholas Kilburn and it furnished an introduction to the first performance of *The Ring* in Newcastle upon Tyne. The other three were given by R. G. Moulton[1] who gave a further three in 1914. There was one

[1] See p. 62

more in 1914: it was by John Talbot and his subject was *The origin of the War*. In 1915 Moulton lectured on three occasions, as he did in the following year and again in 1920. In 1943 the 150th anniversary of the Society's foundation was marked by a special series of lectures which dealt with literature, science, fiction and music in 1793. The lecturers were G. M. Young,[1] J. R. Partington, James Laver and J. A. Westrup. In 1971 Sydney Middlebrook gave his lecture on *The advancement of knowledge in Newcastle upon Tyne*,[2] and in 1979 R. C. Chirnside lectured upon Sir Joseph Swan.[3]

LECTURES IN FRENCH, GERMAN AND ITALIAN
Short courses, each of three or four lectures, were held on Wednesdays. The first of these was in 1899 and the average attendance was 161. Further courses were held, one in each of the following years, until 1912. They were resumed in 1918 and continued until 1922. In that year 362 tickets for the series were issued free to students of high and secondary schools. Some disappointment was felt that, despite this, the average attendance was only 239.

FILMS
In 1933 the Society itself began to hold exhibitions of films, mainly documentary and educational in character, and beginning with John Grierson's *Drifters*. It continued to do so in 1934 and 1935. There was a break until 1944 when they again appeared in the programme as they did in most of the following years until 1957 when they were finally discontinued because of small attendances. There were links between this particular activity of the Society and its lecture programmes. In 1937 there were lectures on the film by John Grierson, Basil Wright, R. S. Lambert and Ivor Montagu. In 1948 Paul Rotha and in 1949 Ralph Bond gave Ernest Dyer Memorial Lectures in conjunction with the Tyneside Film Society.

WIRELESS DISCUSSION GROUPS
In 1930 two of these groups were formed in connection with B.B.C. talks one of which was organised by the Newcastle

[1] The MS of G. M. Young's lecture 'English literature as it was in and about 1793' is held in the Library.
[2] See p. 2 and note.
[3] See note to p. 73.

Economic Circle which was formed, under the auspices of the Society, from the old Newcastle Economic Society. These groups continued to meet until 1933.

MISCELLANEOUS LECTURES 1896-1989

1896

Röntgen's photography of the invisible	A. A. Campbell Swinton
Pan to Pinafore: a history of the flute	John Radcliff
Scenery, customs, folk life and folk lore in Iceland	Jon Stefansson
Holiday geography	H. R. Mill
Albrecht Dürer	J. W. Rowntree
Music in school life	John Farmer
The invaders of Egypt, 3,000 B.C.	W. M. Flinders Petrie
The true use of books	J. Churton Collins
Unfelt movements of the earth's crust	John Milne
The natives of our East African Empire	J. W. Gregory
Some literary associations of the Lake District	Canon Rawnsley
Modern explosives	V. B. Lewes

N.B:— Also in this year are the final 7 lectures listed by Spence Watson.

1897

Wordsworth	P. H. Wicksteed
Life on the surface of the water	L. C. Miall
Schubert	Miss Wakefield
Jean Jacques Rousseau	Walter Emm
The Crown of St. Awdrey and her Minster in the Fens	Dean Stubbs
A medieval abbey	D. H. S. Cranage
Diamonds	H. P. Gurney
How we hear musical tones	J. G. McKendrick
Death and the underworld as seen on Greek monuments	Jane E. Harrison
Travel and exploration in unfamiliar Japan	Walter Weston
Wagner as a mystic with impressions of the Bayreuth Festival, 1897	Alice Cleather and Basil Crump
Joan of Arc	J. R. Baterden
The work of frost and ice in temperate and arctic regions	E. J. Garwood
The modes in which animals conceal themselves from their enemies	E. B. Poulton
Soap bubbles	C. V. Boys
The songs of Schumann	Miss Wakefield
The Malay Peninsula and its people	H. Louis

MISCELLANEOUS LECTURES

1897 (cont.)

Personal reminiscences of exploring service in the China Sea	William Blakeney
The coronation of the Czar	Canon Rawnsley
The geographical distribution of Old English poetry	Israel Gollancz

1898

Musical form	Jas. M. Preston
Old musical instruments	Arnold Dolmetsch
French men and French manners	Albert D. Vandam
Travel and adventures in South Africa	F. C. Selous
The life of a star	A. H. Fison
The tundras and steppes of prehistoric Europe	Jas. Geikie
Haunts and habits of British birds	Richard Kearton
Pre-Conquest architecture in England	C. C. Hodges
Modern developments of photography	J. W. Swan
Durham College: University life before the Reformation	G. W. Kitchin
Medieval architecture	Arnold Mitchell
The world of words and its explorers	J. A. H. Murray
Some living poets	William Archer
Ideals of womanhood	Mrs. Fawcett
Lord Armstrong's experiments in electrical discharge	H. Stroud
English music of the 16th and 17th centuries	Arnold Dolmetsch
Northern Northumbria as revealed to us by excavations	Thomas Hodgkin
Tennyson's *Idylls of the King*	A. B. Boyd Carpenter
The art of Sir John Millais	Whitworth Wallis
The spirit of Greek art	C. Waldstein
A Cistercian abbey in the Middle Ages	D. H. S. Cranage

1899

Readings from *As you like it* and recitations	Mrs. Kendal
Song-form and accompaniment	Miss Annie Glen
The evolution of scenery	R. D. Roberts
The industrial development of the century	W. Moore Ede
Afghanistan and its people	Miss L. Hamilton
Insect architects and engineers	F. Enock
The milky way	A. H. Fison
The process of pattern design	Lewis F. Day
Bacteria, their nature and functions	E. E. Klein
Egyptian art	W. M. Flinders Petrie
The floor of the ocean	Sir John Murray

1899 (cont.)

Old buildings and the story they tell	Arnold Mitchell
The Jenolan caves of New South Wales	Rev. Father Gurrin
Some experiences in West Africa	Mary Kingsley
The Choral symphony	H. H. Champion
The music of Shakespeare	Arnold Dolmetsch
Some further experiences on the coasts of Corea and Japan	Wm. Blakeney
Whales and whale fishing	Frank T. Bullen
The physical nature of vowel sounds as revealed by the phonograph	J. G. McKendrick

1900

Butterflies at home and abroad	Hugh Richardson
An evening with the poets, dramatists and humorists	Ernest Denny
Voyages in cloudland	J. M. Bacon
Dramatic recital	Ernest Denny
Handel's *Messiah*	A. H. Mann
The British Museum Library	Richard Garnett
Tennyson's *Enid and Geraint*	A. B. Boyd Carpenter
Musical evening	Mr. and Mrs. Henschel
Newcastle gilds and trading companies	F. W. Dendy
Arthur Hugh Clough	R. Spence Watson
English poets and the redemption of Italy	Thos. Hodgkin
The philological and ethnological importance of modern English dialects	Joseph Wright
National music, ancient and modern	John Radcliff
English poets and the redemption of Italy, Lecture II	Thos. Hodgkin
The cure of consumption	Sir John Crichton Browne
The national value of science	Karl Pearson
England's debt to Shakespeare	Sidney Lee
William Morris's *Earthly Paradise*	Owen Seaman
"Mere man"	Sarah Grand
Liquid air	Arthur Smithells

1901

Dramatic recital	Mrs. Kendal
England and Europe	Bernard Pares
Sketching and sketchers	Geo. C. Haite
Wireless telegraphy	Oliver Lodge
The Arthurian legend	C. E. Vaughan
Ruskin and his work	R. Warwick Bond

1901 (cont.)

Dramatic recital	Ernest Denny
Some English and French cathedrals compared	Arnold Mitchell
History as saga	Maurice Hewlett
The novelists of last century	Walter Frewen Lord
The future of Russia	Bernard Pares
The natives of South Eastern Africa	Miss A. Werner
The Wallace Collection	M. H. Spielmann
The basis of heredity	Karl Pearson
Amongst the wild hillmen of Northern India	Sir George Robertson
Flemish painters of the fifteenth century	Mrs. Witt
"Flame"	Arthur Smithells
The reform of history	John M. Robertson
Dramatic recital	Ernest Denny

1902

The Simplon Tunnel and its construction	Thomas Oliver
Principles of musical style	W. H. Hadow
Black and White in South Africa	Miss Friend
Dramatic recital	Katherine E. Oliver
Lines of force in a magnetic field	H. S. Hele-Shaw
Bach's well tempered clavier	Ebenezer Prout
Thomas Carlyle	H. C. Shelley
The history of a fly	L. C. Miall
A study of electric fishes	J. G. McKendrick
The legend of Hamlet	Israel Gollancz
The Brontes	Alice Meynell
Character reading: a scientific inquiry as to how far characters can be predicted from externals	Karl Pearson
Insect-borne diseases	Ronald Ross
Caricature in and out of Parliament	E. T. Reed
The natural history of a town garden	L. C. Miall
The Garden City Scheme	John M. Robertson
Newcastle beautiful; or the possibilities of floriculture in a city	W. Errington Cowan
British contemporary sculpture	M. H. Spielmann
Dramatic recital	Ernest Denny
Social life in the reign of James I	G. M. Trevelyan

1903

The British Empire illustrated by its postage stamps for 50 years	Hugh Richardson
Fire and light	J. W. Swan

1903 (cont.)

The glaciers of Kangchenjunga	E. J. Garwood
Dramatic recital	Ernest Denny
Bees and beekeeping	Sidney Smith
Songs of the sea	A. Foxton Ferguson
Newton and his times	R. A. Sampson
The West Indian eruptions	Tempest Anderson
Forgotten cities of Ancient Mexico	Wm. Corner
The Caucasian Alps	H. Woolley
Sir Arthur Sullivan and his music	Bertha Moore
The Field of the Cloth of Gold, Delhi, 1903	E. T. Reed
The Cathedral of Siena	R. Langton Douglas
The songs and ballads of Schubert and Loewe	Wm. McConnell Wood
The art of Turner	Mrs. R. C. Witt
Trinidad and the pitch lake	Henry Louis
The men of the French Revolution	Hilaire Belloc
First impressions of Spain	Canon Bulkeley
A sonata of Beethoven	W. H. Hadow

1904

The Greek statues from a wreck off Cerigotto	E. A. Gardner
Recital of Tennyson's *Enoch Arden*	Mrs. Cumberlege
Dante and the traveller	Maurice Hewlett
The fur seal islands of the North Pacific	G. E. H. Barrett-Hamilton
Natural selection	W. R. Weldon
American democracy	J. A. Hobson
An old gravel bed at Newbiggin	R. G. A. Bullerwell
The Roman desertion of Britain	J. B. Bury
Korea	C. T. Collyer
Music in the home two hundred years ago	Arnold Dolmetsch
The origin of seed-bearing plants	D. H. Scott
The earliest kings of Egypt	W. M. Flinders Petrie
The romance and mystery of India	Sarath Kumar Ghosh
Dramatic recital	Alexander Watson
Wild animals I have known	Ernest Thompson Seton
The pearl fisheries of Ceylon	W. A. Herdman
Radium	W. A. Hampson
Orchids	J. Bidgood
Some aspects of the modern stage	A. B. Walkley

1905

Songs of Northumberland	W. H. Hadow
Dramatic recital	Ernest Denny

1905 (cont.)

The eyes in animals and man	Wm. Stirling
Old English and Scottish ballads	G. K. Chesterton
Three centuries of English song	Bertha Moore
Owls	R. Bosworth Smith
Russia	Bernard Pares
The siege of Port Arthur as I saw it	Ellis Ashmead Bartlett
Egypt and early Europe	W. M. Flinders Petrie
The native races of the British East Africa Protectorate	Sir Charles Eliot
Famous London houses	'John O' London' (Wilfred Whitten)
Across the Pyrenees	T. T. Norgate
Stanley and the development of Africa	J. W. Gregory
The retreat from Moscow	Bernard Pares
Early photography	Walter Corder
The brains and minds of animals	Alex. Hill
The total eclipse of 30th August, 1905	H. H. Turner
Picturesque Morocco	Budgett Meakin
Musical scales and their influence in composition	W. H. Hadow

1906

To Lhasa and the valley of the Brahmaputra	C. H. D. Ryder
Dramatic recital	Ernest Denny
The Bronze Age	Ernest A. Parkyn
The influence of physical geography on the destiny of nations	Hilaire Belloc
Recent discoveries in heredity	Wm. Bateson
The service man afloat	L. Cope Cornford
Jacobitism and Jacobite songs	Mary Wilson
The extermination of disease	C. W. Saleeby
Dramatic recital	Alexander Watson
Bacterial purification of sewage	Gilbert J. Fowler
Bach, with instrumental and vocal illustrations	John E. Jeffries
The origin of life	J. Butler Burke
Bavaria, romantic and paintable	H. von Herkomer
The relation of flies to disease	A. E. Shipley
Water as a sphere of life	L. C. Miall
Ice, water, steam	W. Hampson
Greek classical dress in life and art	G. Baldwin Brown
Dramatic recital	Ellen Bowick
William Tell	G. W. Kitchin
Recent discoveries in Sparta	R. C. Bosanquet

1907

Opera in the 18th century	W. H. Hadow
Dramatic recital	Ernest Denny
Forgotten English composers	R. R. Terry
Garibaldi and the liberation of Italy	J. Holland Rose
Modern nations: a comparison of development	Hilaire Belloc
The paintings of Titian	D. S. McColl
A performance of Mendelssohn's music to *Antigone*	John E. Jeffries
The land of the Black Mountain	T. T. Norgate
Aristotle in literature and history	C. H. Eastwood
Dramatic recital	Ellen Bowick
Sinai	W. M. Flinders Petrie
Buddhist shrines	Gertrude Lowthian Bell
Weather forecasting	W. Marriott
Parody	Owen Seaman
Recent astronomical discoveries	Theodore Phillips
Dramatic interpretation of Shakespeare's *Twelfth Night*	W. J. Morrison
Saxon architecture in Northumbria	G. Baldwin Brown
Volcanoes	W. H. Garrison
Recent developments in the progress of aerial navigation	H. S. Hele-Shaw
The Bacchants of Euripides	A. W. Verrall

1908

Schubert's songs	W. H. Hadow
Edmund Burke	Walter Raleigh
Folk-songs	Cecil Sharp
In the path of the eagles: Elba as it was and is	T. T. Norgate
The Ice Age in the North of England	Percy F. Kendall
The women of Athens	A. J. Grant
Recent advances in the study of heredity	Wm. Bateson
Dramatic recital	Alexander Watson
Alfred Stevens, sculptor and painter	D. S. McColl
Japanese prints	Laurence Binyon
The Frogs of Aristophanes	A. W. Verrall
The Bismarck Archipelago	B. Pullen-Burry
The animals of South Africa, recent and fossil	Richard Lydekker
The literature round Edward III	Geo. Neilson
Christian architecture in Central Asia Minor	Gertrude Lowthian Bell

1908 (cont.)

Thoughts and words: a study in the psychology of expression	Alex. Hill
Early Britain	Sir John Rhys
Border history	Thos. Hodgkin
Among the savages of British New Guinea	A. H. Dunning
Trees, old and new	Wm. Somerville
Anthony van Dyck	Lionel Cust
Christmas and the drama	Israel Gollancz

1909

English folk song	Cecil Sharp
Artillery progress since 1850	Sir Andrew Noble
English town life in the Middle Ages	J. H. B. Masterman
The White City	W. Errington Cowen
A humorist at large	L. Raven Hill
A recital of Sophocles	W. J. Morrison
The arrival of man in Britain	Percy F. Kendall
Discoveries at Memphis and Thebes	W. M. Flinders Petrie
The National theatre	Wm. Archer
The making of Newcastle	F. W. Dendy[1]
Dramatic recital	Ellen Bowick
The origin of the white man	Karl Pearson
Painting in England from Holbein to Hogarth	Herbert Thompson
Chili and the Chilians	G. F. Scott Elliot
Samuel Johnson	E. H. Blakeney
Across the High Carpathians	T. T. Norgate
Dramatic recital	Alexander Watson
The making of prints	Walter S. Corder
Comedy and the comic spirit	J. H. B. Masterman
The sun's surface and surroundings	A. L. Cortie

1910

Robert Schumann	W. H. Hadow
The coming of the aeroplane	Eric Stuart Bruce
The natural history of sea fish in relation to economic problems	A. T. Masterman
Dew ponds	Geo. Hubbard
Secrets in sands	C. Carus-Wilson
The triumph of Athena: Athens and the Panathenaea in the time of Pericles	S. C. Kaines Smith
The senses: newsagents to the mind	Alex. Hill

[1] Published by the Society.

1910 (cont.)

The Panama Canal	Vaughan Cornish
Workmanship in Ancient Egypt	W. M. Flinders Petrie
Euripides	Gilbert Murray
Matavanu: a new volcano in German Samoa	Tempest Anderson
Malaria	Ronald Ross
William Blake	John Masefield
Pioneering in West Africa	Broome P. Smith
The Greek ideal of woman	S. C. Kaines Smith
The life of the deep sea	J. Arthur Thomson
Schumann's songs	W. H. Hadow
Life and way of the Buddha	Reginald Farrer
A night with Irish fairies	Alfred Percival Graves
Wagner	Rutland Boughton
William Hazlitt	Walter Raleigh

1911

Bells and bell tones	W. W. Starmer
The Great Civil War in the North	J. A. R. Marriott
Musical realism	Miss M. M. Paget, assisted by Kenneth Swan
On growing old	Mrs. Mandell Creighton
King Charles I: the last phase	A. J. Grant
Jamaica	Vaughan Cornish
Limestone and coral reefs	C. Carus-Wilson
Cambridge University	E. S. Roberts
Egypt and early Europe	W. M. Flinders Petrie
The gates of North America: a study in social geography	H. J. Mackinder
Music of the future	Rutland Boughton
A plant collector abroad	Reginald Farrer
Christmas carols	W. H. Hadow
The phenomena of splashes	A. W. Worthington
The art of Sir Edward Burne-Jones	Whitworth Wallis
The origin and development of armory	C. H. Hunter Blair
Plant animals	F. W. Keeble
The necessary theatre	Granville Barker
Carillons and carillon music	W. W. Starmer

1912

Cavour and the unification of Italy	J. A. R. Marriott
Old English poetry and the Bible	I. Gollancz
Natural history of spiders	J. Arthur Thomson
Rain and its work	C. Carus-Wilson

1912 (cont.)

The evolution of the printed book	Walter S. Corder
The Blackfeet Indians	Walter McClintock
Star drift	H. H. Turner
Parenthood and race culture	Caleb W. Saleeby
British art of to-day	M. H. Spielmann
Glastonbury lake village	H. St. George Gray
Rembrandt's etchings	Arthur M. Hind
The origin of Alpine scenery	E. J. Garwood
The excavations at Corstopitum	R. H. Forster
The Balkan States	Alex. Taylor
The ancient civilizations of Mexico and Peru	C. Reginald Enock
The Mendelian phenomena	A. D. Darbishire
Radioactivity	W. H. Bragg
Some English song writers	W. H. Hadow
Through birdland byways	Oliver G. Pike
Newcastle Glee and Madrigal Society: a selection of glees, etc	Comments by W. H. Hadow

1913

John Ruskin	Sir E. T. Cook
The landward gate of India	H. J. Mackinder
Stonehenge	T. Rice Holmes
English folk songs and dance airs	Cecil Sharp
Camera adventures in the African wilds	A. Radcliffe Dugmore
Thought and feeling in music	H. Walford Davies
The Pele towers of Northumberland	D. D. Dixon
The romance of the Red Indian	Walter McClintock
Ancient hunters and primeval art	W. J. Sollas
Meroë: four years excavation in the Ethiopian capital	John Garstang
The great observatories of the world	H. H. Turner
Voice and verse	H. Walford Davies
The colours of flowers	F. W. Keeble
The siege of Newcastle	F. J. C. Hearnshaw
The new discoveries at the Pyramids	F. F. Ogilvie
The web of life	J. Arthur Thomson
French music of the 16th to 18th centuries	Arnold Dolmetsch
X-rays and crystals	W. H. Bragg
Political satire and John Dryden	Sir Walter Raleigh
British New Guinea	A. C. Haddon
Newcastle Glee and Madrigal Society: a selection of glees	

1914

Albrecht Dürer	Arthur M. Hind
The early civilization of Northern Greece	Maurice S. Thompson
Curio hunting	Sir J. H. Yoxall
Jonathan Swift	W. H. Hadow
Witchcraft in England	Herbert Hensley Henson
The romance of cave exploration	Ernest A. Baker
The wild life of the Cornish cliffs	J. C. Tregarthen
Northumbrian customs and folk lore	D. D. Dixon
Landmarks in the history of the Eastern question	A. J. Grant
Life in contemporary literature	F. C. Sumichrast
The methods of anthropology as applied to early Mediterranean civilization	L. R. Farnell
Nietzsche	W. H. Hadow
Futurism and form in poetry	Henry Newbolt
The Irishman in English fiction	J. O. Hannay (George Birmingham)
The harpsichord toccatas of Bach	J. A. Fuller-Maitland
Soil bacteria and plant nutrition	W. B. Bottomley
Poetry and patriotism	Henry Newbolt
The natural history of the ancients	D'Arcy W. Thompson
The music of the troubadours	Barbara Smythe
The Great Fire of London as seen by contemporaries	Herbert Hensley Henson
German imperialism as it is to-day	Claude Coffin

1915

The War: its history and its moral	A. F. Pollard
Art and life in Japan	Yoshio Markino
Newcastle as a medieval border fortress	F. J. C. Hearnshaw
The power of poetry in history	R. S. Conway
The making of fiords	J. W. Gregory
The reconstruction of history	S. C. Kaines Smith
The stars and their motions	A. S. Eddington
The structure of metals: some revelations of the microscope	Thomas Turner
Insects and the war	A. E. Shipley
Lister and war surgery	Sir Rickman Godlee
England and Turkey	Sir Edwin Pears
The religion of Russia	Stephen Graham
Mary Stuart and Elizabeth: the first phase	R. S. Tait
To the untrained listener	H. Walford Davies

1915 (cont.)

Modern artillery	A. G. Hadcock
Some problems of the war	John Talbot
The essential quality in art	Clive Bell

1916

Illuminated manuscripts	John A. Herbert
Medieval figure sculpture	E. S. Prior
The stories of Anton Tchekov	W. H. Hadow
The Dogger Bank as a geological study	Percy F. Kendall
Virgil's picture of the after-life	R. S. Conway
Economics of the War	S. J. Chapman
The migration of fishes	Alex. Meek
The tragedy of German history	Edmond G. A. Holmes
Lewis Carroll	A. C. Benson
Unconscious nerves	C. S. Sherrington
English castles and fortified manor houses	E. S. Prior
National England and national Russia	Stephen Graham
Shakespeare as historian	F. J. C. Hearnshaw
Industry and commerce after the war	S. J. Chapman
Music and the war	H. Walford Davies
Napoleon's idea of England	H. A. L. Fisher
The mountains of the moon	A. R. Hinks
Dr. Johnson	John Bailey
The Rising of the Earls, 1569 and the local connection	The Rev. H. Gee

1917

Sea songs and shanties	R. R. Terry
The position of women after the war	John A. Hobson
The original music of Shakespeare's plays	Mr. & Mrs. Arnold Dolmetsch
Education after the War	W. H. Hadow
Plants and the seasons	F. W. Keeble
The place of art in the community	W. Rothenstein
Valasquez and Rembrandt	S. C. Kaines Smith
Birds of Holy Island	E. L. Turner
Recent excavations in Mesopotamia	L. W. King
Melody	H. Walford Davies
Don Quixote	John Bailey
Egyptian jewelry	W. M. Flinders Petrie
The crab and its migrations	Alex. Meek

1917 (cont.)

William of Alnwick: a bishop and his household in the 15th century	A. Hamilton Thompson
Exoticism in British music	W. G. Whittaker
Some mediaeval seals at Durham	C. H. Hunter Blair
English madrigals	E. H. Fellowes
Without the city wall	F. W. Dendy[1]

1918

Astronomy in daily use	A. B. Hinks
Baghdad, Nineveh and Babylon	J. T. Parfit
The British School of Painting	B. Stevenson
The English as seen through the eyes of the enemy	J. W. Oman
Disraeli	Sir W. H. Hadow
Mammals of Northumberland	George Bolam
The women of Rome	A. J. Grant
Creative capital	A Clutton-Brock
Westminster Abbey	J. H. B. Masterman
Phrasing, repartee and word-play in music	H. Walford Davies
Tragedy	W. Macneile Dixon
The spectroscope in some recent astronomical researches	Theodore E. R. Phillips
The mariners of England	A. Corbett-Smith
The Rothamstead agricultural experiments	E. J. Russell
The classical elements in Shakespeare's *Tempest*	R. S. Conway
National humour	J. W. Oman
Literary life in the Middle Ages	G. G. Coulton

1919

What we owe to Greece	T. R. Glover
Illusions of time and space	A. S. Eddington
Modern British folk music settings	W. G. Whittaker
Edmund Burke's social and political philosophy	C. E. Osborne
The rivers of the coal age	Percy F. Kendall
Some aspects of social reconstruction after the war	Stephen McKenna
My four and a half years as prisoner of war	Edgar L. Bainton
Foch	Sir F. B. Maurice
Folk songs of the Southern Appalachians	Cecil Sharp
Old English music, dances and musical instruments	Arnold Dolmetsch

[1] Published by the Society.

1919 (cont.)

The Troubadours	Ezra Pound
Sir Walter Scott	R. S. Rait
Flying and the future of the air	W. T. Blake
Songs of the Hebrides	Mrs. Kennedy Fraser
The organ of hearing from a new point of view	Arthur Keith
The golden eagle and other mountain birds	Seton Gordon
Some people I have known	Henry W. Nevinson

1920

Evolution of history	A. F. Pollard
What the Navy has done in the War	Lt. Cdr. Collingwood-Hughes
Aristophanes	Sir William Hadow
The animal world seen from under the water	Francis Ward
Mediaeval trade gilds	Maud Sellers
Life in fiction	Walter De la Mare
Giant suns	H. H. Turner
Growth and its control	Julian Huxley
Jewish apocalypses	F. C. Burkitt
Songs of the Hebrides	Mrs. Kennedy Fraser
Poetry and commonplace	John Bailey
The recent developments of Mendelism	Wm. Bateson
Some impressions of America	St. John Ervine
Prehistoric invaders of Northern England	Arthur Keith
Extinct giant reptiles	A. Smith Woodward
Is man a gregarious animal?	A. Clutton-Brock
The philosophy of Virgil	R. S. Conway
The subconscious mind	J. W. Oman

1921

The medieval mind in music	R. R. Terry
Venice: a study in oligarchy	A. J. Grant
England and France in the Middle Ages and in modern times	T. F. Tout
Variable stars	H. H. Turner
The origin of the dwellers in Mesopotamia	R. Campbell Thompson
Tales of the North West frontier	J. H. Sims
The animal world seen from under the water	Francis Ward
The making of boundaries	A. R. Hinks
Many inventions: a natural history study	J. Arthur Thomson

1921 (cont.)

Corsica	Alex. Taylor
The English stage	John Drinkwater
The Assyrian sculptured and incised slabs in the vestibule of the Lit & Phil	Nicholas Temperley
The decay of Parliament	Ramsey Muir
Darwin's theory of man's origin in the light of present day evidence	Sir Arthur Keith
Flowers and insects	Frank Balfour Browne
Psychology and the novel	Hugh Walpole
The lost Atlantis in science and romance	Albert Gilligan
Present-day China	J. O. P. Bland
Folk song	R. Vaughan Williams
A theory of art	Lascelles Abercrombie

1922

The present musical horizon	Edgar L. Bainton
Wild bird photography	C. W. R. Knight
The curious, the descriptive and the humorous in music	A. M. Henderson
Style, manner and mannerism in music	Ernest Newman
The great age of art in Ancient Northumbria	G. Baldwin Brown
Afforestation	A. P. Long
The future of the theatre	St. John Ervine
Roman frontiers	R. G. Collingwood
The significance of Russian literature	J. Middleton Murry
Mozart to Scriabin	Edgar L. Bainton
Rivers — from birth to old age	Albert Gilligan
Modern poetry	Lascelles Abercrombie
Mediaeval artists and craftsmen	A. Hamilton Thompson
The two greatest books in English	John Bailey
New views on Shakespeare	J. M. Robertson
Along the Border Line from Solway to the North Sea	J. Logan Mack
Persian painting	Sir Thomas W. Arnold
Mark Twain	T. R. Glover

1923

What is heredity?	Arthur Dendy
Modern astronomical photography	Harold Thomson
The European system before the War	G. P. Gooch
Poetry and life	Wilfred Gibson
Young China	Bertrand Russell

1923 (cont.)

The development of wireless communication	G. W. Todd
Early woodcuts	Campbell Dodgson
The elements of artistic criticism	Percy Buck
Smoke	J. B. Cohen
The courtship of birds	Julian Huxley
Islam in India at the present day	Sir Theodore Morison
The dawn of modern geography	J. L. Morison
Mediaeval contributions to modern civilization	F. J. C. Hearnshaw
The piano and its literature	A. M. Henderson
The romance of Rhodesia	G. de H. Larpent
The Roman Wall from Forth to Clyde	George Macdonald
Three thousand miles on the Amazon	Harold Feber
The inheritance of acquired characters	E. O. MacBride
Jonathan Swift	Sir Henry Hadow

1924

Fear	Sir George Paish
Bird hunting with a bioscope	Oliver Pike
Recent discoveries in plant sensitiveness	Sir F. Keeble
Bismarck	Raymond Beazley
The structure of the atom	G. W. Todd
Petronius and the first realistic novel	J. Wight Duff
Weather forecasting	Lewis F. Richardson
Anonymity	E. M. Forster
The life and work of Sir Joseph Wilson Swan	Kenneth R. Swan[1]
Rock-climbing in the Lake District	Ashley P. Abraham
Modern English domestic architecture	Clough Williams-Ellis
The sunset trail	Harold Feber
Transmission of speech by light	A. O. Rankine
Laughter and song	Charles Tree
Comets	S. Brodetsky
Mostly about caterpillars	Frank Balfour Browne
Wireless	P. T. Eckersley
Wonders of wild nature	Richard Kearton
Northumbrian dialects	W. A. Craigie

1925

How the Roman Wall was built	R. G. Collingwood
Life in motion	W. Stirling

[1] MS held in library.

1925 (cont.)

Reading of verse	Marjorie Gullan
British character as reflected in modern British music	Edgar L. Bainton
Bach's original hymn tunes	C. Sanford Terry
The conquest of Mount Everest	Lt. Col. Pottinger
Louis Pasteur	T. M. Lowry
International intercourse	C. Delisle Burns
French musical art from Lully to Debussy	A. M. Henderson
Beira, the ocean gateway to Rhodesia	G. de H. Larpent
Some aspects of evolution	Julian S. Huxley
Readings from my own poems	Wilfrid Gibson
The building of Gloucester Cathedral	A. Hamilton Thompson
The art of the critic	St. John Ervine
Above the snow line	Ashley P. Abraham
Points about pictures	Frank Rutter
The pageant of Ancient Egypt	Arthur Weigall
Beyond the Amazon	Harold Feber

1926

Heredity in man	J. W. Heslop Harrison
The new-born states of central Europe	C. Sarolea
The power of words	Marjorie Gullan
The origin of continents, mountains and ocean basins	G. A. Hickling
Sea birds and seals	Seton Gordon
The possible future of British broadcasting	P. T. Eckersley
The romance of modern and medieval Mexico	Harold Feber
Popular mythology about food	V. H. Mottram
Musical ideals	W. J. Turner
Northumbrian art in Saxon times	C. R. Peers
Nanda Devi, the highest mountain in the British Empire	T. W. Hodgkinson
The situation of modern art	Roger Fry
Sunlight, artificial sunlight, and health	Leonard Hill
A modern man of letters: Remy de Gourmont	Richard Aldington
Recent discoveries relating to Roman Britain	R. G. Collingwood

1927

Experiments with insects	A. D. Peacock
The worship of Mithras	G. R. B. Spain
A hundred years of Beethoven	Rutland Boughton
Our coming total eclipse of the sun	H. H. Turner

1927 (cont.)

Laurence Sterne	Herbert Read
Mutations: their nature and evolutionary significance	R. Ruggles Gates
El Dorado, the Spanish Main	Harold Feber
Old Newcastle	C. H. Hunter Blair
Rhythm	P. M. S. Latham
Within the atom: the evidence of the spectroscope	W. E. Curtis
Modern poetry	Edith Sitwell
The Aryans: our linguistic ancestors	V. Gordon Childe
Flemish and Belgian art	Mrs. C. Lewis Hind
Psychoanalysis and the artist	Ernest Jones
The lowlands of the Lake District and the uplands of Skye	Ashley P. Abraham
The acoustics of buildings	G. W. C. Kaye

1928

In the jungles of Borneo	Owen Rutter
The drama of animal life	J. Arthur Thomson
Botticelli	Murray Urquhart
A medieval abbey	D. H. S. Cranage
Emily Bronte: the enigma of history	A. M. Ludovici
Shakespeare's London	F. P. Wilson
The higher intelligence of insects	L. E. Cheesman
Reminiscences of Lord Morley	Sir Theodore Morison
The castles of Northumberland	C. H. Hunter Blair
The detective story	Dorothy L. Sayers
In birdland	Oliver G. Pike
The siege of Newcastle upon Tyne in 1644	G. R. B. Spain
Dante Gabriel Rossetti, artist and poet	T. Sturge Moore
The present position of the problems of Hadrian's Wall	F. G. Simpson

1929

Ibsen	Desmond McCarthy
The golden eagle and its neighbours	Seton Gordon
The animals in literature	W. L. Renwick
Winter sports in Switzerland	I. P. Muller
The appeal of Spanish	E. Allison Peers
Television	A. Dinsdale
Schubert	P. M. S. Latham
The enjoyment and preservation of rural scenery	Vaughan Cornish
Spain	Jan and Cora Gordon

1929 (cont.)

Lower Burma and its pearl fisheries	R. N. Rudmose Brown
Tolstoy	D. S. Mirsky
The West Indies	Wilfrid T. Blake

1930

Balzac	Desmond McCarthy
Weighing the earth	G. W. Todd
Music in the twentieth century	Edgar L. Bainton
Abstract and imitative art	E. M. O'R. Dickey
India, past and present	V. A. Haddick
Britain at the Poles	J. L. Cope
The new outlook on science	R. G. Lunnon
Mountaineering in Scotland	E. A. Baker
Wilkie Collins	Dorothy L. Sayers
The science of musical instruments	E. G. Richardson
English carols and Christmas songs	Marjorie Greenfield[1]

1931

Modern architecture in Europe and America	E. R. F. Cole
The psychology of clothes and fashion	J. C. Flugel
Northumbrian dialects	Harold Orton
Persian painting	Basil Gray
The history of the orchestra	Adam Carse[1]
Michael Faraday: his life and work	J. W. Bullerwell
Atlantic seals and sea birds	Seton Gordon
Rock climbing in the English Lake District	J. E. B. Wright
English comic opera	Thomas F. Dunhill[1]
Durham Cathedral	R. A. Cordingley
The first English defence of Gibraltar, 1704−5	G. M. Trevelyan

1932

The tropical forest of British Guiana	A. W. Bartlett
Modern biography	Bonamy Dobrée
The violin: its history, construction and technique	Editha G. Knocker[1]
Iceland: a land of surprises	H. G. Mansfield
The potter's art	Harry Barnard
Mozart	P. M. S. Latham
With the Mounted Police in Canada	H. G. Mansfield
The education of the child a hundred years ago	Frank Smith
Magic through the ages	Rupert Howard

[1] By arrangement with the British Music Society.

1932 (cont.)

Musical America	George Dodds[1]
Wild life at the Farne Islands	T. R. Goddard

1933

Lewis Carroll and his humour	B. J. Collingwood
A brief history of British song	Sir Edward Bairstow[1]
The rise of a new Spain	E. Allison Peers
Is modern art new?	D.M. Lall
The Brahms centenary	Edgar L. Bainton
The National Trust: its work and aims	W. Elliot Dixon
Religion in the machine age: two lectures	L. P. Jacks
Leisure in the machine age	J. MacMurray
Literature in the machine age	Sir John Squire
Art in the machine age	J. E. Barton
Science in the machine age	J. B. S. Haldane
Psychology in the machine age	R. H. Thouless
Social relations in the machine age	C. Delisle Burns

1934

The development of the anthem	Percy C. Buck[1]
What's wrong with the new psychology?	Cyril Burt
What's wrong with the English?	G. J. Renier
What's wrong with modern art?	Stanley Casson
What's wrong with modern novels?	John Middleton Murry
What's wrong with modern science?	J. B. S. Haldane
What's wrong with newspapers?	Kingsley Martin

1935

Pipe making and playing	Margaret James[1]
The control of broadcast music	Basil S. Maine[1]

1936

3,000 miles due west	Claude A. Jones
Development of style in piano music	Edward Mitchell[1]
Nazi Germany explained	Vernon Bartlett
German youth in politics	Lilo Linke
The attack on democracy	C. E. M. Joad
Excavations at Ur and other Mesopotamian sites: four lectures	Sir Leonard Woolley
The romance of song	Steuart Wilson[1]

1937

Cavalcade in music	S. Leslie Russell[1]
Russia to-day	Sir Bernard Pares

[1] By arrangement with the British Music Society.

1937 (cont.)

Spain to-day	Allison Peers
Austria to-day	Hugh Gaitskell
The modern novel	Phyllis Bentley
New reading habits	Denys Thompson
Why read modern poetry?	Michael Roberts
The cinema and society	R. S. Lambert
The film as art	John Grierson
Recent developments in cinema	Basil Wright
Critique of cinema	Ivor Montagu
Canadian music festivals	George Dodds[1]

1938

Queen Elizabeth	G. B. Harrison
George IV	Sir Charles Petrie
Queen Victoria	J. L. Morison
The ivory tower	E. M. Forster
What our children read	E. M. Delafield
Material for fiction	A. E. Coppard
Old English keyboard music	A. M. Henderson[1]
The historical background of 18th century England	Sir Charles Grant Robertson[2]
Social life in 18th century England	R. B. Mowat
The fine arts in 18th century England	R. H. Mottram
The evolution of the oboe	Leon Goossens[1]
Literature in 18th century England	Geoffrey Tillotson

1939

Primitive peoples	M. Fortes
Ourselves	Charles Madge
Critique of Mass Observation	R. W. Firth
Climbing in Britain	G. Winthrop Young
Climbing in the Alps	R. L. G. Irving
Climbing in Greenland	J. L. Longland
Bach's *St. Matthew Passion*	S. T. M. Newman[1]

1940

The war and after	Vernon Bartlett
In enemy territory	"I.K.8"
Shall it be a better peace next time?	Sir Norman Angell
Tschiffely's ride	A. F. Tschiffely
Behind the scenes at the B.B.C.	F. Grisewood
The story of the nebulae	Sir Arthur Eddington

[1] By arrangement with the British Music Society.
[2] MS held in library.

1940 (cont.)

Pianoforte music from Mozart to the present day: four lecture-recitals	S. T. M. Newman

1941

Britons and Romans in Northern England	I. A. Richmond
The coming of Christianity to Northern England	B. Colgrave
The growth of industry	E. Allen
The changing landscape of the North	F. G. Morris
Medieval painted glass in Northumberland	L. C. Evetts
Medieval armory of the North	C. H. Hunter Blair

1942

The evolution of the orchestra: two lectures	J. A. Westrup

1943

Bird life in the Farne Islands	T. Russell Goddard
Life histories of sea-lions and seals	T. Russell Goddard
Birds through the camera lens	H. S. Thompson
English literature as it was in and about 1793	G. M. Young[1]
Science (or natural philosophy) in 1793	J. R. Partington[1]
Fashions and manners in 1793	James Laver[1]
Music in and about 1793	J. A. Westrup[1]

1944

1945

Public schools	C. A. Alington
The new Europe	Bernard Newman
The ballet	Arnold Haskell
Sea birds and seals	Seton Gordon

1946

The country	A. G. Street
Fiction or biography: the modern trend	Ralph Straus
The spirit of English history	A. L. Rowse
Individualism and the film	Forsyth Hardy
The character and achievements of Isaac Newton	A. D. Ritchie

1947

Housman, man and poet	G. B. A. Fletcher
Some tourists and pilgrims of the XV century	H. F. M. Prescott
The creation of character in fiction	Elizabeth Bowen
Odysseus still at sea: on translating the classics	E. V. Rieu
Changes in surgery in the last twenty years	F. H. Bentley

[1] 150th Anniversary celebration lectures.

1947 (cont.)
The North Country during the Puritan
   revolution   H. R. Trevor-Roper

1948
Dr. Johnson   Arundell Esdaile
Victorian architecture   John Betjeman
The growth of commercial printing   John Johnson
Films and the people   Paul Rotha[1]
Artists and engineers: the intellectual
   background to the early railway age   F. D. Klingender
Witches   Margaret Murray
The generation and transmission of
   electrical energy   J. S. Prescott
The nature and vicissitudes of civilization   V. A. Demant

1949
Social surveys and social progress   Mark Abrams
Pre-Raphaelitism in England   Geoffrey Grigson
English-born sculptors, 1550—1800   Katharine Esdaile
The future of British films   Ralph Bond[1]

1965
The plays of W. B. Yeats   Peter Ure[2]

1966
Why the flora of Upper Teesdale should be
   conserved   Margaret E. Bradshaw
The Bayeux tapestry   Miss S. D. Thomson
Prophecy and poetry   Werner Pelz

1967
Outside the temple: an approach to
   profanity   Peter Hamilton
Freedom, morality and the law   D. W. Elliott
An evening with Yeats, Pound and Eliot   Peter Hamilton

1968
Prehistoric settlement in the Border Country   George Jobey
Botanising in Northumberland   W. A. Clark

---

[1] Ernest Dyer Memorial Lecture, in conjunction with the Tyneside Film Society.
[2] This lecture supplemented an exhibition of books by and about W. B. Yeats which had been arranged in the Library to mark the centenary of Yeats's birth.

1969

The medieval religious houses of Newcastle before and after their dissolution	Miss R. B. Harbottle
The literary censorship in England	C. H. Rolph
The government of Tyneside, 1800—1850	N. McCord

1970

Change in the countryside	D. M. Sims
Sewingshields: history and legend	Venetia Newall

1971

William Kennett Loftus, 1820—1858: archaeologist and benefactor of this Society	S. T. L. Harbottle[1]
The advancement of knowledge in Newcastle upon Tyne: the Literary and Philosophical Society as an educational pioneer	Sydney Middlebrook[2]
A quest for Conrad	Norman Sherry

1972

The story of a North Country naturalist: the diaries of Charles Robson	Mrs H. H. Clark
Industrial archaeology and North-East England: a historian's approach	N. McCord
Beamish: a regional museum of social history	Frank Atkinson

1973

The Farnes: some problems of a conservationist	Mrs. G. Hickling
Fairs of the North East of England: their economic and political origins	Constance M. Fraser
The first local railways	L. G. Charlton

1975

A local historian's note-book	W. R. Iley
The ingenious Beilbys — and after	James Rush

1976

The fascination of Northumberland's geology	D. A. Robson

1977

In blackberry time: an approach to writing	Sid. Chaplin
Indian aesthetic theory	P. S. Rawson
Illustration and the future of books	Bruce Allsopp

1978

Literary competitions	J. R. Till

[1] MS held in the Library.
[2] A contribution to the centenary celebration of the College of Physical Science. It was printed by the Society and the MS is held in its Library.

1978 (cont.)

Archaeological excavations at Monkwearmouth and Jarrow: summary considerations	Rosemary Cramp
Thomas Bewick, engraver extraordinary	Arthur Wallace
Music by Bach, Schumann and Franck: a recital	Francesca Uhlenbroek
Brahms for viola and piano: a recital	Marion Hillier, Noel Broome and Christopher Wood

1979

Sir Joseph Wilson Swan	R. C. Chirnside[1]
The living harpsichord: a lecture-recital	John Treherne
Poets and historians: a literary inheritance	Mary Moorman
The 'Rokeby Venus'	R. B. Holland

1980

Wordsworth and his public	R. S. Woof
Some naval scandals of the 1870s	N. McCord
Rescue archaeology in the North East	Colm O'Brien

1981

Unofficial lives: the Rev. William Turner of Newcastle and his family in the early 19th century	J. A. V. Chapple
Political and economic aspects of the energy equation	Ian Fells
The restoration of paintings	R. Hemmett
Capability Brown and the art of landscape gardening	John Cannon

1982

The winter's tale: Shakespeare's artistic manifesto	E. A. J. Honigmann
Keeping your wits in old age	Patrick Rabbitt
The street names of medieval Newcastle	Richard N. Bailey

1983

'Nihon Jin — Ron': Japanese ideas about themselves	Louis Allen
The pen and the sword: generals as authors	Mrs. Joan Taylor
Crime fiction	J. R. Lewis
The Elizabethan portrait miniature	R. K. R. Thornton

1984

Newcastle by gaslight	W. A. Campbell
English misericords	Mrs. Ann Squires
Folk song in the North East mining industry	George Deacon

[1] Printed by the Society.

1985

Grubb Parsons Limited and the making of telescopes	D. S. Brown
The Lit. and Phil.: the building of a library	Charles Parish[1]
The Lit. and Phil.: the development of the library, 1903-1985	Charles Parish[1]
Espionage: the oldest profession: the spy novels of John Le Carré	Peter Lewis
The charm of the Farne Islands	Mrs. Grace Hickling

1986

The modern spirit in Scottish art	Lyall Wilkes
The petroleum potential of Northumberland	J. M. Jones
The King's printer in Newcastle in 1639 and two tracts in the Society's library	John Philipson
Daniel Gooch and the North East	Alan Platt

1987

Evolution as a religion	Mrs. Mary Midgley
Belsay Hall: the restoration of a nineteenth century garden	Stephen H. G. Anderton
Captain George Dixon, circumnavigator and honorary member	Charles Parish
William Bulmer (1757—1830), fine printer and honorary member	Peter C. G. Isaac
The search for blue	W. A. Campbell
H. G. Wells's futures	Max Hammerton

1988

The story of Jesmond Dene	D. F. McGuire
James Hilton: novelist for the eighties	Keith Minton
Capturing intellectual territory: the beginnings of modern physics	D. M. Knight
Semi conductors: experiments, devices and schools, 1900-1919	C. A. Hempstead
Modern uses of early astronomical records	F. R. Stephenson
Current problems on the frontier of theoretical physics	John Barrett

1989

A little light on the power of darkness: Boulton and Watt's activities in the North East	Jennifer Tann
Natural history in Malaysia	A. J. Richards
What went wrong with the French Revolution?	Norman Hampson

[1] Printed by the Society.

CHAPTER SIX

Robert Spence Watson Lectures

1914 Some aspects of English poetry	Israel Gollancz
1915 Ballad literature	Sir Henry Newbolt
1916 The ethical idea in Shakespeare	Sir Henry Jones
1917 Literature as revelation	Gilbert Murray[1]
1918 Literature and society in the 18th century	John Bailey
1920 Charles Lamb	T. R. Glover
1920 Technique in poetry	Walter De La Mare
1921 English satire and English character	Sir Henry Hadow[2]
1922 Place names and history	Allen Mawer
1923 The creation of Falstaff	J. Middleton Murry[3]
1924 The study of poetry	H. W. Garrod[2]
1926 Milton, the man and the poet	H. J. C. Grierson[2]
1927 Carlyle and history	G. M. Trevelyan[2]
1928 The muse of history	Philip Guedalla
1928 John Bunyan	Ernest De Sélincourt[2]
1929 Drama in the North of England in the Middle Ages	D. Nichol Smith[2]
1931 Robert Bridges's *The testament of beauty*	J. H. B. Masterman[2]
1931 Books in ana	F. P. Wilson
1932 Sir Walter Scott	R. S. Rait[2]
1933 Poetic reputations	Edmund Blunden[2]
1934 William Morris	Arthur Compton-Rickett
1936 Strachey and the art of biography	Desmond MacCarthy
1936 The meaning of *The Tempest*	J. Dover Wilson[1]
1937 Samuel Johnson	R. W. Chapman
1938 An addition to Byron's biography	Harold Nicolson[2]
1941 Some minor eighteenth century poets	W. L. Renwick[2]
1942 Hamlet	H. B. Charlton[2,4]
1943 Shakespeare's earlier history plays	E. M. W. Tillyard[2]
1945 The moral poetry of Pope	Geoffrey Tillotson[1]

[1] Printed by the Society.
[2] MS held in the Library.
[3] Published in *Discoveries*, by John Middleton Murry. 1924.
[4] A revised version of H. B. Charlton's "Hamlet" was published in the *Bulletin of the John Rylands Library*, Vol.26, No.2, May-June, 1942.

Year	Title	Author
1945	Boswell	G. C. Abbott
1947	The colloquial element in English poetry	C. Day Lewis[1]
1948	Keats's *Ode on a Grecian urn*	C. M. Bowra[2]
1949	Chaucer the rhetorician	Nevill Coghill[2]
1950	History as a branch of literature	Herbert Butterfield[2]
1950	Herman Melville	Montgomery Belgion[2]
1951	Dickens's *Christmas stories*	John Butt[2]
1952	Queen Elizabeth I and the English historians	A. L. Rowse[3]
1953	Sentiment and drama in the 18th century	J. Isaacs
1954	Wordsworth and the human heart	James Sutherland[2]
1955	Shakespeare in the theatre	Clifford Leach[2]
1956	The art of translation	F. L. Lucas[2]
1957	Joseph Conrad	F. R. Leavis[2]
1958	Robert Burns	David Daiches[2]
1960	How Shakespeare got his plays on	Ivor Brown[2]
1960	Rudyard Kipling: poet or versifier?	Bonamy Dobrée[2]
1961	The words of English folk songs	James Reeves[2]
1962	Language and style	Angus McIntosh[2]
1963	The English of two islands: Pitcairn: Jamaica	Alan S. C. Ross[2]
1964	Why we should read some Browning	Geoffrey Tillotson[2]
1965	Genius befriended	Douglas Hubble[2]
1966	The landscape of T. S. Eliot's poetry	Helen Gardner[2]
1968	Othello, Iago and the critics	John Wain[2]
1970	Virginia Woolf	Angus Wilson
1973	Objects in novels	Barbara Hardy[2]
1974	The young Thomas Hardy	Robert Gittings[2]
1977	Samuel Beckett	Christopher Ricks[2]
1978	Dickens	Kathleen Tillotson[2]
1980	Emily Dickinson	L. C. Knights[2]
1982	John Webster and the Overbury murder	M. C. Bradbrook[2]
1984	Blake and the city	Kathleen Raine
1986	The English hymn: its lines and landscapes	J. R. Watson
1988	The trouble with Keats	John Bayley[2]

[1] Printed by the Society.
[2] MS held in the Library.
[3] Published in *An Elizabethan garland* by A. L. Rowse, 1954.

CHAPTER SEVEN

BIOGRAPHICAL ESSAY I

Unofficial Lives: Elizabeth Gaskell and the Turner Family*

J. A. V. Chapple

About the year 1830 Elizabeth Stevenson, then in her late teens, made one or more long visits to her relation William Turner (1761-1859), Unitarian minister at Newcastle-upon-Tyne. She was of course to become a well-known novelist in later years, but this is an obscure period of her life.[1] Her biographers either copy each other uncritically or with some justification make raids upon a book she published in 1853, *Ruth*, often called her 'Newcastle story'. A great deal more is known about the Reverend William Turner about this time. His name appears frequently in the *Reports* of the Newcastle Literary and Philosophical Society. (He had been a founder-member and one of its Secretaries.) Similarly, the Church of the Divine Unity in Newcastle possesses a number of documents of his old Hanover-Square congregation and a splendid scrapbook[2] about the celebration of his fiftieth year in the city, when on 21 December 1831 nearly one hundred people sat down to a dinner in the new Assembly Rooms.

All these records relate to the public man, the honoured citizen and minister, and it is information of this kind that forms the substance of the most extensive account of his career. Its title is significant: *The Christian Character, the Union of Knowledge and Benevolence, Piety and Virtue, as Illustrated in the Life and Labours of the late Rev. William Turner* (London and Newcastle 1859). Its author, George Harris, could hardly have neg‒ lected Turner's part in founding the Bible Society, Natural History Society and Mechanics' Society in Newcastle, his

* Lecture to the Society in 1981.

efforts for education and prison reform, his campaigns against slavery and capital punishment. But one eventually longs for something less official and less hagiographical, something that conveys a sense of what private life was like in the little house where Turner lived with his unmarried daughter Ann and which Elizabeth Stevenson visited after the death of her father in March 1829.

Fortunately, Newcastle institutions have been sentimental and sensible enough to preserve less formal documents, the kind that allow us to look behind the scenes of public life. First in importance is a hitherto unknown letter to William Turner from Elizabeth Gaskell (though an early one, her married name is now appropriate), kept in the Moor Collection of the Literary and Philosophical Society.[3] Written soon after her marriage to William Gaskell, junior minister at Cross Street Unitarian Chapel in Manchester, it shows the simple warmth of her connection with William Turner and his younger daughter Ann:

No 1 Dover Street   Oxford Road,
Saturday Morning [6 October 1832]

My dear Sir,

I received your most kind & welcome letter on Thursday when we arrived here; and we have been so busy ever since that I am literally seizing the first leisure moment to write my very warmest thanks for all the good wishes expressed in it, and for the kind interest you take in me. Pray thank Anne [sic] for all her nice messages in it.

I have been so completely in a 'whirl' these two days that I feel as though I could hardly arrange my thoughts enough to give you an account of the few plans we have formed with regard to our future proceedings. Mr Gaskell has promised as soon as the *formal* bridal calls are made, to go with me and introduce me to most of the families under his care, as their minister's wife, and one who intends to try to be their useful friend. My dear colleague too has promised her assistance and advice with regard to my duties. I like my new home very much indeed — for Manchester it is very countrified, and is very cheerful and comfortable in every part. I was detained by a sore throat on the road, or else we had intended being at home last week; as it was, and we had dipped into another week, we staid a few days longer in my old home, and saw Aunt Lumb's almost daily improvement in health, spirits, and strength. She promises to come and pay us a visit very soon, and I enjoy the idea of receiving her in a house of my own, and where I can in some measure provide for her comforts, as she has so often done for mine.

I have just received on the part of Mr Gaskell & myself, a very handsome fish-slice and a very kind note from Mr James Turner.

Pray tell Anne I can fully sympathise with her in the troubles of removing, for I am just now feeling so doubtful as to the success of my housekeeping, and little *daily* cares, that the very idea of a removal sounds alarming. I am very glad however that you are going to leave your present house for one so much pleasanter in situation if I remember rightly.

I have been on the watch ever since I received a very charming little note from Mrs Greenhow, for an opportunity to Newcastle by which I might answer it, and acknowledge the receipt of a very pretty pair of little glass vases for flowers. I am half tempted to write by post; it seems so long since I received them. Will you give my kind love to Anne, the Rankins[,] the Eldonites, Mrs Welbank, Allhusens, Mortons & Carrs if they are returned;

And ever believe me to remain
My dear Mr Turner's very affec[tionate] & grateful
E. C. Gaskell

The 'dear colleague' who was to help her in Manchester was in fact Turner's other daughter Mary, sister of Ann and wife of the senior minister at Cross Street, John Gooch Robberds, said to be a kind and genial man 'ever inclined to pass a favourable judgement and to look on the bright side of things'.[4] A degree of idealisation seems to be common to all these nineteenth-century memoirs — or did the optimistic attitudes actually *create* brighter lives?

Both ministers at Cross Street Chapel therefore had wives who had been educated by William Turner. A long letter from him to Mary[5] is worth quoting from here. It is annotated (ironically?) 'My Father's Pastoral Epistle':

Newcastle. Jan.29. 1812

Though I have followed you in idea, my dearest Mary, almost from hour to hour since you left us, amidst the various scenes through which I pleased myself with supposing you to be passing. I have not thought it necessary or even season-able to trouble you with either my good wishes or my advice; because I was sure you would give my affection full credit for the former; and because I had no doubt of your conducting yourself, through the various circumstances attendant on your change of character, with that modest and unaffected propriety, which would render the latter quite unnecessary, had I been qualified to offer it in this stage of your proceedings. But now that the ceremonials attending your first introduction are over, and you are beginning to think of settling upon a plain domestic plan, will you allow me to pour forth some of the overflowings of a Father's heart, which has often of late engaged the head to meditate on your future duties and prospects?

On the qualities which a man of sense will most regard in the choice of a wife, you have read the judicious remarks of Dr Aikin; on the general duties of a wife you have availed yourself of the advice of Mr Gisborne; and you have perused the strong and often coarse, though too often well-founded, strictures of Mrs Wollstonecraft. I need not, therefore, say any thing to you on the general rights and obligations of Husband and Wife: you are neither of you, I trust, disposed to be jealous of each other's rights, or grudging in the discharge of mutual obligations.

And so the letter flows on, in lines of tiny, elegant handwriting beautifully spaced and set out on the large folio pages: a mellifluous and balanced piece of eighteenth-century prose totally sure of its form and values.

William Turner's advice is detailed and clear-cut. A minister's wife at Manchester must make 'a limited income support a respectable appearance'; 'set an example of attention to religious duties, and of general decorum and propriety of conduct'; prepare to educate her own children, who will one day be 'almost exclusively the objects of their Mother's attention' during their formative years, by giving 'an active attention, in the mean time, to the religious and other instruction of the lower classes of the congregation, either in charity or Sunday schools, or otherwise'; 'always study the things which make for peace'; avoid squabbles and meddling, gossip and mischief . . . So much decorum and good sense becomes rather tedious, but we eventually come to a joke about the length of the epistle and then a far more colloquial postscript:

> '. . . You have not answered *one* of our queries, Whether your things [,] among the rest the Ham [,] got safe; and what they (*I* particularize your Mother's preparations for you) have been tho[ugh]t of? Whether you have bought and sent off the Calico Sheeting? . . .'

This is William Turner, but the point is picked up in a much less formal — indeed, slightly illiterate scribble round the edge of the letter:

> I cannot see you in your new habitation yet. you will think us sad discontented mortals — but we have lost you, crampetes! send Ann the large sheet you promised with plans & drawings & then I will fill you one with pretty agreeable small talk without the least bit of a lecture. I shall have plenty to say for Miss Aikin is coming on friday morning. I hope you will get me the sheeting before Cotton is ris.

Could this be the hand of Mary Robberds' step-mother, née Jane Willetts, herself the daughter of yet another Unitarian minister?[6] The lively minded Elizabeth Gaskell was not unique, perhaps, in this kind of society. She might have been following a feminine tradition: a sharper, more sprightly set of attitudes, Regency rather than proto-Victorian. Such a background — the second Mrs. Turner had died a few years before Elizabeth arrived in Newcastle to stay with William Turner and his daughter Ann — *could* have been transmitted in informal, domestic ways to help nurture what I myself believe lies close to the heart of her genius as a writer, her 'vital sense of laughing, earnest middle-class life'.[7]

By sheer good fortune a copy has survived of some reminiscences by Mary Robberds.[8] They reveal the *tone* of the household quite plainly:

> [1799] Then my father married again, & we had a kind & good mother — She taught us how to employ our time usefully, & not waste it in nonsense, & yet she liked fun as well as any body, & was very entertaining; she encouraged us in learning to draw, & often read to us while we were at work.

> But she often locked up the book when she had done, till the next evening, because, she said, it was an idle habit interrupting our work to finish a story, & it was a good exercise of patience to wait; we rather rebelled at this, but I daresay she was right. In this manner we went on for several years very happily: when I was about eighteen years of age [c.1804], I went several pleasant & improving journies. First, to London for three months, during which time I was a guest six weeks at Mr John Wedgwoods...

It is hardly necessary to stress that about twenty-five years later Elizabeth Stevenson went on 'a pleasant & improving' visit, to Newcastle. The mixture of fun and work would surely have been very similar. As Mary Robberds wrote,

> On my return home, I was so happy as to be able to make my drawing lessons useful to my dear father; for he had been appointed lecturer to the "Literary and Philosophical Society" [in 1802] and my mother encouraged me to draw the diagrams on the black board, which he wanted as illustrations of his subject. As I could do them privately before the lecture there could be no objection, & I quite enjoyed the work; it also enabled me better to understand the lecture. — This was a very pleasant part of my life as my brothers were clever & amusing companions and my cousin Henry Holland, who lived some years with us [1799—1803], was a great favourite, & his sisters also paid us long visits... My little sister Ann was quite a little child & very delicate & required a great deal of care; but my mother made even this entertaining. One day when she was standing at the window reading, she said 'Mother, who are my fellow creatures?['] 'Why look out of the window, & whoever you see are your fellow creatures.' 'What! those lime people, Mother?' 'Yes, certainly!' said my Mother. 'Not fellows like stockings['] replied Anne [sic]. My cousin Mary Holland, whom you now know as Cousin Mary at Knutsford staid a year with us, and was then as now, very amusing.

And so it continues. They may have had to write 'a remembrance of the sermon on a Sunday', but father and mother 'always made the evening pleasant... by singing & talk'.

How conscious these families were of themselves and their values can be shown by contrast. Mary Robberds and

Elizabeth Gaskell both reacted strongly against the austerity of a mutual acquaintance in Manchester, Mrs. F. W. Newman.[9] On 18 October 1840 Mary Robberds wrote to her father,

> Tell Ann we have called on Mrs Newman, and been received very graciously, indeed kindly, but we are told that we must not expect the visit to be returned. She is an interesting woman and, I doubt not, sincerely pious, but I am sorry that her creed is so narrow. There is a text in one of the Epistles of St John about not bidding Godspeed to an unbeliever, which she thinks forbids her to associate with those who she considers to have an erroneous creed. In her apartment there are various texts framed like Samplers and hung on the walls; but they reminded me so much of the scripture denunciations which were placarded on the walls of Albion Street in the Race week, that I had no very pleasant or hospitable association with them. I would rather fix the text in my mind than on the walls, and prefer the Heywood plan to that of the Plymouth Brethren.

On 25 November 1849, Elizabeth Gaskell wrote about Francis Newman and his wife:

> He dresses so shabbily you would not see his full beauty, — he used to wear detestable bottle green coats, wh. never show off a man. Mrs Newman is a Plymouth Brother which is a sort of community-of-goods-and-equality-of-rank-on-religious-principles association and *very* calvinistic.

Newman, brother of the future Cardinal, lectured at Manchester New College, as did J. G. Robberds and William Gaskell. His association with Unitarians was a complicated one, well worth further study.[10]

(ii)

Just how worldly were these Unitarian ministers and their families? In Turner's 'Pastoral Epistle' to Mary Robberds, we notice the stress on 'the arts of frugal but decent housekeeping' and the neat arguments that a minister's wife should purchase from his congregation:

> For, certainly, all other things being equal, or even nearly so, it is a reciprocity which is only fair and reasonable that you should lay out among the congregation that income which you

receive from them. You will thus, as well as by a mutual interchange of good offices in other respects, strengthen your husband's interest with his people.

Yet there is a good deal of evidence to suggest that in practice William Turner did *not* intertwine commerce and pastoral care so ingeniously, but was generous to the point of foolishness. Mrs Chadwick reported the tale current in Newcastle that beggars would manage to obtain one gift, take another route and reappear a little later with 'a still more pathetic story' to 'open his heart and also his purse for a second time' (p. 102). It sounds as if we are once more amongst the Lives of the Saints (the absent-minded ones). However, the documents preserved by the Church of the Divine Unity provide supporting evidence. The Secretary's Minute Book of the Hanover Square congregation shows that on three occasions Turner attempted (but was not allowed!) to give up his retirement pension — in 1844, 1847 and 1851, when the death of his unmarried daughter Ann brought the proposal that he should give up 'half of its former Amount, viz 30 Pounds per Annum'. Or there is an earlier letter from his nephew, James Aspinall Turner,[11] a typical philanthropist and business man:

Manchester 27 May 1834

My dear Uncle,
 . . . In reply to the other Business part of your Letter, I assure you, my dear Uncle, I have much pleasure in sending you the sum you mention, and now enclose a Bank Note No. 1126 for £50 — dated Manchester 15 Feb. 1834. Nothing can at any time be more gratifying to me than to contribute in any way to your comfort, but you must allow me to say, that it would have pleased me much more if I could have thought that the sum now sent was intended to add to your own personal or domestic comforts, or even to aid your plans for the good of others — but I fear from the account you give me, that it will only assist in enriching some Knave, who has imposed upon your good-nature, and I certainly regret much that it is not better employed — I really feel very much disposed to *preach* to *you* a little, my dear Uncle — I know it little becomes me to do so on every other subject — but in wordly wisdom, and business-like prudence, perhaps I

may, without much vanity, profess myself your superior —
Do, pray, then learn to say — No . . .

A letter from Ann Turner in the Moor Collection is most valuable of all in this context, since it not only reveals more about William Turner but also throws a flood of light upon his little known daughter Ann, who, Mrs Chadwick claimed (p. 104), was the original of the character Faith Benson in Elizabeth Gaskell's novel *Ruth*. This letter from Ann Turner to her father in fact reveals a relationship that (with all the usual qualifications) resembles the fictional one between Faith Benson and her brother, a Dissenting Minister of the most charitable type:

Saturday morning May 21st [?1836]

My dear Father,

I am afraid that I am going to do, and to own that I have done, what you may consider very impertinent, but I hope that you will forgive me if you *do* think me so. I went yesterday (as you once gave me leave to do at any time) to look for the date of some engagement in your pocket book; and there I saw an account of some transactions with regard to the New York Stock, which, together with a letter which was on your table (and which I acknowledge I ought not to have looked at as I saw you put it into your pocket without saying what it was about) leads me to fear that you have been obliged to sell this Stock, and, from your having transacted this business not through Mr Rankin or Mr Carwell, but through a person of the name of Bell, whom I do not know, I fear that it is sold to enable you to answer some obligation which he or some other needy person has prevailed upon your kindness to take upon yourself. If this be so, there will only be the money in the Society's hands remaining of what you had, and I cannot help looking forward with some anxiety; not, my dear Father, in my own account but in yours. Should your life be prolonged as we *earnestly pray* that it may be for *many* years to come; and you should feel your duties in the chapel too much for you, how grieved would your children be to see you compelled to continue them because you cannot do without the income arising from them: yet if you suffer unworthy or at best improvident persons to find that they can prevail upon you to pay their debts out of your own property, it will all dwindle away: and then what is to make your latter years comfortable.

I know too well that I am far from being as good a manager as my dear Mother was, and that she would from her notable habits have saved you many expenses which I have put you to: I have followed her example in almost the only way in which I ought not to have done so, in not keeping regular accounts and therefore I cannot be sure how far this has been the case: but I cannot think that our expenses can have *much* exceeded that they were during her life. My own dress, though I am aware from the same want of management costing more than it ought, has not been at your expense. I think therefore your money can only have gone in the way I have alluded to for except perhaps a few more books and subscriptions than are absolutely necessary I am *sure* it does not go in any expenses of your own. Will you therefore excuse me for suggesting that it would lessen the difficulty to you of refusing requests of this kind; (which I know it is painful to your kind feelings not to comply with), if you would transfer to my Brother [William Turner (1788-1853)] the shares in the Society and the remainder (if there be any) of this Stock. You know *him* too well to doubt for a moment that he would be strictly honourable about it: and also that should you want any part of it for *yourself*, it will always be forthcoming: but you could then say with truth that it was not in your power to undertake to be answerable for *any* debts or bonds of any sort. If you are only selling this Stock because the time is approaching when it must be paid off, I shall feel much relieved. Still I cannot but think some plan like the one I have ventured to suggest would be desireable [sic]: for I know how you are teazed by persons who ought to know better than to work upon your kind feelings as they do.

Excuse me dearest Father if you think I am presumptuous: I fear you will, because letters about money are the only ones you never shew me and I thought too that you thought me impertinent when I tried (at Catherine's [her sister-in-law's] desire) two years ago to find out how the 300£ had gone.[12] I again repeat that it is not on my own account (at any rate much more on yours) that I feel anxious. I know indeed that in her ever kind thoughts for me as unmarried: my Mother once said something of considering this Stock as mine, but *that* I would never have considered it: but should insist upon an equal division between my brother, my two sisters and myself, of anything that may remain of your property: and should there not be enough to supply my wants I can by some

means add to it. But I *cannot* bear the thought of *your* wanting the comforts which your advancing years will require, or being dependent for them on the kindness of your friends: who will I know never suffer you to want for comforts, and will have a pleasure in contributing to them: but still they would blame me, and I fear even you my dear Father, that better care had not been taken of the money which ought to have supplied them. I have taken this way of addressing you because I feel that I can do it better than by speaking. I have only again to entreat your forgiveness and subscribe myself your ever affectionate and grateful daughter
Ann Turner

Ann Turner was then in her early forties, born according to her father's Register on 21 October 1796. She comes to life as one whose 'excellent practical sense, perhaps, made her a more masculine character than her brother.' I say 'brother' and not 'father' because I am actually quoting from *Ruth* at this point. The novel tells of the numerous small economies made by the minister and his sister; his salary was £80 a year augmented by thirty or forty more from canal shares. It also describes the minister as 'just the man to muddle away his money in indiscriminate charity' — at least that is how he appeared to the severer type of business mind. *(Ruth,* ed. A. W. Ward, 1906, pages 203, 132, 364—5, 392.) Of course, Elizabeth Gaskell invented a very different set of circumstances for her novel and, in any case, there have been the usual displacements and redistributions of fact for the purposes of fiction. Nevertheless, I think the letter from Ann Turner reinforces the claim that some of this novel stems from Newcastle experience and certainly gives us our first insight into the very positive character of one who (apart from the slight but important part she plays in Harriet Martineau's *Autobiography)* has been till now a very shadowy being. She moved to Manchester with her father on his retirement in 1841 and died unmarried in 1850.

(iii)

Nothing so far discovered has a *direct* bearing on Elizabeth Stevenson's days in Newcastle. The most disappointing document of all is a letter from her cousin Henry Holland to William Turner, dated 16 December, kept in the scrapbook I have mentioned. The year must therefore be 1831. Holland apologises for his inability to attend the celebration dinner and goes on to write at some length about the Asiatic cholera then sweeping across Europe.[13] As a physician appointed to the Central Board of Health set up in June 1831 to advise the Privy Council about the disease, then quite mysterious in its causes and uncertain in its cure, he was naturally eager to discuss with his old tutor the first cases in England — at Sunderland across the Tyne in the previous November:

> The rate at which the disease may spread in Newcastle, as regards the number attacked & the proportion of deaths, becomes a very interesting question . . . It will further be an object of deep interest to know, whether your medical men can devise & apply any happier mode of treatment, than has yet been ascertained.

But there is not a word about his young cousin Elizabeth. One might plausibly say that in these circumstances a young female is unimportant, but it is also obvious from his later autobiography, *Recollections of Past Life* (1877), that even as a famous novelist she had principally existed as one of *his* relations.

The cholera epidemic is said to have driven Elizabeth and Ann Turner to Edinburgh, though the disease reached the city's crowded tenements soon enough. *Ruth,* too, has its epidemic, of typhus fever rather than cholera. We must remember the state of medical knowledge then, for as Henry Holland writes,

> We shall be anxious for the opinions of your intelligent medical men in Newcastle; as to the relation which some have judged to exist between this disease, & some forms of congestive Typhus. As you still have some Typhus in the Town, the comparison may be made in the most favourable way for truth. I have no doubt myself of the Cholera being a specific infection.

The distance of the fiction from fact may not therefore be as great as we might suppose, but it can never compensate a biographer for the absence of solid external evidence.

One must, I suppose, keep following clues. Who, for instance, are all the people mentioned at the end of the very first letter I quoted? William Turner's 'Book of Names' shows that many of them were Unitarian families — Greenhows, Rankins, Welbanks, Allhusens, Mortons and Carrs — just as one might expect. The name of Carr is very interesting indeed, because five early letters (18 June 1831 to 6 August 1832 'where dated') sold at Sotheby's on 13 December 1977, which I have not been able to see, were written by Elizabeth Stevenson to a Harriet Carr. In the scrapbook about Turner's fiftieth year in Newcastle is a letter from a George Carr of Clavering Place, dated 5 December 1831. He lived, that is, in a 'spacious and splendid' part of the town,[14] and I have discovered that he was Agent or Manager of the Bank of England branch that opened in Bailiffgate in 1828. His salary was rather more than a minister's — £1000 per annum, no less.[15] But was he Harriet Carr's father? And did she marry a Mr Anderson, as seems likely from the description in Sotheby's Sale Catalogue? All this I have still to find out. At times it seems an endless process, but one thought sustains me. Even if I have not stumbled upon absolutely solid evidence of Elizabeth Gaskell's presence in Newcastle circa 1830, there is now much more known about the *unofficial* lives of those she met, their sense of values and way of life.[16]

FOOTNOTES
1. The earliest details are given by Mrs Ellis H. Chadwick in *Mrs Gaskell: Haunts, Homes and Stories* (rev. edn 1913), pp.99-117, 249-50. She undoubtedly traced original sources, though she was not always cautious in her use of them. Margaret Emily Gaskell, for instance, was undoubtedly baptised by Turner (p. 109) but it was at Cross Street Chapel in Manchester, according to its Register.
2. This material, formerly kept at the Church of the Divine Unity in Newcastle, is now deposited with Tyne and Wear Archives. I must express my gratitude to Mrs. H. M. Claxton, who arranged for me to see it all and showed me great personal kindness, and to the Chief Archivist, Mr. B. Jackson.
3. The Collection, donated by Miss Amelia Moor of the Isle of Man, contains letters relating to William Turner from over fifty correspondents. I am indebted to the Society for permission to quote and to the Librarian, Mr Charles Parish, and his staff for their many courtesies.

4. Memoir by J. J. Tayler in *Christian Festivals and Natural Seasons: Discourses [by the] Rev. J. G. Robberds*, ed. M.R. et al. (1855), p.18. Mary Turner had married the reverend J. G. Robberds on 31 December 1811.

5. This document, formerly in the possession of the Misses Hartas Jackson, is now in Mrs. H. M. Claxton's possession. Turner probably refers in the portion quoted to John Aikin's *Letters from a Father to His Son* (1793), Thomas Gisborne's *An Enquiry into the Duties of the Female Sex* (1797) and Mary Wollstonecraft's *A Vindication of the Rights of Women* (1792).

6. He married as his second wife Jane, daughter of the Reverend William Willetts, in 1799. The *DNB* states she died in 1855 but William Turner's funeral sermon (published in 1827) gives the date as 25 December 1826. I cannot explain the strange word 'crampetes'.

7. See J. A. V. Chapple and John Geoffrey Sharps, *Elizabeth Gaskell: a Portrait in Letters* (Manchester U.P. 1980), pp. xiv—xvi, 24—25, 107.

8. Hartas Jackson document now in Mrs. H. M. Claxton's possession. A portion was quoted in J. A. V. Chapple, 'William Stevenson and Elizabeth Gaskell', *Gaskell Society Journal*, Vol. 1 (1987), p.7.

9. The letter from Mary Robberds, together with one from Ann Turner to Mary Robberds dated 10 October 1835, which contains some account of the reception of George Combe's lectures introducing 'the properly phrenological subject', was owned by the Misses Hartas Jackson and is now in Mrs. H. M. Claxton's possession. See also *The Letters of Mrs Gaskell*, ed. J. A. V. Chapple and Arthur Pollard (Manchester U.P. 1966), p.88.

10. See especially his sinewy, subtle letter of 21 December 1841 to J. H. Thom refusing to write for the *Prospective Review* on a regular basis. The letter is in Liverpool University Library and I owe thanks to Mr. M. R. Perkin, Curator of Special Collections, for sending me photocopies of Newman correspondence in the Rathbone papers there.

11. Four letters to William Turner from his nephew James survive in the Moor Collection of the Newcastle Literary and Philosophical Society, dated 24 October 1823, 27 May 1834, 8 August 1836 and 7 November 1838. The third supplies an illegible name: 'Mr Merz, a very amiable and clever man who is raising a very excellent school in our neighbourhood'. Cp. *Letters*, p.47.

12. On 9 January 1832 the Hanover Square congregation invested £300 in securities for him. (John Sykes, *Local Records; or Historical Register of Remarkable Events*, 1833, II.334.) In a letter of 7 June 1833 (Moor Collection), the Reverend George Cook mentions that William Turner had given money to a John Williamson.

13. See R. J. Morris, *Cholera 1832: the Social Response to an Epidemic* (1976), pp.26, 32-3, 50, 60-66.

14. S. Middlebrook *Newcastle upon Tyne: Its Growth and Achievement* (Newcastle 1950), p.147.

15. Information kindly supplied by Mr. E. M. Kelly, Curator of the Bank's Museum and Historical Research Section. I owe the late Professor W. Chaloner thanks for assistance in this matter.
16. The Brotherton Collection of Leeds University now possesses the five early letters, some of which are addressed to Harriet Carr at George Carr's, Clavering Place. Finally, I must thank Miss Ruth Green of the Hull University English Department for invaluable assistance in both research and preparation.

CHAPTER SEVEN

BIOGRAPHICAL ESSAY II

Captain George Dixon

Circumnavigator and Honorary Member of
The Literary and Philosophical Society
of Newcastle upon Tyne*

Charles Parish

In its early years the Literary and Philosophical Society of Newcastle upon Tyne elected many honorary members in the hope that communications would be received from them that would contribute to the interest and usefulness of its regular monthly meetings. Over one hundred were elected in the years 1794 and 1795, many of them distinguished in the field of knowledge in which lay the Society's main interest: that of natural philosophy, pure and, particularly, applied.[1] Among them were those bearing great names : Sir Joseph Banks, Matthew Boulton, Erasmus Darwin, Joseph Priestley and Sir John Sinclair are examples; but there were other names less well known one of them being that of the man who is the central subject of this paper: Captain George Dixon. In recording his election the Society's minutes provide only his name and his place of residence which was then Bermudas. At that time Dixon was known as a man who had sailed around the world on two great voyages: once

* Lecture to the Society in 1987.

[1] In 1797 a new class of honorary members was formed. It was limited to four, and these had the privileges of ordinary members, unlike the earlier class. It was a means of recognising local merit. At the present time (1988) honorary members (not limited in number) are, in practice, chosen from those members of the Society who have distinguished themselves in literature, science or art, or who have rendered outstanding services to the Society.

as one of that truly remarkable body of men who had accompanied Cook, and once as captain of the *Queen Charlotte* in a voyage of which he had published an account entitled *A voyage round the world; but more particularly to the North-West coast of America: performed in 1785, 1786, 1787, and 1788 in the King George and Queen Charlotte, Captains Portlock and Dixon.* London, Geo. Goulding, 1789.

The question of the book's authorship is a matter for conjecture. It is written in the form of letters, the majority of which are signed 'W.B.', the initials of William Beresford who was supercargo on the *Queen Charlotte.* Dixon himself writes: 'It yet remains for me to bespeak the candour and indulgence of the reader in perusing the following work as it was written by a person . . . totally unused to literary pursuits, and equally to a seafaring life. However, to obviate any objection that might possibly arise from his deficiency in nautical knowledge I have been particularly careful in correcting that part of the work, and, by way of appendix, have given everything of the kind which, in my opinion, can be any way interesting to a seaman; as also a short sketch of the subjects we have met with in natural history that are likely to engage the attention of the curious; and I hope that a plain narrative of facts . . . will prove interesting though deficient in smoothness of language, or elegance of composition.' The *D.N.B.* takes Dixon's word for it and credits the writing to William Beresford but Rüdiger Joppien and Bernard Smith in their *The art of Captain Cook's voyages. Vol.3. The voyage of the Resolution and Discovery, 1776-1780.* 1988. Text, p.212, Note 6, state that Dixon wrote the account under the pseudonym 'W.B.' Whatever the truth there can be no doubt that a substantial part of the work was written by Dixon and that a great deal of the information in it was copied from his journal. It is apparent that Dixon was a man of ability and attainments, a keen observer, a first class navigator, and also the possessor, if he wrote the whole of his book, of some literary ability and the gift of imagination for he 'became' Beresford in many parts of his narrative. Nathaniel Portlock also wrote an account of the voyage, with the same title as Dixon's. It was published by John Stockdale and George

Goulding, London, 1789. The two books are complementary and may be regarded as a two-volume account of the same voyage.

Dixon's book was dedicated to Sir Joseph Banks who was President of the Royal Society (of which the Literary and Philosophical Society of Newcastle upon Tyne was designed as a provincial model) and filled the office from 1778 until 1820 during which time he exercised extraordinary power and influence. He had been with Cook on the navigator's first great voyage[1] and thereafter took the liveliest interest in all matters concerning exploration and scientific discovery. In the last quarter of the 18th century, using as his agents scientists, seamen and merchants, he directed, more or less on his own authority, most of the British voyages of discovery and trade. The voyage made by Portlock and Dixon was one of them. These two men had been shipmates on Cook's third and last voyage. Portlock, in 1776, was entered on *Discovery* where he was rated as master's mate. In August 1779 he was moved into *Resolution*, Cook's second ship, and there joined George Dixon who was armourer, per warrant, aboard her. The story of Cook's voyage is told in his journal: *A voyage to the Pacific Ocean. Undertaken . . .for making discoveries in the Northern hemisphere, to determine the positions and extent of the west side of North America; its distance from Asia; and the practicability of a northern passage to Europe . . . in the years 1776, 1777, 1778, 1779 and 1780.* It was published in 1784. There are occasional mentions of Dixon and Portlock in this journal which make it clear that both were trusted men of ability and character. Cook had as his principal object the discovery of a navigable

[1] One result was his advocacy for the establishment of a penal colony in New South Wales. His interest in the colony was maintained and he corresponded frequently with its early governors. The second of them, John Hunter, was another honorary member of the Society. There is an account in Spence Watson's *History* of a gift to the Society of two 'hitherto nondescript animals lately found in New South Wales'. They were the duck-billed platypus and the wombat. They reached the Society in Newcastle via Sir Joseph Banks in 1799. Drawings and descriptions of them were inserted in the new edition of Bewick's *General history of quadrupeds* 'now just published.' The wombat may still be seen in the Hancock Museum, Newcastle upon Tyne.

passage from the North Pacific to the North Atlantic. He failed in this but in the course of his quest he explored parts of the North American coast of which little was known. The principal places he investigated were Nootka, or, as he called it, King George's Sound, Prince William's Sound, and Cook River, named after him. The Russian navigator Bering had fallen in with the land in this region in 1741 and had made a partial survey; the Spaniards and the French had also explored parts of the coast from 1775 onwards, but their records were partial and of doubtful accuracy. Cook was of the opinion that the Russians, for example, had never reached Nootka for had they done so, he thought, 'the natives would hardly be cloathed in such valuable skins as those of the sea beaver; the Russians would find some means or other to get them all from them.' It was from the furs Cook found in the harbours he explored that the trade was first set on foot. He wrote: 'There is no doubt but a very beneficial trade might be carried out with the inhabitants of this vast coast, but unless a northern passage is found it seems rather too remote for Great Britain to receive any emolument from it.' J. C. Beaglehole in his edition of the *Journal* of Cook's third voyage (Hakluyt Society, 1967) notes: 'Nevertheless there were British sailors anxious to reap an emolument, starting with Cook's own men.' G. T. Gilbert, midshipman in *Discovery*, in one of the supplements to Cook's *Journal*, wrote: 'We sold the remainder of our furs to much greater advantage [at Macao] than at Kamchatka; the Chinese being very eager to purchase them; that is from £11.5s to £15.15s. for what we bought with only a hatchet or a saw.' The possibilities of profit were also seen by the British commercial interests in Asia. A brig of sixty tons under the command of James Hanna was despatched from Canton in April 1785 and reached Nootka Sound in August. Hanna went again in 1786 and, in the same year, merchants from Bombay and Bengal sent ships to the same area and they were followed by the Portuguese from Macao. Also in 1786 at least five ships from England were on the coast in the fur trade, the first of these being those commanded by Portlock and Dixon. However, Cook's assessment of the long term possibilities so far as

Great Britain was concerned proved afterwards to have been sound, for, in the long run, as Beaglehole points out, it was the Americans and the Russians who made the most of the trade on the Pacific coast; the British trade continuing to be the inland one of the Hudson's Bay Company.

The first expedition from Great Britain with the primary purpose of trade in furs was mounted in May 1785 when Richard Cadman Etches, a London merchant and his associates entered into a commercial partnership under the title of the King George's Sound Company for carrying on a fur trade from the Western coast of America to China. For this purpose they obtained a licence from the South Sea Company of which company Portlock observed 'without carrying on any traffic themselves [they] stand in the mercantile way of more adventurous merchants.' A similar licence was procured, also with some difficulty, from the East India Company which, at the same time, engaged to give them a freight of teas from Canton. The difficulty with the East India Company was caused by the Company's initial opposition to the scheme which it regarded as an intrusion into its own sphere by independent merchants. Ultimately the Company gave way but imposed restrictions on the sale of the fur cargo which were to be imposed by the Company's super-cargoes at Canton who would also dictate terms for the return freight to London. While these negotiations were proceeding the King George's Sound Company purchased a ship of 320 tons and another of 200 tons, ships of a size and burden which Cook had recommended as the fittest for distant employments. These vessels were immediately put into dock in order that they might be fitted for so long a voyage and on 8th July 1785 they were moored at Deptford for the convenience of fitting rigging, engaging seamen and taking on stores and provisions. Dixon writes: 'In addition to the provisions usually allowed in merchants service (and of which the greatest care was taken to procure the best of every kind) a plentiful stock of all the various antiscorbutics was laid in which could be thought of as a preservation of health. These and an unremitting attention to the rules observed by Captain Cook have, under Providence, been the means of preserving the health of the people in every variety of climate; for during the present voyage, which has been more than three years continuance, the *Queen Charlotte* lost only one person.' Despite these measures scurvy was a constant menace and on one occasion when it struck Dixon himself was a victim. Portlock writes: 'Notwithstanding every precaution, the scurvy made its appearance among us, and the boatswain in particular was so bad that I had almost despaired of his recovery; but it fortunately happened that some salad, such as mustard and cress which I had sown in several casks of mould procured at Falkland's Islands was now in great perfection. I planted some horse-radish in a cask before we left England, which was in an improving state and some potatoes planted since we left Falkland's Islands, began to sprout very finely. These things were given to the boatswain and they had every good effect that could be wished; they checked the disorder and he began to recover his health daily. This unwholesome weather had likewise affected the health of several seamen on board the *Queen Charlotte* and Captain Dixon, in particular, being very bad, I went on board the *Queen Charlotte* and found his disorder to be the scurvy. At my return I sent him a cask of fine mould with salad growing in it together with some krout, garden seeds and a few bottles of mineral water . . . We frequently caught turtle which was constantly served out amongst the ship's company and I sent some on board the *Queen Charlotte*. This, with the addition of krout, portable soup and sweet-wort, contributed greatly to preserve the health of the ships' crews.' In fact many of these things were ineffective in combating scurvy. All were used because they had been used by Cook. The value of lemon juice seems not to have been fully recognised despite the experience of Banks who, on Cook's first voyage, had suffered scurvy and had been cured by its use.

'In the meantime', writes Portlock, 'the owners appointed me commander of the larger vessel, and of the expedition, and George Dixon of the smaller, both of us having accompanied Captain Cook in his last voyage into the Pacific Ocean were deemed most proper for an adventure which required no common knowledge and experience. Other officers of competent talents were at the same time appointed in order that they might know each other . . . The novelty of the enterprise attracted the notice of several persons who were eminent either for talents or station, and who promoted the voyage by their countenance or strengthened the company by their approbation. When Sir Joseph Banks and Lord Mulgrave, Mr. Rose and Sir John Dick came on board the Secretary of the Treasury named the larger vessel the *King George* and the President of the Royal Society called the smaller the *Queen Charlotte*.' The Secretary of the Treasury was George Rose. Constantine Phipps, Lord Mulgrave, was an Oxford friend of Banks who became a naval officer. Banks sailed with him to Newfoundland in 1766 in the *Niger*, a naval vessel on the North American fisheries patrol. Later he became a member of the Board of Control. Sir John Dick was a diplomat who had a considerable knowledge of Russian expansion, a matter which had already attracted the notice of Cook and which was of considerable interest to the promoters of the present enterprise. Portlock continues: 'Exclusive of the profits of trade, or the advantages of discovery, this voyage was destined to other national objects. Several gentlemen's sons who had shown an inclination to engage in a seafaring life were put under my care for the purpose of initiation into the knowledge of the profession which requires length of service rather than supereminence of genius. I engaged William Philpot Evans and Joseph Woodcock, two of the pupils of Mr. Wales, the master of the mathematical school in Christ's Hospital, who were at once able to assist in teaching the boys the rudiments of navigation and might be usefully employed in taking views of remarkable lands and in constructing charts of commodious harbours.' William Wales (1734? - 1795), F.R.S. and also an honorary member of the Society, was engaged by the Board of Longitude to accompany Cook on his second voyage and to make astronomical observations. He also went on Cook's third voyage. The *King George's* company comprised fifty-nine officers, men and boys, some of the boys mere children, plus the tutors Evans and

Woodcock. The *Queen Charlotte* had thirty-three officers and men plus one supercargo, William Beresford, described, as were Evans and Woodcock, as Assistant Trader.

There was a slight delay before the voyage began. Dixon writes: 'Our pilot being come on board and everything being ready for sailing we weighed anchor and stood down the river for Gravesend . . . Though we were got thus far yet our voyage had like to have been greatly retarded on the following account. The articles of agreement being read to the people this evening they refused to sign them without a greater advance of wages than is usually given; but this Captain Portlock absolutely refused to comply with and after reasoning with them some time they cheerfully agreed to proceed on the voyage . . . In the morning the people of both ships were paid what wages were due to them, together with a month's advance which they presently laid out in purchasing necessaries of the slop-boats that came alongside us, and who never fail to attend on these occasions, well knowing that a proper sailor can never go to sea with a safe conscience while he has any money in his pocket. The tide serving we stood for the Downs.' On 9th September 1785 the two ships were at Spithead, leaving there on the 16th for Guernsey where they lay waiting for a fair wind. They departed from there on 26th September and touched at Madeira, the Cape Verde Islands and the Falklands, doubled Cape Horn and reached the Sandwich Islands at the end of May 1786. From there they sailed on 13th June and made the coast of America, near the mouth of Cook River, in latitude 59°N. on 18th July. In that neighbourhood they remained some weeks and then worked their way southwards towards King George's or Nootka Sound off which they were on 24th September, but, being prevented by baffling winds and calms from entering the Sound, they returned to the Sandwich Islands where they wintered. On 13th March 1787 they again sailed for the coast of America and on 24th April anchored off Montague Island where the search for furs began. On 14th May the two ships separated, it being considered more likely to lead to profitable results if they worked independently. During the next three months Dixon was busily employed southward as far as King

George's Sound, trading with the natives, taking notes of their manners and customs, as well as of the trade facilities, and making a careful survey of the several points that came within his reach. Cook had already denoted the general outline of the coast, but the detail was still wanting and much of this was now filled in by Dixon, more especially the important group of islands discovered and named by him the Queen Charlotte Islands. Nearer the mainland, inside the Dixon Entrance to Hecate Strait, he called one of the larger islands he discovered there after Banks. He also collected specimens of natural history and many artefacts including a canoe from Port Mulgrave and an Indian lip piece which came into Banks's collection. Dixon, it appears, also collected for himself, for Rüdiger Joppien and Bernard Smith, in the book cited earlier in this paper, record, with an acknowledgement to their informant Jonathan King, the existence in the Keswick Museum of an undated MS catalogue which records that the Crosthwaite Museum in Keswick, founded by Peter Crosthwaite (1735-1808) and opened in 1780, had a number of objects from George Dixon's collection. The catalogue also mentions 'a most ingenious machine which the late Captain Dixon invented for measuring Deapth of the Sea, when lead and line will not answer; after getting to a certain depth with lead and line the pressure is so great upon them that you lose the weight and cannot tell when the lead reaches the bottom; this curious and ingenious little model was made by Captain Dixon and is very much admired; it answers at all times if there are no currents.' The Crosthwaite Museum was disposed of in 1870.

The Charlotte Islands, as Dixon wrote: 'surpassed our most sanguine expectations and afforded a greater quantity of furs than perhaps any place hitherto known.' He noted, on one occasion in July 1787 that 'there were ten canoes about the ship containing as nearly as I could estimate, 120 people; many of these brought most beautiful beaver cloaks; others, excellent skins and, in short, none came empty handed, and the rapidity with which they sold them was a circumstance additionally pleasing; they fairly quarrelled with each other about who should sell his cloak first; and some actually threw their furs on board, if nobody was at hand to receive them; but we took particular care to let none go from the vessel unpaid . . . In less than half an hour we purchased 300 beaver skins, of an excellent quality; a circumstance which greatly raised our spirits, and the more as both the plenty of fine furs, and the avidity of the natives in parting with them, were convincing proofs that no traffic whatever had recently been carried on near this place and, consequently, we might expect a continuation of this plentiful commerce.'

On leaving King George's Sound the *Queen Charlotte* returned to the Sandwich Islands. On 18th September she sailed from there for China where it had been agreed that she was to meet her consort. On 9th November she anchored at Macao where it was learned that a permit from the customhouse was required before she could proceed to Canton. On 16th November the *Queen Charlotte* came to anchor in Whampoa Roads and Dixon went in a Chinese passage-boat to Canton to seek the East India Company's supercargoes. From them he learned that no steps could be taken to dispose of the furs until the Superintendent of the Chinese customs had been on board to measure the vessel. On the 25th the *King George* arrived in the river 'and anchored near us; bringing all her people in good health and spirits.' On the following day both captains went to Canton. 'Mr. Browne (President of the Supercargoes) assured them that the Superintendent of the Customs (or John Tuck, as the Chinese commonly called him) would come to measure both vessels very shortly, and that immediately afterwards, our business should be expedited without delay . . . At ten o'clock in the morning of the 2nd December we were honoured with the presence of John Tuck on board. He was attended by a numerous retinue, who paid him a princely respect, saluting him at his coming upon deck with a bent knee. This visit' continues Dixon, 'seems to be a mere matter of form, as they only measure from the foremast to the taffrel, and then athwart near the gangway, which certainly can give them but a very imperfect idea of a vessel's burthen; however they demand (I am informed) no less than a thousand pounds sterling as a port charge for this piece of mummery ... His Excellency made us a present of two poor buffaloes, eight jars of Samshu (a spirit so bad that we threw it overboard) and eight bags of ground rice, about forty pounds each. This necessary piece of business being over, proper measures were taken to get our furs to Canton. We learnt on enquiry that a Custom-House boat must be procured at Canton for the cargo of each vessel, the expense of which would be fifteen dollars each; however, as the *King George's* cargo was considerably less than ours, we judged that by taking their furs on board our vessel, the expense of a boat might be saved.

From our first arrival till now, the people had been employed in overhauling the rigging and repairing whatever was defective ... These different employments engrossed the greater part of this month; and indeed we were in no particular hurry as none of our furs were yet disposed of and ... we could not take in any cargo for the East India Company. Whilst everything on board our vessel was getting forward ... our business at Canton was totally at a stand ... In order to form some idea of the probable reasons for this delay, it may perhaps be necessary to say a few words respecting the consignment of our skins, the methods taken by the persons they were consigned to for the disposal of them, and the various impediments raised by the Chinese to prevent their being sold to advantage. No sooner were our skins landed ... than a particular account of them was taken by a set of merchants belonging to the Customs and who (I understand) give security to the Emperor for the duty being paid: another account was taken by people employed by Mr. Browne. Our skins being properly assorted the quantity fixed on to be disposed of by Mr. Browne was 2,552 sea-otter skins, 434 cub, and 34 fox skins. The remainder of our cargo: beaver tails, pieces of beaver skins, fur seals, and marmot, racoon, lynx skins, etc. were left to be disposed of by our captains in the best manner they were able; probably for no other reason than to furnish them with money for their current expenses and no doubt, expecting what they had left would be surely sufficient for that purpose. In regard to the sale of our furs I should first observe that there is at Canton a Company of wealthy merchants called the Hong-Merchants with whom our East India Company transact all their business and purchase from them the whole of the tea and China-ware sent to Britain. To these people our furs were offered with an expectation of their immediately taking them off our hands at an advantageous price; but here we were woefully disappointed ... for the moment these Hong-Merchants had looked the skins over and fixed a value on them, no other merchant durst interfere ... In this poor situation were we ... during the month of December and the greatest part of January: either we must close with the paltry offers which the Hong-Merchants had made to the super-cargoes, or be under the necessity of leaving our furs in their hands undisposed of ... Meanwhile some of the refuse which they had left for us to dispose of, sold to considerable advantage.' The furs were sold at last on 26th January for 50,000 dollars, roughly one third of the sum hoped for, it having been found impossible to get a better price. By this time, too, the cargoes of tea were on board and it was time to think of sailing. The venture, in terms of trade, had not fulfilled, indeed had fallen far short of, the high expectations of the King George's Sound Company; nevertheless a profit had been made — some thousands of pounds according to Portlock. The two ships dropped down to Macao and sailed on 9th February 1788 for England. In bad weather off the Cape of Good Hope they parted company and, though they met again at St. Helena, they sailed from there independently. The *Queen Charlotte* arrived off Dover on 17th September having been preceded by the *King George* by about a fortnight.

There remains to be told what else is known and what may be conjectured about the lives of Nathaniel Portlock and George Dixon. Portlock was born about 1748 and entered the Navy in 1772 as able seaman. He was soon made midshipman. Before this he may have been mate, or possibly master, of a merchantman. In 1776, as mentioned already, he was master's mate on Cook's *Discovery* and was moved in 1779 into *Resolution*. On returning to England at the end of Cook's last voyage he passed his examination for lieutenant. This was on 7th September 1780 when he was officially stated to be 'more than 32'. On 14th September he was promoted lieutenant. In May 1785 he was appointed to command the expedition described in this paper. In 1791 he was appointed to command the brig *Assistant* going out as tender to the *Providence* which was commanded by William Bligh on the second breadfruit voyage of 1791-3. The breadfruit voyages, initiated and planned by Banks, had the object of introducing breadfruit trees from the Society Islands to the West Indies as a reliable source of food for the slave population there. The first, in 1787, was in the *Bounty*, also commanded by Bligh. It failed because of the mutiny. The second was successful. In 1793 Portlock was appointed Commander and in 1799 he was advanced to post rank. His health was much broken in later years and he does not appear to have had further service afloat. In 1816 he was admitted to Greenwich Hospital where he died on 12th September 1817. His son, Joseph Ellison Portlock, was born in 1794 in Gosport. He, after passing through the Royal Military Academy at Woolwich, was commissioned as second lieutenant in the Royal Engineers in 1813. He rose to major-general and was an eminent geologist who became President of the Geological Society and did distinguished work on the Geological Survey of Ireland. He died in 1864.

Much less is known about George Dixon, partly because he seems never to have held commissioned rank, the title by which he is known deriving from his command of the *Queen Charlotte*. Joppien and Smith have identified him with a George Dixon who was a native of Kirkoswald in Cumberland and who was baptised on 15th September 1727. Their source was the Cumbria County Council Archive Department from where they gained the additional information that brief mentions in county directories indicate that he may have died about 1791. The disappearance of Dixon's name from local directories, if it was from this that the inference was drawn, may mean only that he left the county at about that time. It lends some support to his identification, mentioned in *D.N.B.* as based on insufficient evidence, with a George Dixon who taught navigation at Gosport and published there, in 1791, the *Navigator's assistant*. The Kirkoswald identification is supported by the inclusion in the Crosthwaite Museum of the items from George Dixon's collection and the description of him in its catalogue as 'circumnavigator, a native of Cumberland, he sailed twice round the Globe, once with Captain Cook, and once with Capt. Pocock [Portlock].' But, accepting that the identification is correct, it would seem that Dixon was about fifty years of age when he sailed with Cook as a petty officer and approaching sixty when he made his own voyage as captain of the *Queen Charlotte*. Cook, certainly, was an older man than Dixon but, even so, there is cause for surprise.

Of Dixon's early life, education and early career nothing is known, his first appearance in the annals of exploration and discovery being in Cook's journals. In August 1784,[1] the year before his departure on the voyage I have described, he put before Banks a scheme for an expedition to the North-West coast of America by way of a land crossing along the string of lakes westward using Indian guides. He proposed that thirty subscribers should finance the expedition which would be directed by three scientists: David Nelson, assistant surgeon on Cook's *Resolution* was the botanist, William Ellis, another surgeon, the draughtsman, while Dixon himself would take command and do the astronomical work. He had several meetings with Banks to get support but Banks was doubtful. He admitted that the unsettled state of relations between Britain and America 'furnishes excuses for every act of irregularity', but thought the scheme impracticable. Nothing came of it. Towards the end of 1784 Dixon was approached by William Bolts, the Dutch adventurer who had been deported from India by the East India Company and who was then supervising the construction of a ship at Marseille for a voyage to the North-West coast of America planned by the Imperial Asiatic Company of Vienna. This also fell through. Early in 1785 Dixon, with the aid of Banks,

[1] For this and for much subsequent information on Dixon's activities in 1785 and in 1789 and 1790 I am indebted to Mackay, David. *In the wake of Cook*. London, 1985.

engaged the interest of Richard Cadman Etches in the scheme which resulted in the voyage of 1785-1788. On his return to England Dixon busied himself with his book which was published in 1789. Later in that year Alexander Dalrymple, hydrographer to the East India Company published his *Plan for promoting the fur trade* for which he drew heavily on Dixon's experience. He advocated co-operation between the East India and the Hudson's Bay companies in which the former would send their ships from China to collect furs on the North-West coast of America which had been gathered by agents of the Hudson's Bay Company. Soon afterwards Dalrymple and Dixon submitted a plan to the Home Office for crossing America by way of Quebec or Hudson's Bay. This was a revised version of Dixon's scheme of 1784. In July Dixon conceded that it was too late in the season for a crossing of the continent from the East but suggested that the government should send a ship via Cape Horn to make a settlement on the North-West coast so as to avoid the possibility of the engrossing of the fur trade by the many foreigners then operating in the North Pacific. In 1790 a scheme, based probably on Dalrymple's and Dixon's plan, was proposed which involved the sending of two overland parties from Hudson's Bay. Dixon, who would then have been sixty-three years of age, was chosen to lead one party. Events in 1790 which caused naval and diplomatic clashes with Spain resulted in the shelving of this plan too.

At the beginning of this paper it was mentioned that when Dixon was elected an honorary member of the Society he was living in Bermuda. The discovery of this fact led to correspondence with Bermuda Archives and the St. George's Historical Society in Bermuda which established that he was living there in 1794, for there, on 27th May, died Mrs. Dixon, wife of Captain George Dixon of St. George's. She was, reported the *Royal Bermuda Gazette,* 'lately from England.' The records of St. Peter's Church, St. George's, Bermuda show that she was buried on 28th May. They also record the baptism of Marianne, daughter of George and Ann Dixon on 6th May, 1794 and in the following year, on 12th November, the burial of George Dixon. The *Gazette* published an obituary: 'Captain George Dixon . . . died on 9th November after a short illness. He was celebrated for having sailed several [sic] times around the world, the last of which he performed in the ship *Queen Charlotte*. He was by profession a jeweller which he latterly followed, more for amusement than for emolument.' He would have been about sixty-eight years of age. His daughter Marianne lived on in Bermuda and married there. She had three daughters, the first of whom was named Georgeanne. None of them married and with their deaths the Dixon family's connection with Bermuda came to an end.

SOURCES:

The Literary and Philosophical Society of Newcastle upon Tyne. *Minutes* for 1795.

Correspondence, filed by the Society, with Bermuda Archives and the St. George's Historical Society, Bermuda.

Carter, Harold B. *Sir Joseph Banks, 1743-1820*. London, 1988.

Cook, James. *A voyage to the Pacific Ocean in the years 1776-1780*. London 1784.

Cook, James. *A voyage to the Pacific Ocean in the years 1776-1780*.
Edited by J. C. Beaglehole (Hakluyt Society). London, 1967.

Dictionary of National Biography.

Dixon, George. *A voyage round the world* . . . London, 1789.

Joppien, Rüdiger and Smith Bernard. *The art of Captain Cook's voyages.* Vol.3. London, 1988.

Mackay, David. *In the wake of Cook.* London, 1985.

Portlock, Nathaniel. *A voyage round the world* . . . London, 1789.

CHAPTER SEVEN

BIOGRAPHICAL ESSAY III

William Bulmer (1757-1830)

Fine Printer and Honorary Member*

Peter C. G. Isaac

Without any previous indication in the Minutes of the Council of the Royal Society that anything like this was about to happen, one of the Minutes of the meeting of the Council for the 22 December 1791 reads

> Resolved,
> That in consideration of the avowed superiority of Mr Bulmer's printing he be for the future employed in printing the transactions of the Society ...

And so, perhaps for the first time, two of our distinguished Honorary Members came together — Sir Joseph Banks, President of the Royal Society, and the subject of my talk this evening, William Bulmer, the Newcastle-born fine printer. Banks, who, as we shall see, was 'into everything', was elected Honorary Member of our Society in 1794, while Bulmer was elected in 1797.

Bulmer set up the Shakspeare Press on Lady Day 1790, and, as we can see from this Minute, he seems to have been recognized as a 'fine printer' from the outset of his career. How did his background and training equip him for this?

BULMER'S START IN LIFE

William was the seventh child of Thomas Bulmer, a member of the House Carpenters' Company, and was born in Newcastle upon Tyne towards the end of 1757, being baptised on the 13 November in St. John's Church. It is worth noting parenthetically that the second son was

---

* Lecture to the Society in 1987.

Sir Fenwick Bulmer, some 12 years older, who became successful as a druggist in the Strand, and who must have played a part in introducing his younger brother to the 'right people'.

We have contemporary mentions of Bulmer in Thomas Bewick's posthumous memoir and in the near-literate 'Biographical sketch of three Newcastle apprentices', written no later than 1828, by Robert Pollard, the little-known copperplate engraver, who was an apprentice in Newcastle at the same time as Bewick and Bulmer. The sketch was published by the radical editor, William Mitchell, in his *Newcastle Magazine* for October 1830[1], the issue carrying Bulmer's obituary. Neither is much more than anecdotal, although Bewick tells us that Bulmer helped to take proofs of his early wood-engravings.

The printer seems to have been apprenticed to Isaac Thompson, a Quaker master printer who died on the 6 January 1776, just before Bulmer was out of his time. His indentures must have been transferred to Isaac's son, John, since William Bulmer was admitted to Freedom of Newcastle by patrimony at the Guild in January 1778. The general standard of printing in Newcastle at that time was not high — even in a book which may be carrying our printer's name as editor[2] — so that it seems likely that Bulmer can have learnt no more than the rudiments of his craft. His ambition demanded more.

Although he was admitted to the Freedom of the City in January 1778 he was not sworn until September 1780. This suggests that Bulmer had left Newcastle by the end of 1777. J. B. Nichols, in his unsigned obituary of the printer in the *Gentleman's Magazine* for October 1830[3], writes that our printer was employed by John Bell, who had strong connexions with France. Further, Robert Pollard, in his sketch, says that Bulmer went to that country to improve his skills, and on returning to England attracted the attention of George Nicol, bookseller to the King. (It is no more than a conjecture on my part, but service to the King may have been the means by which Fenwick Bulmer drew the attention of the Royal Bookseller to his brother's talents. The older brother was a member of the Honourable Band of Gentlemen Pensioners, who waited on the King on ceremonial occasions, from 1785 and William from 1790.)

On the face of it there is a gap in our printer's history between his leaving Newcastle in 1777 and his working for George Nicol — to be mentioned in a moment — in 1787. My attention has very recently been drawn by Miss Mary Pollard, formerly of the Library of Trinity College, Dublin, to a William Bulmer who was a printer at 2 Church Lane, Dublin, and who printed the *Volunteer Evening Post* in that city from the 10 November 1783 to the 19 May 1785. The printer is listed in Wilson's *Dublin Directory* for 1785 and 1786, and in Pendred (1785). 'The paper was funded by the Administration as part of their propaganda battle with the Dublin newspaper press, and payments to Bulmer, ostensibly for advertisements and proclamations, are recorded in the *Journals of the House of Commons of Ireland.*' There are no records of payments to Bulmer after May 1785.[4] It seems more than likely that such a printer would not be Irish; is this our printer on his way up?

THE BOYDELL SHAKSPEARE

Since Bulmer was launched on the book-loving world of his time by his commission to print the great illustrated Shakspeare of Alderman Sir John Boydell, it is worth a moment to glance at the genesis of this project.

Boydell, who had been Master of the Stationers' Company and was Lord Mayor of London in 1790, was one of the leading print-sellers of the late eighteenth century and was a patron of artists. At that time portrait painting, at which British artists excelled, had less prestige than historical painting. Boydell, therefore, wished to stimulate the start of a school of British historical painting. A meeting to discuss this was held at the house of his nephew, Josiah, in Hampstead on the 4 November 1786.[5] Amongst the artists present were Benjamin West, George Romney, William Hayley and Paul Sandby. A grandiose scheme was proposed:

1. to commission two series of oil paintings of Shakspearian scenes;
2. to build a gallery for their permanent exhibition;
3. to publish, without text, a collection of engravings from the larger pictures;

4. to publish a folio edition of Shakspeare's plays, illustrated with engravings from the smaller pictures.

George Nicol, who was also at the meeting, and who seems to have been one of the prime movers in all this, undertook the oversight of the publication of the plays. In an advertisement, dated 4 June 1791, that he prepared for this publication, after mentioning type-founding, paper and ink he wrote[6]

> The last object was still the most important — the making proper use of all these materials. For that purpose a printing-press had been erected in my house; but it was soon foreseen, that my numerous and unavoidable avocations would prevent me from paying that unremitting attention to the executive part of the printing, which in a great work is absolutely indispensable. In the meantime a gentleman offered his assistance, whose talents, industry, and skill, left nothing further to be desired; and I will venture to say, that the specimens of typography which will soon appear from the Shakspeare Press, will convince all Europe that Mr. Bulmer is second to no man in his profession.

This strongly suggests not only that Bulmer was working for him, perhaps in his house in Pall Mall, from 1786 or 1787, but also — and very importantly — that our printer was recognized, as early as 1786, as a skilled craftsman and (?) as a 'gentleman'.

SIR JOSEPH BANKS AND THE ROYAL SOCIETY

Sir Joseph Banks was at the centre of scientific and related public affairs for the whole of Bulmer's working life at the Shakspeare Press, and Bulmer printed for many of his associates. The Banks family, originally from Yorkshire, held Revesby Abbey in Lincolnshire. Joseph was born in London in 1744, and was schooled at Harrow and Eton, where he had shown a keen interest in natural history. As a gentleman-commoner at Christ Church, Oxford, in 1760 he had engaged a lecturer in botany to instruct him in it. In 1763, after his father's death, he inherited the large Revesby estate. Here he continued his scientific studies, and gave much attention to agriculture (reflected later in his contributions to the

Board of Argiculture), to the development of his property and to the raising of stock.[7] He made the acquaintance of Lord Sandwich, First Lord of the Admiralty, and this friendship later helped him when he proposed voyages of discovery in both northern and southern polar regions.[7]

Banks was elected a Fellow of the Royal Society in 1766. The Society's attempt to make scientific observations of the transit of Venus across the sun's disk in 1761 at St. Helena had proved unsuccessful because of bad weather, but another opportunity offered in 1769. The Royal Society persuaded the Government, once again, to finance an expedition to the Pacific. The Astronomer Royal, Dr. Nevil Maskelyne FRS, who had been balked by the weather at St. Helena, prepared the instructions for the observers. Those in the Pacific were to be Lieut James Cook and Charles Green.[8]

Banks wrote to the Council of the Royal Society, asking them to apply to the Lords of the Admiralty for permission for him to accompany Cook in HMS *Endeavour* at his own expense. This was agreed, and Banks, with his staff including Dr. Solander, a Swedish botanist, two draughtsmen and four servants, joined the expedition, which sailed from Plymouth on the 26 August 1768. Travelling by way of Rio de Janeiro and Cape Horn, they reached Otaheite on 13 April 1769.[9] 'The transit was successfully observed, and the ship returned by way of Batavia and the Cape of Good Hope, reaching Deal on the 12 July 1771. The voyage had been most successful, for besides the observation of the transit of Venus important additions were made to our knowledge of Australia as well as of the fauna and flora of the coasts and islands.'[10] Banks made valuable collections of natural-history specimens, and this expedition left him with a lasting interest in the plants and animals of the Pacific and Asia, which resulted in the production of several rare illustrated books, for which Bulmer was responsible. An example is *Plants of the Coast of Coromandel,* three folio volumes published between 1795 and 1819 by William Roxburgh and Sir Joseph Banks. This has 300 splendid plates.

It was in the spirit of enquiry adumbrated by Francis Bacon, of experiment into natural (as opposed to metaphysical) knowledge, that a small group of natural philosophers, many hailing from the University of Cambridge, met at Gresham College in London during the Commonwealth to pursue their learned discussions and studies. Out of this Society of Philosophers grew the Royal Society of London for Promoting Natural Knowledge. From the first men of substance and influence, who could provide the necessary patronage to practising scientists, were admitted to the Society. From 1660 until the middle of the nineteenth century slightly over two-thirds of the Fellows of the Royal Society were non-scientific, and this proportion is reflected in the membership of Council until about 1820.[11] It happened, therefore, that the President was not always an eminent scientist.

In 1778, following a disagreement between the Society and the King about the design of lightning-conductors, the President, Sir John Pringle, physician to George III, did not stand for the annual reelection. After much discussion Council recommended Joseph Banks as President; this was a considerable departure from previous practice, since he was only 35 at the time. He was reelected annually until his death in 1820.[12] There must have been some canvassing for the post for Nichols reproduces a letter from Banks to Richard Gough, soliciting his support.[13] In view of the Royal Society's desire to heal its estrangement from the Court the choice of Banks as President seems to have been wise. On his return from the expedition in HMS *Endeavour* he had become George III's chief adviser on science, persuading him 'to turn Kew Gardens into a centre for cultivating exotic botanical specimens'.[14] He 'took no part in the politics of the day, and identified himself with neither of the principal parties, nor would he stand for election as a Member of Parliament, all of which qualities were in his favour'.[15] 'A man of so forceful a personality and such exceptional ability would soon make himself familiar with the business of the Society and would then control to a great extent the activities of the Council'.[16]

Although Banks was a wealthy landowner he seems to have been regarded as one of the scientific Fellows, and is supposed to have wished to limit the Fellowship 'to those who had either successfully cultivated the sciences or who were rich enough to become the patrons of those who did'.[17] This, as may be imagined, produced dissension in the Society.[18] Although, for example, Sir Charles Wilkins was elected FRS in 1788 for his pioneering work in Sanskrit, the Royal Society seems to have reduced its support for antiquarian research and other non-scientific pursuits from the end of the eighteenth century.[17]

Lyons, writing as an able treasurer and administrator in the Royal Society, is very critical of Banks's unbusinesslike handling of the Society's finances.[19] Having gone over the records of several organisations of which Banks was an officer, it is clear to me that Sir Henry Lyons has projected back over one and a half centuries the more democratic manner in which learned bodies are now run. It is anachronistic to do so; Sir Joseph Banks saw the Royal Society, like Revesby Abbey, as his fief — to be run efficiently by himself without much explanation to those he may have regarded as subordinates. And this is the purpose of my lengthy discursus on the Royal Society — to show how Sir Joseph Banks, by taking firmly into his own hands the affairs of those organisations which he led, was able to patronise those tradesmen and craftsmen, whose work he valued and whom, like Bulmer, he wished to support. His position as PRS resulted in his being called on to support, and advise on, the establishment of many new scientific and related activities.

Perhaps the earliest result of Bulmer's being brought to the attention of Banks (presumably through George Nicol) was the resolution of the Council of the Royal Society on the 22 December 1791, with which this talk opened.[20] This resolution seems to have come out of the blue, in so far as there is no relevant discussion recorded in earlier minutes. Nichols[21] quotes a letter from Banks (whom he supplied with information about Lincolnshire) explaining that it was only Bulmer's reputation as a fine printer that had caused the

Society to change their printer. Nichols adds an illuminating and ironic footnote in extenuation

> Mr. Bulmer has the credit of first bringing into extensive use what is technically called *Fine Printing;* which had been previously carried on in Paris by the celebrated Didot; at Birmingham by Baskerville; and still earlier in London (on a small scale) by Dryden Leach... — — It consists in new Types, excellent Ink, improved Printing Presses, a sufficient time allowed to the Pressman for extraordinary attention, and last, not least, an inclination in the Employer to pay a considerably advanced price. — Mr Bulmer's example was succesfully followed by Mr. Bensley; and *Fine Printing* is now performed by every Printer of respectability in the United Empire.

In fact an analysis of the costs of printing the *Philosophical Transactions* from 1780 to 1822 does not show any sudden increase when Bulmer took over.[22]

Before he died at Heston, Middlesex, on the 19 June 1820,[23] in which year Bulmer retired from active control of the Shakspeare Press, Sir Joseph Banks had helped Bulmer to get commissions from several other societies.

BANKS, BULMER AND THE OTHER ORGANISATIONS

Another corporate customer, for which Bulmer came to print as a result of Sir Joseph Banks's intervention, was the African Association. The two men who took the lead were Henry Beaufoy and Banks. Beaufoy, the son of a Quaker wine-merchant, was an MP and opposed the slave trade; he became the Secretary, while Banks became the Treasurer, and it is out of the duties of this office that the Association's first printer was changed for Bulmer — once again![24]

The Association's earliest printer was Colin Macrae of Orange Street, Leicester Fields. He seems to have been a less than satisfactory businessman, since he was bankrupt in 1795,[25] but he clearly fell out with Banks over his account for the Association's printing.[26] The Banks papers in the Sutro Library naturally show mainly one side of the correspondence, but is is clear that Banks thought that the Association had been overcharged for printing and sewing. There is a sworn deposition, dated 1 July 1790, about the affair.

The early volumes of the Minutes of the African Association are in the Cambridge University Library.[27] There are several references to arranging for papers to be printed, but the printer is in no case mentioned except in relation to accounts being presented for payment. It seems clear, therefore, as I have suggested above, that Banks, as Treasurer, acted on his own authority to engage (and discharge) the printers.

Bulmer printed the Association's *Proceedings* from no later than 1792, and, although these do not carry his name, it seems that George Nicol acted as the Association's bookseller.[28] In March 1808 Nicol gave an account of the Parts held by him, and at the same meeting Bulmer presented an estimate for reprinting 750 copies of the papers to date in one quarto volume.[29] Bulmer also printed such papers for the Association as James Rennell's *Elucidations of the African Geography* (1793), and such major works as the journeys of Park and Hornemann.

It was not until the Association recruited the young Scottish surgeon, Mungo Park, in 1794 that it can be said to have successfully begun its exploration. Park's *Travels in the Interior of Africa, 1795-1797* (1799), in two volumes was a success and had run into six editions by 1810, four years after his death on his second expedition, which was not under the aegis of the Association. The later expedition and the two journeys together were published by John Murray, and the details may be found in that firm's archives.[30] It goes without saying that Bulmer printed all of them.

There are many other ways in which the influence of Sir Joseph Banks helped Bulmer in his career, particularly in developing his market. It is noticeable, for example, that two members of Council of the Royal Society, who attended most meetings of the Council in Bulmer's early days as printer to the Society, were James Rennell and Joseph Planta. Rennell was active in the African Association, that we have already discussed, and Bulmer also printed at least six of his geographical books. Planta had been appointed Assistant

Librarian at the British Museum in 1773, becoming Principal Librarian in 1799. His own *History of the Helvetic Confederacy* (2 vols. 1800) was printed by Bulmer, and no doubt he had a hand in guiding in our printer's direction the Museum's splendid illustrated descriptions of its marbles and terracottas. (Incidentally, it is worth remembering that Banks bequeathed all his books and other collections to the British Museum.)

Of the Societies for which Bulmer printed the last to be founded with a Banks connexion was the Horticultural Society of London, the lead being taken by John Wedgwood, of the pottery family. In this case Bulmer did not work for the Society from its very earliest days, perhaps because we find the bookseller John Hatchard associated with the enterprise rather than George Nicol.

The inaugural meeting of the Society was held on Wednesday the 7 March 1804 — in the house of the bookseller, John Hatchard, in Piccadilly, London. Seven attended this meeting: Wedgwood, who took the chair, William Forsyth (gardener to the King), Banks, the Rt. Hon. Charles Greville, R. A. Salisbury, W. T. Aiton and James Dickson.[31]

Periodical meetings were held, at which papers on horticultural subjects were read, and minutes of these meetings are in the archives of the Royal Horticultural Society. From about 1807 these papers were printed and issued in periodical parts, five or six making up the first volume. These first five or six parts were printed by William Savage, of Bedford Bury, London,[32] but Bulmer seems to have become the printer by 1812, when the first volume of collected parts was published. From then onwards he printed the *Transactions* and such other publications of the Society as lists of members etc.[33] The manuscript minutes of the early meetings of the Council of the Society mention accounts for printing from William Savage on the 5 May 1807, 3 May 1808, 2 January 1810, 9 February 1810, 5 June 1810 and 15 May 1811. The first mention of an account for printing from Bulmer was the 7 April 1812. It looks, therefore, as if the Society's printing was transferred to him in 1811.

The Society's second President, T. A. Knight, younger

brother of another of 'Bulmer's authors', Richard Payne Knight, issued his *Pomona Herefordiensis,* in ten bi-monthly parts (each containing three coloured plates), beginning in October 1808,[34] and the letterpress was printed by Bulmer, the work was published by the Agricultural Society of Herefordshire. Nevertheless there was, once again a close connexion with Sir Joseph Banks: the engraver of the splendid plates was William Hooker, often employed by Banks.[35]

BULMER AND BEWICK

Meeting as we are within a stone's throw of Bewick's workshop we must take account of the working relationship between Bulmer and that other of the Northeast's famous sons, the wood-engraver Thomas Bewick — a relationship that was not always easy.

One of Bulmer's early productions, and the first in which he ventured as his own publisher, was the *Poems of Goldsmith and Parnell* (1795), with splendid wood-engravings by the brothers Thomas and John Bewick. This is, perhaps, the most successful contemporary showing of Bewick's wood-engravings. It was very profitable for the printer, but caused some friction between him and the Bewick family, who thought that the engraver had been inadequately rewarded for his work.

That Bulmer gave detailed oversight to all aspects of this work is shown by instructions in his hand accompanying proof pulls of three engravings: The Traveller (p. 3), The Departure (p. 29) and the Hermit, Angel, and Guide (p. 72).[36] The first of these is well worth quoting

> Mr. Westall, you will see has drawn an outline to this painting, which will assist you very much. Be very particular in finishing this block, and above all things preserve the characteristic sentiment of the face, which so happily accords with the language of the poet. Without this, the whole force of the drawing will be lost. The Shrub, too must be exactly copied. Omit the W.R.W. at the corner.

In April 1794 Bulmer issued a prospectus[37] about the *Poems,* which starts in the same vein as his much-quoted

Advertisement to the first edition. The fourth paragraph is very germane to the Bewick thesis

> The Price of the Work in boards, to Subscribers, will be One Guinea. And as this publication is undertaken with the laudable ambition of exhibiting the abilities of the different Artists, without the most distant regard to emolument on the part of the Printer, two hundred and fifty copies only will be taken off.

It seems highly unlikely that the run was as small as 250, and there is a note in Jane Bewick's hand on the letter from Bulmer to Bewick, which will be discussed in a moment, 'Bulmer told us he soon sold 1000 copies at one guinea each he wd. not tell us where the cuts now are.' Timperley[38] also records 'This volume was highly appreciated by the public; two editions of it, in 4to. were sold, and they produced a profit to the ingenious printer, after payment of all expenses, of £1,500.'[39]

The next, and last, paragraph in the prospectus shows how important the engravings were to the enterprise

> Gentlemen wishing to be possessed of this Specimen of the Art, are requested to leave their names, as early as possible, at the Shakspeare Printing Office, Cleveland Row, St. James's, where the Engravings on Wood, and the Letter-press, may be seen.

A letter from Bulmer to Bewick, dated 20 January 1794, gives his answer to the engraver's accusations.[40]

> Why you should obliquely hint a doubt of my honor, or the expressions of friendship which I had frequently professed for your fame, & for your welfare, I know not — neither will I trouble myself with the enquiry — & retrospect of my conduct to you, since our earliest acquaintance, will, I presume, be the strongest confutation on that head. We are now at issue concerning a business in which I employed you near 2 years ago, & the sooner that is settled, the more agreeable it will be to my feelings; for you may rest assured it is contrary to my inclination to enter a correspondence of disputation with any person, but more particularly with a man for whom I have invariably held the highest respect & esteem.

The printer then goes on to list the engravings involved, and the prices that the two of them had agreed, drawing up a final account showing that he owed Bewick £37.7.0.

For this sum you may draw on me at 6 days or 6 weeks, as Mr. Beilby & yourself may think proper, sending me a receipt in full of all demands for the business done. There are 4 large drawings in my possession, *which cannot be used,* but which I am of course ready to deliver whenever you shall call for them [The letter is endorsed, in Bewick's hand,' Ansrd. 29 Jany 1794']

In spite of such strains in their relationship, the two Novocastrians remained on reasonably friendly terms, helped, no doubt, by the distance between them. The extensive series of letters from Robert Pollard to Thomas Bewick, now in the Library of the Victoria and Albert Museum, includes friendly mentions of the printer. For example, in a letter of the 1 June 1821, Pollard mentions a recent invitation from Bulmer to Bewick to come to London, presumably to stay with him in Clapham.[41] We also know that, on his last visit to London in August 1828, the year of his death, Bewick dined with Bulmer.[42]

In a letter from Bulmer to Bewick, dated 10 December 1795 and printed at the end of his posthumous memoir,[43] the printer expresses sincere regret at the early death of Thomas's younger brother, John, a few days earlier, but — for modern taste, at least — spoils the tone by going on to discuss the engraver's work for G. L. Way's *Fabliaux* (1796).

After his death subscriptions were raised for a marble bust of Bewick, which now stands in our rooms here. Bulmer was one of the subscribers.[44]

I believe that the acrimony between Bewick and several of those for whom he worked was overemphasized by his daughters after his death. He was a notable success in his own lifetime, as was Bulmer. Both were good businessmen; perhaps Bewick's provincial milieu allowed him to be somewhat sharper than would have been possible for Bulmer. One must conclude that the printer was not unfair, but believed in striking a good bargain.

BULMER'S PUBLISHERS

The launch given to Bulmer by George Nicol and the Boydells, together with the support of Sir Joseph Banks, gave him a flying start. His clientele slowly increased and his annual production grew steadily from the six books in 1792, to eleven in 1793, to 21 in 1794, reaching a peak of 35 in 1802. This was exceeded only in 1812 with 36 and in 1814 with 47 (ten of which were editions of Byron's topical *Ode to Napoleon Buonaparte*, a small pamphlet printed, every few weeks, for John Murray in 'batches', initially of 1000, reducing to 750 and, by the fifth edition to 500).

Robert Faulder, bookseller in New Bond Street, was the publisher of one of the books printed by Bulmer in each of the years 1792−7. Maxted[45] shows that, in 1799, he was bookseller to the King. He may, therefore, have had some association with George Nicol; at least, he must have been well known to him.

While his prinicpal publishers, in the early years, were Nicol and the Boydells, others were beginning to use Bulmer's services. In 1793 the Society of Antiquaries commissioned him to print Major-General William Roy's *Military Antiquities of the Romans*, a large folio. Roy was a pioneer of the Ordnance Survey, a project with which Banks was closely concerned.[46] In that same year Bulmer printed *The Peerage of Great Britain and Ireland* for Robert Pollard, a copperplate engraver and life-long friend of the printer from the time that they were apprentices in Newcastle upon Tyne. There were also two books for James Rennell.

In 1794 Bulmer printed Kindersley's *Specimens of Hindoo Literature*, which was dedicated to the Directors of the East India Company, and is our printer's first contact with the Company. This association afterwards produced many books for authors employed by the Company, some using various exotic typefaces. In the same year he also printed Major Dirom's *Narrative of the Campaign in India in 1792*.

Also in 1794 Bulmer printed eight of ten *General Views* of county agriculture. The ninth (Walker's *Hereford*) came out in 1795, and the tenth (Young's *Lincoln*) in 1799.

For the first few years that Bulmer printed the *Philosophical Transactions* of the Royal Society, the name of Peter Elmsly, the Strand bookseller, appears in the imprint. In 1795 Bulmer printed Sir William Drummond's *Philosophical Sketches* and Skrine's *Three Successive Tours in the North of England* for Elmsly. There were also at least three other reports for the old Board of Agriculture. In that year Bulmer felt sufficiently confident to publish, on his own account, the *Poems of Goldsmith and Parnell,* that I have already mentioned as a source of friction between the two eminent Novocastrians.

By 1796 we find the names of Cadell and Davies, and of James Edwards on the imprints. In 1797 Bulmer started printing the *Communications to the Board of Agriculture,* and the first of his publications for the Society of Dilettanti *(The Antiquities of Ionia,* part ii) — this Society was another of Banks's activities.

You may be amused if I read to you part of a letter of the 21 May 1798 from George Nicol to Philip Metcalfe, Treasurer of the Society of Dilettanti, about Bulmer's charges for his work.[47]

> As it is my duty to take care that nobody shall cheat you but myself, I have made Bulmer make out his account a little more explicitly, which I have now examined — I confess if Bulmer printed no better than he writes — few would employ him.

Although the range of his publisher clients had grown considerably by the end of the eighteenth century, it was not until 1805 that we find the name of Longman in a Bulmer imprint. In that year was issued the four-volume edition in octavo of the *Plays* of Massinger, edited by William Gifford. The Longman Impression Books, now in the Library of Reading University, show that the total cost of the edition of 750 was £897.18.0, of which printing cost £372.0.0. and paper £296.16.0. Eight other booksellers were associated with Longmans in this publication.[48] To judge from the study of these Impression Books that I made over twenty years ago, with the help of the late Cyprian Blagden and Mrs. B. M. Hurst, Bulmer did not, in fact, print very much for Longmans.

It was not until he moved from Fleet Street to 50 Albemarle Street, in 1812, that John Murray employed Bulmer. At this time John Murray seems to have changed his emphasis, as is shown by a bound set of his catalogues, ranging from 1774 to 1824.[49] While in Fleet Street he seems to have concentrated mainly on bookselling, and the books had a medical and similar emphasis. After his move to Albemarle Street he made a substantial entry to publishing, with works of literary and general interest. He was, for example, as is well known, Byron's publisher, and issued the later editions of Mungo Park's two expeditions.

It was not until 1808 that that most irritating of bibliophilic writers, the Rev. T. F. Dibdin, first commissioned Bulmer, and by that time it is arguable that the printer's most attractive typeface was already in the past. In that year Bulmer printed for Dibdin More's *Utopia* and the bibliophile's own *Lincoln Nosegay*. There followed another half-dozen works, several of which were very substantial and printed in more than one colour.

BULMER'S ACHIEVEMENT

In the prefatory 'Advertisement' to the *Poems of Goldsmith and Parnell* Bulmer says that the work is 'particularly meant to combine the various beauties of PRINTING, TYPE-FOUNDING, ENGRAVING, AND PAPERMAKING'. He then goes on to extol William Martin for the type, the Bewicks for the wood-engravings, and Whatman for the paper; what he does not mention is ink. This matter is well put into context by Iain Bain in his note on Bewick's engraving in the 1975 edition of the engraver's *Memoir*.[50]

> Much of the trouble he [Bewick] had with the quality of printing stemmed from the poor inks that were used (not to mention the effect of frost on them during the winter months) ... When the *Fables of Aesop* was printed in 1818, although a fine quality stiff ink was bought in for the job, the pressmen in Walker's newspaper office were quite unused to it and applied it far too thickly.

Hansard[51] devotes a whole chapter to printing ink, and says 'Few printers, of any eminence, in this country attempt to be the entire makers of their own ink ... with the exception of Mr. Bulmer'.[52] Several paragraphs later he asserts that Baskerville was the first printer to turn his attention to 'this most essential article', and goes on

> It was reserved for to him to discover ... a superior kind of black for the purpose required, and to this success may be attributed, in a great measure, the superiority of his printing.

Hansard attributes the 'discovery' to 1760, and suggests that, from the time of Baskerville's death in 1775 to 1790, the technique lay dormant. In that year, through Robert Martin,

> A considerable quantity of this fine black, which had been collecting, for a length of time, from the glass-pinchers' and solderers' lamps, was bought by him, at an almost unlimited price, and was supplied to Mr. Bulmer for his experiments in fine printing. But the difficulty of obtaining any regular supply by these means, and the adulterations practised by the workmen when they found a demand for the article, induced Mr. Bulmer to erect an apparatus for the purpose of making it, for his own use; and he succeeded in producing a very superior black.[53]

The work was slow and unpleasant and, in consequence, Bulmer did not produce the ink commercially, but used it to good effect in some of his finest books.

Hansard especially commends the quality of the ink in Bulmer's printing of the *Anacreontis Odaria* (1802), with fine engravings by a Miss Bacon (afterwards wife of the editor, the Rev. Edward Forster) and printed in a splendid Greek face, and also of a number of wood-engravings in volume 2 of Dibdin's *Bibliographical Decameron*. These had a very dense black background and were printed on the same page as footnotes that can have been in type no larger than brevier (say, 8 point); the black ink admirably fulfils the two different functions.[54] (It is just possible, however, that the text and wood-engraving were printed at separate pulls; red was used on other pages, and this must have called for a second pull.)

I have dwelt on this at some length to illustrate how Bulmer's achievement, immediately recognized, resulted from the kind of attention to detail that George Nicol, in his advance notice for the Shakspeare, says is 'absolutely indispensable'.

BULMER'S TYPOGRAPHY

If, in fact, Bulmer worked for John Bell, after he left Newcastle in late 1777, he was in the right shop to acquire the skills of, and a feeling for, 'fine printing'. As the late Oliver Simon pointed out Bell 'did much to popularize

'Fine Printing', as many of his prospectuses and books bear witness. His work and influence as a typographer were important.'[55] Indeed, Bulmer used his types very widely, especially in his earlier books, when they probably predominate over those of William Martin. Nevertheless, it may be said that our printer not only practised what he had learnt, but also carried the craft to a high point in the very early years of the nineteenth century. Marrot,[56] who was writing at a time of inter-war renaissance of typography, is enthusiastic about the achivement of Bulmer and Bensley; he writes of them

> They were, indeed, not far from being model printers. Common sense, tact, perception, mechanical knowledge and skill, a sense of balance and proportion, energy and enterprise — the equipment, in a word, of the artist and man of affairs — all these are necessary to such a being; and by the quality and quantity of Bulmer's and Bensley's output they are attested.

Marrot was, no doubt, overstating the case, but when one considers what went before and what followed in the Victorian crepuscule, it will be recognized that their achievement was noteworthy.

Since the early 1930s, when Marrot was writing, and even since the late 1940s, when Oliver Simon wrote his splendidly stimulating article, our knowledge of Bulmer's output has increased so much beyond the fine books, so flatulently mentioned by Dibdin in his *Bibliographical Decameron,* that we can make a more informed judgement.

When we compare, say, *Poems of Goldsmith and Parnell* and a piece of jobbing printing such as Dimsdale's *Extract from an Account of Cases of Typhus Fever,* a small pamphlet printed for the Society for Bettering the Condition of the Poor about 1803, and intended to sell for 1s. for a dozen copies, we can see that Bulmer quite properly devoted less attention to more everyday bread-and-butter work. Bulmer was a commercial printer — and a very successful one at that, as his will shows[57] — not a private press. He had to provide what his customers wanted and were prepared to pay for. Marrot[58] puts it in this way

It is clearly unreasonable to expect of the commercial printer that his work should be as consistently good as that of the private presses, but what one may, and should, ask is, that he show equal enterprise and intelligence *within the limits of his narrower orbit.*

An examination of William Bulmer's output over his thirty years at the Shakspeare Press shows that he satisfied Marrot's criterion.

A MAN OF SUBSTANCE

Dr. Johnson, on being taken to dinner in Kensington in Mr. Strahan's coach, remarked that this showed that the printer was a man of substance and mentioned Hamilton[59] 'who had arrived at grandeur before Strahan'.[60] This comment suggests that prosperity and status were not common for printers in the eighteenth century. Bulmer was clearly a man of substance. His carriage is mentioned by Robert Pollard in a letter to Bewick,[61] his will demonstrates that he was prosperous,[62] and he was a member of the Honourable Band of Gentlemen Pensioners from very early in his printing career.

It would be otiose to go into Bulmer's will here, since it has been published elsewhere, but we may usefully glance at the property, aside from money, because this may help to show where he lived in London at various times.

He leaves, to his brother Ralph, houses and other premises near Parsons Green, Fulham, and also at 12 Park Street, Islington. He also mentions at length his share in Fulham Bridge, which he bequeaths, after a life interest to his wife, to the illegitimate children of his brother Fenwick and to their children.

The poor-rate books for the Parish of Fulham[63] show that Bulmer paid a poor rate from the first half of the year 1805-1806 (having taken over the house of the 'late Cording') until the second half of the year 1809-1810. It seems likely, therefore, that he lived in Broomhouse Lane in Parsons Green from the later months of 1805 until the early months of 1810.[64]

We know that Bulmer was living in Clapham Rise when he died. The printer's house was actually in the Parish of

St. Mary, Lambeth, and the poor-rate books for that parish demonstrate that he took over the house of a Julius Schroeder from the third quarterly collection in 1816.[65] A glance at a map of London does not suggest that Park Street, Islington, was a likely residential stage between Parsons Green and Clapham. He may have lived 'over the shop' from 1790, or soon afterwards, but Islington does not seem to be conveniently located either for Cleveland Row — or for the Strand, if Bulmer did, in fact, work for John Bell.

John Nichols quoted several *jeux d'esprit* from William Gifford, editor of *The Anti-Jacobin*, to Bulmer and these show that both were members of the Honourable Band of Gentlemen Pensioners. Indeed Gifford was Paymaster and Bulmer printed some of the payslips for the Band.[66] What was this Band? And what does membership of it tell us about Bulmer?

A complete run of the *Royal Kalendar*, in the Institute of Historical Research of the University of London, shows that, rather astonishingly, William Bulmer was a member of the Gentlemen Pensioners from 1790 until his death in 1830; he must have been commissioned within a few months of setting up in Cleveland Row, St. James's. His elder brother, Fenwick, was a member of the Band from 1785 until he died in 1824. Robert Pollard, in a letter of the 6 August 1821 to Thomas Bewick wrote[61]

> This being the "Grozer" season according to annc. custom I Recd. from his [Fenwick's] brother Willm a few weeks before An invitation to go & dine with him. I happened to go the Sunday after the Coronation [of George IV, 29 July 1821] for that purpose when I got to Willms. Residence He was engaged out to Dinner but as the Gentleman he was going to was an intimate friend of his & with whom I was not quite a stranger to be in a friendly way inforced me to go with him & Sir Fenwick was invited before Therefore in Wms. Carriage we all set of[f] accompanied by Mrs. Wm. Bulmer The new Knight was as easy & free as before & we had a very pleasant excursion on the whole tho a 6 o clock Dinner & attended by two Servts. in handsome Livery . . . He [Fenwick] had the Honour conferred on him in right of Custom of being the oldest or Senr Gentleman Pentioner — & if a Chapter is held soon to make any additional Knts. of the Garter his Brothr.

William on his Seniority will probably be Knighted also...[67]

As to Pollard's last suggestion it must be said that William was no more than the fourth senior Pensioner at that time. He is listed as the most senior for the first time in the *Royal Kalendar* for 1826.

The English Sovereign had for long had a close personal guard in peace and war, but it was Henry VIII who, on his accession in 1509, formed the Honourable Band of Gentlemen Pensioners, on the pattern of the French Pensionnaires established by Louis XI in 1474. Henry VIII required his Pensioners to be of noble blood, and the horses, arms and servants that they were required to provide meant that they also had to be wealthy.

The commission in the Band was paid, and soon came to be sold — at some times by the Captain, who was invariably a peer after the second Captain, Sir Anthony Brown, and at some times by the member himself. In early years the Band was a crack fighting body, but by the reign of George III its duties were entirely ceremonial, and Brackenbury (1905) remarks that when George IV came to the throne 'the Corps was composed, almost if not quite without exception, of civilians untrained in the use of arms.'

It seems that the reputation of the Band had dropped by the end of the eighteenth century, and as early as 1782 Burke had tried to suppress the practice of selling places, but without success. At that time the place of a private Gentleman in the Band cost on average 1000 guineas, while the annual income, after deducting land tax and other outgoings, amounted to only £76 per year.[68] (It was not, in fact, until 1862 that the Corps was reconstructed on its present lines as a Corps of senior retired Service officers with distinguished careers.) The Captain, whose appointment by Bulmer's time was political, received £1000 per year, the Paymaster £300 and the ordinary members £100.

Reading the names of the Gentlemen Pensioners in the *Royal Kalendars* from 1784 to 1831 does not immediately suggest aristocratic family names, but they were all treated as gentlemen, being graced with 'esquire' in the lists. It almost looks as though William Bulmer had achieved — or bought — that status by 1790.

However that may be, there a few conclusions that we may tentatively draw from this. Clearly his elder brother, Fenwick, must have been a helpful connexion. William's location, so close to St. James's Palace where the Prince of Wales lived, is much to the point, especially since the Band became attached to the Prince, rather than the King, after the latter became mad. It has been remarked to me that Bulmer became as nearly the King's personal printer as anyone ever has, and some colour is given to this by Dibdin's circumstantial story of the 'Bodoni Hum'.[69] As I suggested earlier, William Bulmer's connexion with the Crown, through the Gentlemen Pensioners, must have been assisted by his older brother, Fenwick, and may have led to his being introduced to George Nicol. Further, if it was indeed our William Bulmer who was working for the Dublin Administration, he may well have been in favour with the Government all those years before.

Even if Bulmer was no scion of a noble family, he must have been wealthy enough by 1790 to buy a place in the Gentlemen Pensioners, and have been an acceptable companion to gentlemen and wealthy tradesmen like his elder brother. His joining such a group so early in his career as a master-printer says much for his ambition and for his opinion of himself.

I like to think that Bulmer always retained a kindly feeling for his native town — certainly he remembered his family in Newcastle in his will — and, no doubt, his native town enjoyed his fame. A similar kind of bookish interest that enabled him to find customers for his fine printing led, three years after his establishment in Cleveland Row, St. James's, to the foundation of our own Society. Our predecessors invited Sir Joseph Banks to accept Honorary Membership in the Society's first year, and our printer likewise three years later. The Society possesses two letters from Bulmer to the Rev Anthony Hedley, Secretary from 1821 to 1825. In these he presents a number of his books to the Library and belatedly acknowledges the honour of his election in these words.

> With respect to the distinction paid to me by the Literary and Philosophical Society of Newcastle, by electing me an honorary member of their Body, I have found myself awkwardly situated, for never having conceived myself officially informed on the subject, I could not under such circumstances send a formal letter of thanks, & have of course remained a stranger to the Institution. (Letter dated 25 June 1821).

(The correspondence is clearly incomplete, and he seems to have presented two lots of books.)

CONCLUSION

Even Homer nodded or — to use a more appropriate metaphor, since Bulmer was printing for profit, not for pleasure — because our printer did not feel obliged to supply a Rolls-Royce when he had been paid only for a Mini, not all his work was of the standard of the Milton. I am happy to echo the words of Marrot in his summing up of the achievement of Bulmer and Bensley[70]

> In their choice of the best types, paper, and ink that circumstances would permit, in their active researches after every kind of improvement in material as in method, they were worlds removed from that ordinary docile beast of burden, the 'commercial' printer . . . It is, of course, not implied that they were infallible nor that their books were all faultless . . . The two men are specially remarkable for the way in which they understood their types — performed, that is, exactly the primary and most essential duty of the printer.

In his early days especially, Bulmer had the better of it in William Martin's transitional face, which he generally handled in masterly fashion in prose text, while Bensley was more successful in his title-pages. 'Fine printing' was being striven for by the very few cognoscenti before Bulmer, but he gave it consistent form and impetus.

Updike says of the best printing of Bulmer's time

> Whatever may be the opinion of the light, open types and widely spaced and leaded pages of volumes by the best printers in these last years of the eighteenth century, they seem to me to be very sincere and workmanlike solutions of

problems which the printer worked out in the manner of that time. Such books were part of the life about them. They accorded admirably with the cool, sedate interiors in which they were housed. It was printing faithful to the best standards of its day, and because of this I think it will live.[71]

To this development the Newcastle apprentice who became a prosperous 'gentleman' made a major contribution, and I hope that I have shown that William Bulmer was indeed a Fine Printer — and worthy Honorary Member of this famous Society.

NOTES

1. pp 464-6, and there signed R.P.H.
2. BULMER, William [Ed] *Wit's Repository.* Thomas Robson, Newcastle upon Tyne, 1777.
3. The file copies of the *Gentleman's Magazine,* made by the Nichols family are in the Folger Library, Washington, and this obituary carries an annotation that it was written by J. B. Nichols.
4. Personal correspondence, August 1987. Miss Pollard points out to me that she knows no other imprint of his in Dublin.
5. See, for example, the accounts given in BALSTON, Thomas 'John Boydell, publisher, the commercial Maecenas.' *Signature,* NS 8, pp 3-32, and FRIEDMAN, Winifred H *Boydell's Shakespeare Gallery,* New York, 1976, Part I.
6. A copy is in the St. Bride's Printing Library.
7. LYONS, Sir Henry (1944) *The Royal Society: a History of its Administration under its Charters.* Cambridge University Press, p. 187.
8. LYONS pp 183-7.
9. LYONS pp 187-8.
10. LYONS p 188.
11. LYONS Appendix ii.
12. LYONS pp 193-4 and 197-8.
13. NICHOLS, John and J. B. (1817-1858) *Illustrations of the Literary History of the Eighteenth Century.* 8 vols, London, vol 4 p 693.
14. Exhibition catalogue *Apples to Atoms* p 43.
15. LYONS p 197.
16. LYONS p 198.
17. EVANS, Joan (1959) *A History of the Society of Antiquaries.* Oxford University Press, p 179.
18. NICHOLS vol 7 p 460.
19. LYONS p 202.

20. This transcription has been made from an early manuscript copy of the Council Minutes in the Archives of the Royal Society, with the permission of the Librarian.
21. NICHOLS vol 4 p 697n. It must be remembered that this was published in 1822, with the judgement of hindsight.
22. See ISAAC, P. C. G. (1984) *William Bulmer, 1757–1830, 'Fine Printer'*. Sandars Lectures, University of Cambridge, p 17.
23. CARTER, H. B. (1981) Sir Joseph Banks — the cryptic georgian. *Lincolnshire History and Archaeology*, 16, 53-62.
24. LUPTON, Kenneth (1979) *Mungo Park the African Traveler*. Oxford University Press, p 20.
25. MAXTED, Ian (1977) *The London Book Trades, 1775-1800*. Folkstone, Dawson, p 145.
26. The episode may be followed in the photocopies, in the Library of the Royal Geographical Society, of the Banks papers in the Sutro Library of the California State Library, San Francisco — see sheets numbers 111-128.
27. CUL Add. MSS 7085, 7086 and 7087.
28. See, for example, CUL Add. MSS 7085 fo. 116-117.
29. CUL Add. MSS 7085 fo. 117v.
30. John Murray ledger B fo. 1 and 2, and daybook (1811–17) fo. 133.
31. FLETCHER, H R (1969) *The Story of the Royal Horticultural Society, 1804-1968*. London, p 22.
32. The bound copy of Vol. 1 of the *Transactions* (shelfmark 25.1.A) in the RHS Library carries the imprint of William Savage, in various forms, on pp 70, 111 and 169. There is no imprint at the supposed ends of Parts 4-6. The end of the Appendix carries Bulmer's imprint, as does the title-page. See also *Flora Malesiana Bulletin*, 1 ser, no 4, March 1954 for a discussion of the dates and pagination of the Parts. Three editions of the early volumes of the *Transactions* seem to have been published.
33. A lengthy list of members for 1820 is in the John Johnson Collection in the Bodleian Library.
34. According to a pencil note in a modern hand in one copy (shelfmark 86bis.E.2b) in the RHS Library, which also shows the price of each part as 8/- and indicates that the information came from an original wrapper. Another copy (shelfmark 86bis.E.3) has uncoloured plates, printed in green in both copies. The latter copy has on the top board a small printed label in a border of flower ornaments, showing that the price was £4 4s plain and £6 6s coloured.
35. Personal communication from Mr. H. B. Carter, the historian of Banks.
36. Item no. 61 in the Pease Collection of Bewick material in the Newcastle Central Library. It is interesting to note how Bewick was acting as a trade engraver, working from another artist's painting — and that Bulmer seems to have wished to suppress that fact!

37. In the collection of the late John Hack.
38. TIMPERLEY, C. H. (1842) *Encyclopaedia of Literary and Typographical Anecdote.* London.
39. p. 912. In fact the second edition (1804) is in octavo.
40. This letter was published as Plate 8 by Iain BAIN (1970) *Checklist of the Manuscripts of Thomas Bewick,* Pinner, reprinted from *The Private Library.* I quote it here from a xerox copy kindly provided by him.
41. Shelfmark 86.JJ.18B; letter no. 89
42. See, for example, Montague WEEKLEY (1935) *Thomas Bewick* pp. 187-8. At the time Bewick was already failing, for when 'Bulmer took him for a drive to the new splendours of Nash's Regent's Park, he did not even bestir himself to get out of the carriage in order to look at the Zoo, which had been established there in that year.'
43. pp. 337-8.
44. There is a list of the subscribers and an engraving of the bust in item 184 in the Pease Collection in the Newcastle Central Library. The bust is illustrated in Iain Bain's edition of Bewick's *Memoir,* facing p. 211.
45. MAXTED (1977).
46. Roy was also FRS.
47. The records of the Society of Dilettanti are deposited in the Library of the Society of Antiquaries of London. This letter is on folio 494 of a bound collection of manuscripts (D MSS Vol 1).
48. Impression Book 2, folio 130r.
49. In the archives of the present firm at 50 Albemarle Street. In working on these archives I was greatly assisted by Mrs. Virginia Murray, Archivist to the firm.
50. BEWICK, Thomas *A Memoir of Thomas Bewick, written by himself.* Edited by Iain Bain, London, 1975, p. xxxi.
51. HANSARD, T. C. *Typographia.* London, 1825, pp. 715-33.
52. p. 716.
53. HANSARD *op cit* p.718.
54. *idem* pp. 718-9.
55. SIMON, Oliver English typography and the industrial age. *Signature,* NS 7, p. 22, note 1.
56. MARROT, H. V. *William Bulmer, Thomas Bensley: a study in transition.* London, 1930, p. 13.
57. DREYFUS, John and ISAAC, P. C. G. William Bulmer's will. *Studies in the Book Trade in Honour of Graham Pollard.* Oxford Biblographical Society, 1975, pp 341-9.
58. MARROT *op cit* p. 8.
59. Presumably Archibald Hamilton (*c* 1719-1793) who, on moving to London from Edinburgh, became associated with Strahan (PLOMER, BUSHNELL and DIX (1968) *A Dictionary of Printers and Booksellers who were at work in England Scotland and Ireland from 1726 to 1775).*

60. KNIGHT, Charles (1865) *Shadows of the Old Booksellers.* London, p. 231.
61. Letter no. 90 in the Pollard-Bewick correspondence, Victoria and Albert Museum Library shelfmark 86.JJ.18B.
62. DREYFUS and ISAAC (1975).
63. The Fulham Parish records are in the Shepherds Bush Library shelfmark PAF/1/36-37. These rate books also mention the Bridge, which was also rated. The first reference to WB is on folio 12 of PAF/1/36 and the last on folio 8 of PAF/1/37. The Library also has a number of deeds, deposited by a firm of London solicitors, which include several dealing with Bridge transactions, in which WB was concerned.
64. The will gives the address as Broom house Lane. An eighteenth-century map of London shows Broom house Lane running down to the Thames through market gardens just to the east of Fulham Bridge.
65. Minet Library, Lambeth, shelfmark P2/133 pp. 339 and 461. The printer's name is, in fact, spelt 'Bulmore'.
66. NICHOLS (1817-58) vol. 6, pp. 1-36.
67. Grozers is Northumbrian dialect for gooseberries. BRACKENBURY, Henry (1905) *'The Nearest Guard': The History of the Honourable Corps of Gentlemen-at-arms* wrote of George IV's coronation

> the Pensioners made a more splendid appearance than at any time since when, selected from her personal friends, they escorted Queen Elizabeth on her numerous progresses, or, in the reign of her father, they had added brilliancy to the Field of the Cloth of Gold.

Brackenbury (p. 177) further tells us that the Gentlemen Pensioners wore a 'Tudor' dress of great magnificence, provided at the King's expense at £200 each. Pollard mentions having seen Sir Fenwick's dress, in which he was knighted.

One of the duties of the Gentlemen Pensioners was to wait on the Sovereign at the Garter installations; it is not to be assumed that Pollard is making the highly unlikely suggestion that William Bulmer was to be made a Knight of the Garter.
68. BACKENBURY (1905) pp. 170-9.
69. DIBDIN, T. F. (1817) *The Bibliographical Decameron.* London vol.2 p. 396 and vol. 3pp. 483-4.
70. MARROT *op cit* pp. 12-14.
71. UPDIKE, D. B. *Printing Types: their history, forms and use.* Cambridge, Massachusetts, 1951, vol. 2, p. 147-8.

CHAPTER SEVEN

BIOGRAPHICAL ESSAY IV

W. K. Loftus

An Archaeologist from Newcastle*

Stephen Harbottle

William Kennett Loftus was born on 30th November, 1820, possibly at Rye, Sussex, but more probably at Linton, near Maidstone.[1] His father William was a Newcastle man. I have not been able to discover the maiden name of his mother, Ann, though I think it a reasonable assumption that it was Kennett. There are a number of Kennetts recorded in the Land Tax Assessment for Rye in 1820, Ann was to be buried there, and two of William Kennett's sons carried the name.

Loftus came on the male side from a line of innkeepers. His great grandfather William had the White Hart Inn in the Fleshmarket, Newcastle. His grandfather, the younger son, was born about 1760 and became a well-known and highly successful coach owner as well as hotel owner. He was also Clerk of the Newcastle Racecourse for many years. In 1801 he was running three coaches (to York, Leeds and Edinburgh) from the Shakespeare Tavern, Mosley Street. From here he moved via the Turks Head to the Turf Hotel, Collingwood Street, on the site of which Lloyds Bank now stands. In 1825 he had nine coach services from here, adding to the earlier routes two to London, a second to Edinburgh and local services to Lancaster, Carlisle and Sunderland. He was admitted as a Merchant Adventurer in 1786.

I have gone into this detail about Loftus's grandfather because in the event it was to be he and not Loftus's father

---

[1] Venn

*Reprinted from *Archaeologia Aeliana*, 5th Series, Vol. 1. Lecture to the Society in 1971.

who was to exercise the decisive influence on Loftus's upbringing. Loftus's father had joined the Durham Militia some time before 1809, which might I suppose have been regarded as not wholly inconsistent with an intention to carry on the family business. In April 1809, however, he volunteered for the 68th Regiment (the Durham Light Infantry) and transferred to them with the rank of ensign.[2] This was a decided blow for freedom. The regiment went abroad in July 1809 on the ill-fated expedition to Walcheren, where they saw little fighting but contracted malaria on a large scale. In January 1810, they returned to Kent and were stationed there until June 1811.[3] It is to me an irresistible inference that Loftus's father and mother first met in this period. Whether they then married I do not know. I can only observe that William went out with the regiment to the Peninsula still as an ensign, in June 1811, and then, before the regiment had been in contact with the French, resigned his commission on 29th August.[2] Welford described William as having "served with his regiment in some of the stirring scenes of the Peninsular War". This seems rather to dignify what was a very temporary visit.

When and where Loftus's parents married I have not been able to discover. When he was five years old his mother died, aged 39, and was buried at Rye. A fortnight later, on 23rd March 1826 he was baptised, also at Rye.[4] His first known school was the Grammar School at Newcastle, of which Dr. Mortimer was then headmaster. It seems reasonable to suppose that his mother's death broke up his father's household and that he must from this time have begun to live with his grandfather in Newcastle, either at the Grandstand, where his grandfather had a house, or at the Turf Hotel. Some time later his father remarried. I would suppose from the terms of the grandfather's will that the remarriage probably took place before 1830, and since the will throws some light on the family attitudes, I turn to it now.

The will was made on 10th June 1830. It is what I would describe as a strong document, which showed very definite

[2] Army List.
[3] Ward.
[4] Register at St. Mary the Virgin, Rye.

views about both son and grandson. The grandfather appointed John Brandling, his solicitor William Carr, and his nephew James Radford as his trustees and gave them all his property on trust, first to pay an annuity of £60 to William Loftus the son for life and subject to that to hold the whole estate on trust for his grandson, on attaining twenty-one absolutely. If his grandson did not reach twenty-one the property went (subject to some legacies) to James Radford. He committed "the care instruction and bringing up" of his grandson to his trustees and so far as he had power (which he probably had not) appointed them as guardians. Finally, to make matters clear, he directed that if William Loftus in any way interfered with the trustees' care or bringing up of his grandson the annuity was to cease. One is left in no doubt that William Loftus was regarded as an undesirable influence.

His grandfather confirmed the will in February 1833. Later that year he gave half the coach business to Radford, and in February 1834, he died.[5]

Loftus was now 13. After the Grammar School he went to an establishment known as Old Park, Durham, under a Mr. Gillespie, and later to the Twickenham Academy under Rev. Dr. Nicholson. In April 1840, he was admitted as a pensioner at Caius College, Cambridge, where he matriculated in October of that year.[6]

Loftus's University career is not easy to follow. He was obviously a highly intelligent undergraduate with a gift for making friends which was to serve him well later. He was elected a Scholar of Caius in March 1841. His interest in geology attracted the attention of Professor Adam Sedgwick (the Woodwardian Professor of that time) who secured his election to the Geological Society of London in January 1842.[7] This was a considerable achievement for an undergraduate without influential connections. I do however find it inconsistent that he went down in 1843 without taking a degree.

Welford says that on his permanent return to Newcastle Loftus took up residence at his grandfather's old house at the

[5] York Probate Court.
[6] Venn.
[7] Welford.

Grandstand. The Grandstand itself was burnt down in 1844 but the house called Stand House was evidently not destroyed as his paper for the Tyneside Field Club on "Evidences of Diluvial Action at Belsay" is dated from there in 1848.

He lived in Newcastle for nearly six years. After that period he came back only on visits, and I think it clear that he had no business ties with the town. He had of course inherited from his grandfather the half of the coach business which his grandfather had retained, but what had been a flourishing enterprise in 1825 must have looked very different twenty years later. The railway from London reached Gateshead in 1844 and that must have finally destroyed the old coaching days. No doubt the Turf Hotel was still open, and perhaps a true Loftus could have managed it with care and built it into a triumphant success, but his tastes did not lie that way. This period in Newcastle was only preparatory to the real career that he had yet to find.

In the meantime he joined local societies and read papers to them, and he got married. The first activity is well enough recorded; the second is ignored by both the *D.N.B.* and Welford. To deal first with the societies, there was the Natural History Society, to which he was elected when still an undergraduate. He delivered a number of papers to them such as, in October 1847, "An Account of the Occurrence of the Glowworm near Gibside". He was soon on their committee, coping with the awkward question of the Curator, Mr. King, who had been detected in dealing in objects of natural history, and sitting on a sub-committee to enquire what the Curator's duties *"should be"*. This unfortunate incident terminated in the dismissal of Mr. King, who then refused to deliver up the keys of the collection and for some months set the Committee at defiance. Loftus was a founder of the Field Club, to whom he gave other papers, and his name appears regularly in their accessions book. The tertiary fossils from the Isle of Wight and Belgium recorded for 1844 and 1845, and the Devonian fossils from the Eisel which he and an old Cambridge friend, Glossop, presented in 1846 hint at summer geological expeditions.[8]

He joined the Literary and Philosophical Society in 1845, and its Committee in 1848, so establishing a connection which was to have an unexpected sequel.

There is no reference to Loftus's marriage in the printed accounts of his life, for reasons which its circumstances probably explain. The facts are simply that on 7th July 1846 he married Charlotte Thulbourne at St. Pancras, Middlesex. The marriage took place by licence and the witnesses do not seem to have been related to either family. Loftus was described as resident in St. Pancras and Charlotte in All Saints, Newcastle. On 21st September 1846 a son, Frederick, was born at Richmond Street, Newcastle (though Loftus was living at Stand House). In later documents Frederick appears as the second son, and Alfred Kennett as the eldest. All in all the affair seems to have been too much for the writer of Loftus's obituary on which later biographers relied, and though Charlotte was to bear him five children, and live with him until his death, neither she nor they are mentioned in the *D.N.B.* or Welford.

While Loftus was then engaged in or about Newcastle some extremely protracted negotiations between Turkey and Persia, which had arisen out of actual hostilities in 1839-1840 were in progress. The conference had the benevolent assistance of Russia and England, who were no doubt in this way demonstrating that they were Great Powers. Out of the eventual treaty there emerged a requirement for a commission to arbitrate on the rival frontier claims to which one Colonel W. F. Williams, Royal Artillery, was appointed in 1843 as the English commissioner. From arbitration the Commission moved with deliberation to contemplating an actual survey of the frontier.[9] By the early summer of 1848 Col. Williams was in consultation with the Foreign Office on tents and surveying equipment and the actual composition of his party.[10]

An obvious companion for him was Henry Layard, who had just returned to England after some sensational

---

[8] NHS Minutes and Accession Book. [10] FO Corr 78 : 762.
[9] Waterfield.

discoveries during excavations at Nineveh, and who was qualified by first hand knowledge of the frontier with Sir Stratford Canning, the British Ambassador at Constantinople. Layard, three years older than Loftus, was at this age at any rate an ambitious and hasty man. Equality with Col. Williams at least was his private requirement if he was to join the commission. At first things went smoothly. At his request Williams asked Palmerston to be allowed to employ a naturalist to accompany the commission to the "interesting and unexplored regions" of the frontier, as well as a naval officer to carry out the necessary survey. Palmerston approved of the plan (though wishing "first to be informed what amount of remuneration this person would expect") and it was left to Layard to find the man. Williams had left for Constantinople before Palmerston wrote that, on Layard's recommendation, he had consented to the attachment of one G. F. Angus, who possessed according to Layard not only experience of South Africa, New Zealand and New South Wales and a knowledge of natural history, but also great taste and skill as a draughtsman. Angus lasted only two months in Constantinople, and had barely time to account for an advance of salary to cover his expenses of travel before he had resigned through ill health. Layard too had fallen by the wayside. After innumerable extensions of leave due to ill health, his forthcoming book and his desire to help in arranging the Nineveh exhibits, he had finally asked to be attached to the Embassy at Constantinople and to be relieved, because of illness, of his obligation to join Williams on the frontier. Palmerston agreed. Williams reported Angus's resignation in November and his letter carried a faint suggestion that Angus's departure was not unwelcome. "As the recurrence of fever on the march," wrote Williams, "seemed to weigh so heavily on his mind I do not regret his determination to abandon the expedition".[11]

Layard's withdrawal also permitted Williams more freedom on the subject of naturalists. "Mr. Angus," he went on, "at once confessed to me his slender knowledge of geology which is a very severe deficiency as our route lies through

[11] FO Corr 78 : 762.

little known mountains. I therefore hope that any future appointment may be made on reference to the Geological Society . . . I cannot doubt that young men of high talent will present themselves". Loftus's opportunity had arrived.[12]

Palmerston had little time in which to act, for the Commission were due to set out in January 1849. He applied to Sir Henry de la Beche, then head of the Geological Survey, for advice offering a salary of £100 a year, which was what Angus had received for the post. Sir Henry replied promptly that Loftus would be suitable, but that his salary ought to be £200. The Foreign Office agreed with equal promptness. It was desirable, Addington wrote on 3rd January, that Loftus should set out as soon as possible and, he added, "although Lord Palmerston has no desire inconveniently to hurry him, His Lordship thinks it as well that he should be apprised that a Steam Vessel will leave Southampton direct for Constantinople on 29th of this month". By 5th January Loftus was writing from Stand House to accept the job. By 23rd he had got an advance of half a year's salary for his outfit and passage. Sir Henry made an attempt to secure the delivery of geological specimens obtained by Loftus direct to himself, but was firmly repulsed by Palmerston. By 29th Loftus had conferred with officials of the British Museum and set sail. The most remarkable feature of the whole affair is the confidence with which Sir Henry turned to Loftus. Not only his ability, but also his availability were well known. The geological holidays and the membership of the Geological Society of London seem the likely reason.[13]

We hear of him next at Constantinople, where he found that Colonel Williams and his party had already left on Christmas Day 1848. Angus had deposited here for his use various articles provided by the British Museum Trustees, and he carried a letter from the Foreign Office authorising their collection. Sir Stratford Canning detained him here until the roads through the Turkish mountains, which had been blocked by heavy snow, had improved. On 7th March he set out again, first by steamer along the Black Sea coast and thence over the mountainous interior to Mosul where he

[12] *Ibid.* [13] FO Corr 78 : 811; IGS Corr.

joined the British party on 5th April. They did not neglect the opportunity to visit the mounds made famous by Layard of Kuyunjik, Khorsabad, Karamles and Nimrud. Five years were to elapse before Loftus himself did any excavations here, but it is fair to suppose that the three days' journey round the sites of Nineveh inspired him with the wish to find for himself an untouched site in this antique land where for all that was known discoveries of a brilliance equal to those of Layard were waiting to be made.[14]

The Near East *c.* 1850

He was not however forgetting his appointed duties. It is evident from his book that as the party made their way south he cast a keen and appreciative eye on the flowers, the insects and the birds which flourished in profusion on the banks of the Tigris. The rendezvous with the other parties to the Commission was at Baghdad, which was reached on 5th May. However, for one reason and another the Commission remained there, doing very little but having an agreeable time, until December 1849. They stirred out only once, in September, for a jaunt to Babylon, again a site to which

---

[14] *Travels* pp. 2-5.

Layard had been. Loftus clearly enjoyed himself. His book offers historical commentary mixed with a dispassionate but not unkindly view of the present primitive inhabitants and their corrupt rulers which seems well suited to contemporary English views.[15]

The Commission were to start work at Mohammerah, that is at the South end of the disputed frontier, and the main party were to travel there from Baghdad by a river steamer provided by the East India Company. The servants and animals were however to go overland by the Jezireh, and Loftus eagerly seized on the chance of traversing an area largely unvisited up to that date by any European. Official interests were to be served by an examination of the geology of the Chaldean marshes; he also wanted to see Warka, which he believed to be the birthplace of Abraham. Col. Williams consented, and on 27th December Loftus set out with H. A. Churchill, the assistant surveyor of the British party and a competent Oriental linguist, with whom he had evidently struck up a close friendship. It was a considerable caravan. There were not only the Commission's servants and animals, but an escort of four light guns and a hundred Turkish cavalry, as the ruling Turks regarded the native Arabs to the South with justified distrust.[16]

This arrangement did not last long. After three days the escort received orders to take the caravan down the West bank of the Euphrates and not across the Jezireh. To follow this route would have deprived Loftus of his chance to enter the unknown area and he was not to be put off. He and Churchill therefore engaged an escort of eight Bashi Bazuks, irregular horsemen, and taking a few of the servants split off from the main party at Hillah and entered the desert on 30th December. After three days spent in crossing some featureless sands and marshes and making an unsatisfactory visit to a local Sheikh, the party reached the mound and ruins of Niffar, where again Layard had been previously. They returned from there to the left bank of the Euphrates to find the Pasha of Baghdad engaged in dam building. Elaborate negotiations were necessary before permission could be

[15] *Ibid* pp. 9-71.   [16] *Travels* pp. 72-76.

obtained to proceed to Warka, but eventually, by display of "European obstinacy", success and a new escort were obtained. On the morning of the fourth day's ride the great mound of Hamman, enlarged by the intervening mist and the shimmer of the air, came romantically into view. The battered remains of a statue were found nearby, and its pieces were promptly packed up by Loftus, to be subsequently brought on the backs of the party's mules to Basrah, and later to be shipped to England. It was his first find.[17]

Some hasty measurements were taken of the ruins, and Churchill did a watercolour sketch but there was no time for more. Loftus never returned to Hamman, for Warka (now known as Uruk or Erech) which he reached the next day, and where nearly two days were spent, clearly gripped his imagination. While no more could be done on this occasion than to make a map and some drawings he left, certain that a thorough exploration was required, and determined to return. A visit to the site at Mugeyer (that is Ur) which they again sketched and surveyed and a long ride across more desert were the only memorable events of the next week, at the end of which on 18th January Loftus and Churchill rejoined the Commission at Mohammerah.[18]

He was quickly able to persuade Col. Williams that he should be allowed to return to Warka to conduct some excavations, particularly with a view to obtaining specimens of the coffins there (Loftus's obsession with the Warka coffins led in the end to a remarkable misapprehension as to the nature of the Warka site). The Commission were locked in local political disputes which made the ascertainment of the boundary at this point unusually difficult, and we may suppose that since there was no surveying to be done Loftus could be more easily spared.[19]

He was back at Warka within two or three weeks, with some servants but without an escort of troops, having deliberately decided to rely on direct approaches to the Arabs. A visit to the Sheikh of the Muntefik obtained him a letter of protection and in bitter winter weather he set to work. The

[17] *Travels* pp. 78-116.
[18] *Travels* pp. 116-138.
[19] *Travels* p. 139.

camp was first six miles from the site, where there was no water, and later nine, to be near the tent of the local Sheikh. The workmen came from the local tribe of the Tuweyba, some of whom were already practised ransackers of the site in search of gold. The dig lasted a month, but what precisely was done on this occasion is obscure in Loftus's book, as he runs the account of his discoveries into one with those made on his return four years later.[20]

From Warka he seems to have moved to the mound at Sinkara (better known as Sankara, its ancient name being Larsa) some fifteen miles to the South, where proceedings were enlivened by the discovery of a lioness and two cubs among the ruins who demoralised his workers. How long he was there, and what was done, is not clear from his book. Probably the results he describes were mostly obtained in 1854, though he seems to have brought away some inscribed tablets and cylinders. Very soon the annual flooding of the delta commenced and stowing his horses, mules, grooms and finds aboard two native vessels, he set sail for Mohammerah and the Commission.[21]

The first steps had been taken in his archaeological career. It was now necessary to record them. The finds were packed up and despatched to the British Museum in the "Apprentice" from Basrah at the end of April. There were ten packages in all, nine containing articles from Warka and Sinkara, including the inevitable coffins, and one holding natural history specimens. There was also a report to write on the overland journey from Baghdad, complete with compass bearings and estimated distances, and illustrated with watercolours by Churchill, but this did not reach the British Museum until June of the following year (a delay not uncommon in excavation reports).[22] Finally for the Natural History Society of Northumberland and Durham there was a miscellaneous collection of curiosities, ranging from three bats and five desert mice to a brick with a cuneiform inscription.[23]

When the finds had been despatched Col. Williams asked

[20] *Travels* pp. 140-154
[21] *Travels* pp. 240-278.
[22] BM Corr.
[23] NHS Accession Book.

him to go to Susa, an ancient site inside Persia, to try to make some excavations, and Churchill was given permission to go with him. They went via Shuster and Dizful, with Loftus taking specimens of the changing vegetation for his herbarium, noting the lizards and birds, discussing enthusiastically the geological characteristics of the mountains of Luristan and accompanying Churchill on an obligatory diplomatic visit to the Governor of the province at Shuster. However, after about a week, the party reached Susa and set up its tents on the mound. Trouble immediately arose with the local Muslims, as the mound adjoined the Tomb of the prophet Daniel, and the presence of Christians near the tomb was unwelcome. Loftus's reasonable argument that Daniel was esteemed as a prophet by the Christians also was of no avail. As a result no workmen could be obtained, and no trench was opened, though he and Churchill produced a plan of the mound. One evening out riding they met a herd of wild pig, and in the course of an over-enthusiastic chase Loftus fell from his horse, severely injuring himself. They were forced to withdraw from the mound, and Loftus spent a month's frustrating convalescence at Dizful, apparently fighting a continuing fever. About June 1850, they were joined here by Col. Williams and the rest of his party, seeking some respite from the heat of the plains, and all went up to Mungerrah, in the mountains.[24]

The summer of 1850 was spent here, and Loftus took the chance of making some geological observations. The party then set out on a journey north to Kermanshah and from there in a wide circle through the Persian highlands to the East and South as far as Shiraz. The days were rainless and Loftus and Lt. Glascott were able to fix the true position of each night's camp, evidently by sights of the sun or stars, as there is later a reference to a chronometer being delivered in the diplomatic bag. In the meantime Col. Williams had with the help of the British Ambassador obtained permission from Tehran to excavate at Susa, and the whole English party arrived there, to camp on the mounds, in January 1851.[25]

[24] *Travels* pp. 287-332.   [25] *Travels* pp. 333-4. FO Corr 248 : 139. GS

Excavations were at once begun, using the under-servants of the Commission, who on the very first day opened a trench forty feet long and nine feet deep directed to "the very heart of the mound". The few Arabs who watched were much astounded at the audacity of the Firenghi, and well they might have been. Later some workmen were obtained but after a few days during which thieving broke out at night they departed. The party, thrown back on their own resources, luckily stumbled on a series of column bases, though their exact layout eluded discovery. A month was all that could be spared, and in February the Commission regathered at Mohammerah to spend the whole of the rest of the year in painful delimitation of the frontier.[26]

The dullness of this occupation which even Loftus, a congenital optimist, undoubtedly felt, must have been slightly relieved for him by the prospects of a possible return to archaeology. Col. Rawlinson, who as the British Consul in Baghdad controlled the British excavations in the area, wrote to him in March to ask whether, as Layard was leaving the country, Loftus would be disposed to carry on the general excavations in "Assyria, Babylonia, Chaldea and Susiana". Loftus did not get the letter until May. His reply was clear. He concluded from Rawlinson's letter, he said, that "Layard has finally abandoned the work, and has no intention of resuming it. Under such circumstances", he went on, "I should be happy to undertake the task but if it is required of me merely to act in Layard's absence I should of course decline altogether having anything to do with it." Col. Williams, he added, was willing to release him and to put servants and mules at his disposal as he could still continue his geological investigations. The double duties which would result entitled him, he hinted broadly, to some addition to his salary of £200.[27]

Rawlinson took this reply back to England in July, and, against a background of new excavations being started by the French, produced it to a sub-committee of the Trustees of the British Museum at a meeting with Layard and himself. By the beginning of August their report was ready. They

[26] *Travels* pp. 349-55.   [27] BM Corr.

thought it desirable to undertake experimental excavations at new sites in Babylon, and that the task might be properly confided to Loftus under the superintendence of Rawlinson. They estimated that, including the cost of an artist to draw the finds and of the transport of the finds to England, the expense would be £1500 a year for two years. Rawlinson had got his way and was soon back at Baghdad.[28]

The machinery to give effect to the decision — the initial grant from the Treasury of £500 for a dig at Susa and the formal approach to Lord Palmerston to authorise Col. Williams to release Loftus — moved slowly throughout the autumn, but by early January 1852, when Stratford Canning in Constantinople was beginning to grapple with the problem, Rawlinson had already extracted Loftus from the Commission and set him to work. Rawlinson required a practice dig to begin with, at an unidentified palace of Nebuchadnezzar about 10 miles from Baghdad. The intention was that, unless the results were very promising, Loftus was to leave after about 10 days for Susa and work there during the Spring. Rawlinson's plans extended on into the autumn, when he wanted Loftus to be ready "to break ground at Senkerah or Niffer" or anywhere that the French were not.[29]

Loftus did his ten days near Baghdad, and was then despatched to Susa, with Rawlinson reporting to the Trustees that he trusted that before April Loftus would have laid the great mound of Susa completely bare. That Rawlinson, an able Assyrian scholar, seriously contemplated that one man could excavate a mound containing thousands of years of history in two months is a striking commentary on what archaeology was then expected to achieve.[30]

Loftus reached Susa in the middle of February, having circumvented with some adroitness the rapacious attentions of an Arab tribe on the way. He carried the firman of the Shah authorising the excavation and was this time able to hire seventy labourers. He viewed the vast area of mounds almost with the feeling that his enterprise was a hopeless one

[28] BM Min.
[29] BM Corr.
[30] BM Corr.

(thereby incidentally showing more sense than Col. Rawlinson) but decided to start operations beside the site of columns found by Col. Williams. Aided by good fortune, an intelligent calculation of distance between column bases, and some knowledge of the Great Hall at Persepolis, he verified the layout of an area some 250 feet by 350 feet either by direct excavation or by inference.[31]

On two of the column pedestals appeared trilingual cuneiform inscriptions regarding the completion of the building by Artaxerxes. There were numerous finds — terracotta figures of Venus, enamelled bricks, coins from the seventh century A.D., alabaster vases but all of Greek or Persian times and therefore of a comparatively late date. All this was done despite interference from aggrieved Arab tribes, the general disorder created by the workmen themselves who were increased in the end to 350 and quarrelled incessantly, and a visit by Col. Williams and his party when they had two horses stolen.[32]

Loftus stopped work about the middle of April, having added to his archaeological discoveries a plausible identification of the rivers now existing with those described by the Greeks. He then set out to rejoin the Commission now in the Northern section of the frontier.[33]

He had reported on his results to Rawlinson who wrote to Layard in July that Loftus had "turned the mound of Susa topsy-turvey without finding much", a comment which was, I suppose, consistent with his original intention to have the mound laid bare in no time at all, but showed no other appreciation of the problems involved. On the same day he wrote to the Museum Trustees advising in view of the financial position against the employment of Rassam, a former assistant of Layard, as an additional excavator. Loftus, he said, was "active, intelligent, and thoroughly in earnest, and will do all in his power to compensate for not being gifted with ubiquity".[34]

In London, however, matters were proceeding on different lines. On 26th June the Trustees had already agreed to

[31] *Travels* pp. 357-368
[32] *Travels* pp. 374-405.
[33] *Travels* pp. 423-433.
[34] BM Corr.

engage Hormuzd Rassam to work under Rawlinson and Rawlinson was to be asked "to communicate to Mr. Loftus that that gentleman's further assistance beyond what he may be at present engaged upon, will not be required".[35]

Since Loftus had been promised permanent employment, this strikes one as a pretty cool performance. Rawlinson's reaction was cooler still. If, he wrote to the Trustees, on hearing of the change, Loftus did not get Rawlinson's letter he would try to employ Loftus in South Babylonia for the winter. "Loftus being of independent means will not raise money difficulties but will see that Rassam's engagement entails the use of economy". Loftus got no chance to comment. The news in fact did not reach him as he was by now far to the North and got none of Rawlinson's letters.[36]

He had been noting carefully the geological features of the frontier, discussing with Mr. Perkins of the American Mission the saltiness of Lake Urumia and investigating with Lt. Glascott the fluctuations in level of Lake Van. It seems however that he had a severe illness about this time so that his exploration of Mount Ararat itself was never finished. It was some time during the summer, too, that the work of the Commission was completed.[37]

Early in October 1852 he came down from the hills to Cizre, some 90 miles North of Mosul. He pitched his tent near the bridge of boats over the Tigris there, and was unexpectedly joined by Rassam on his way to Mosul from Iskenderun and carrying with him the instructions of the Museum Trustees. It was the first information that Loftus had had of the change of plan, and he was according to Rassam not a little surprised at the news. They travelled down the river together to Mosul, and Loftus visited the site at Kuyunjik in Rassam's company.[38] After that he went on to Baghdad to see Rawlinson and evidently to refuse to do any further work on Rawlinson's terms. The Colonel reported grumpily to London that Loftus could not work in South Babylonia because of the disturbed state of the country and also that the funds would not permit it, so that Loftus had

[35] BM Min.
[36] BM Corr.
[37] GS Proc.
[38] Rassam pp. 3-4.

better return to England.[39] Little time was lost because he was evidently back in London by the middle of December. He had been absent for very nearly four years.[40]

He must early have decided to abandon Newcastle and set up his household in London because by April 1853 he was writing letters from Clifton Road, St. John's Wood, and this remained his address during the year. After he left again for Babylonia his wife moved to Moreland Cottage, Norwood, and this became his permanent residence for the rest of his time in London.[41]

It was of course in London that his future most obviously lay. To begin with, there were the various botanical and zoological specimens he had collected to deliver to the British Museum (though the birds in one of the boxes had been entirely destroyed by water). Then there was a report to be made to the Trustees on the excavations at Susa. After a couple of requests for an extension of time he delivered his report at the beginning of April 1853 with some drawings and "photographic representations" of some inscriptions. (Incidentally this must be one of the earliest records of the use of the camera in archaeology). On 9th April the Trustees conferred with him upon the subject of discoveries and conveyed to him their "especial thanks". I confess to great pleasure at the discovery that among the many eminent personages present there was the Rt. Hon. T. B. Macaulay.[42]

There was no security however in relying on the British Museum and he was soon casting around for other support. Ten days later he was writing to Sir William Hooker at Kew Gardens enclosing seeds of plants collected by him in Persia in 1851. It is the letter of a man who despite no previous acquaintance with the addressee is confident that what he has to offer is of interest. "As [the plants] may assist in throwing light on the gum-resins of the East they may prove an interesting addition to the Royal Gardens". Sir William's reply is not known but by September Loftus is promising to deliver personally some dried plant specimens and the correspondence develops a warmer note and becomes a

[39] BM Corr.
[40] BM Min.
[41] Kew Corr.
[42] BM Min and Corr.

regular feature of the next three or four years.[43]

However for Loftus the really important event of the year was the founding of the Assyrian Excavation Fund about July or August, 1853. The real promoters of the Fund, or "Society for Exploring the Ruins of Assyria and Babylonia with especial reference to Biblical Illustration" have not been identified, though Dr. Gadd surmises that certain London publishers were concerned.[44] The Prince Consort headed the subscription list. Layard became a member and was on the Committee. So also was Col. Rawlinson, which is hardly consistent with his later behaviour.[45]

The purpose of the Fund was to make good "the limited means hitherto at the command of the British Explorers in Assyria which have prevented their carrying on their researches in a systematic manner and on an adequate scale". The Society aimed to obtain material for completing the history of Assyria and Babylonia rather than bulky sculptures, and for this they wanted £10,000 to spend over three years.[46] In the meantime they had to engage an excavator. The choice in a sense was obvious. Layard had now turned to politics and in particular to encouraging the defence of the Turks against the Russians. Rassam was already in Assyria for the British Museum. Whether the Fund invited Loftus, or he came to them I do not know, but by August he had accepted the appointment.[47] The salary was £500 a year, which was by no means ungenerous, and in fact beyond the Fund's resources.

Before he set out he made a will. He signed it in London but it shows his strong attachment to Newcastle and his family. His executors were Edward Mather (a founder of the modern firm of Ingledew Botterell) and John Gray, an innkeeper of Rosemary Lane. He appointed them, with his wife, as guardians of his three sons, Alfred Kennett, Frederick and William Kennett. He left his wife an insurance policy of four hundred pounds, and legacies of ten pounds to buy mourning rings to James Radford (who had been his own

[43] Kew Corr.
[44] Gadd p. 95.
[45] Fund I.
[46] Fund I.
[47] BM Corr.

guardian), to Benjamin Green, the architect (who designed the Theatre Royal) and to Glossop, his friend of Cambridge days, who had gone on geological expeditions with him and now lived in Middlesex. He then directed the provision of two annuities, one of £300 for Charlotte for so long as she remained his widow and the other, to begin after his father's death, of £60 to his step-mother Elizabeth. This was evidently intended as a continuation of the £60 annuity which his grandfather had directed to be paid to his father for keeping away, but whether his grandfather would have approved of it is another matter. Finally the residue of the estate was left to Charlotte for her life, and after her death, by an arrangement much beloved of the draftsmen of wills, equally between such of his children as should attain the age of 21 or, being female, marry under that age. It was an excellent and comprehensive document, but it could only work if the necessary funds were available.[48]

On 5th October he left for the East via Marseilles. Three weeks later he was writing from Constantinople to Kew, this time on the subject of gum-resins, while at the same time retailing political gossip about the Turko-Russian dispute and speculating on the cold ride ahead over the Taurus. Early in November he left by boat for Samsun on the Turkish Black Sea coast and from there must have ridden south over the mountains to Baghdad, meeting Rassam on the way.[49]

He had as companion William Boutcher, an artist engaged by the Fund to draw and photograph any finds, so that he was better equipped than on his previous excavations. On the other hand he could expect no encouragement from his former director, Col. Rawlinson, who thoroughly disapproved of the establishment of the Fund. Loftus might have been appointed to go when the Museum Trustees' work had stopped, said Rawlinson, but "that he should appear as a competitor is objectionable". Rawlinson promised the Trustees to check any attempt by Loftus to excavate in Assyria. The inconsistency of his attitude in one who was a Committee Member of the Fund is indeed so great that one suspects that Rawlinson's name had appeared as a

[48] Principal Probate Registry.   [49] Kew Corr.

Committee Member without his authority. However, the Fund was tactful enough to ask Rawlinson's help for Loftus, and the Colonel accordingly offered a choice of sites South of Baghdad where no conflict of interest could arise. Loftus's earlier experience had been in this area and he may not have been dissatisfied with the result.[50]

He was in Baghdad by 6th December and had travelled South and established a camp some three miles from Warka, and near wells dug for the occasion, by the middle of January 1854. His account of this and of the start of his excavations is contained in two letters written by him to the Fund in January and February which were published with an appeal for financial support as their first report.[51] It is hopeless to attempt any coherent description of the excavations from these sources, which were undoubtedly written with one eye on the public. His discovery of a wall decorated with terracotta cones, which from later discussion by the Germans who now excavate at Warka seems to have been a significant find, evidently occurred in February 1854.[52] He also recovered numerous clay tablets for decipherment by Rawlinson. At the same time Boutcher was busily drawing both plans and elevations of walls, but not plans or sections of trenches. Loftus also had time to write to Kew and to head the letter "Ruins of Warka (Ur of the Chaldees)". "From the date of this note" he goes on, "you will observe that I have reached my destination and that I am once more on classic ground — at the birthplace of Abraham."[53] He was of course wrong about Ur (though to be fair not by more than twenty five miles) but evidently in high spirits.

He continued at Warka until April 1854 by which time the position in the North had completely altered. While Rassam had made a remarkable new discovery at the turn of the year, of the North-West Palace of Ashur-Bani-Pal at Kuyunjik, this coincided with the crippling illness of his artist, Hodder. By the middle of January Hodder was being removed in a litter and Rawlinson was already trying to persuade Loftus to send Boutcher up to Mosul. The problem was that there

[50] BM Corr.
[51] Fund I.
[52] North p. 214.
[53] Kew Corr.

were immense numbers of slabs being unearthed but no-one to draw them. Rassam could draw plans of the site, but very wisely no-one was prepared to entrust the finds to the uncertain waters of the Euphrates for transmission to Basrah without some previous record of what was being sent. A further trouble was that the Museum's funds were running out, so that late in March 1854, Rawlinson had to order Rassam to cease work by the end of the month as he was overspent.[54]

The opening for Loftus and Boutcher was obvious and the Fund Trustees were naturally keen to seize it. The characteristic of Assyrian excavation was large and spectacular finds. For all the Fund's announced devotion to the task of collecting historical material, the clay tablets of Warka were not to be compared as money-raisers with the winged lions and hunting scenes of Nineveh.

So Boutcher was sent on ahead to Kuyunjik in early April to draw the uncovered sculptures while Loftus delayed at Akher Koof near Baghdad waiting for confirmation that the Museum Trustees had finally abandoned Assyria. Rawlinson disapproved of this dilatoriness but as had happened three years before when he was asked to take over from Layard, Loftus liked to be certain who was in charge.[55] While he waited through May 1854, he wrote again to Hooker saying that he proposed to collect some plants and drugs by purchase in the bazaar and discussing how to obtain other specimens. He considered that his "First Campaign against the Mounds in Chaldea" had been tolerably successful because of the tablets he had discovered which had provided much information for Rawlinson. The hot weather was starting. "I do not relish" he said, "the summer's prospect before me".[56] At the beginning of June he received formal authorization from Rawlinson to excavate Kuyunjik and Nimrud at the expense of the Fund, and went up there.

He had hardly begun before receiving a severe letter from Rawlinson pointing out that his work did not confer any title to the property in the antiquities discovered by him. They

[54] BM Corr.
[55] BM Corr.
[56] Kew Corr.

belonged to the Museum Trustees who alone had been granted rights by the Turkish Court. At the same time Rawlinson wrote to the Trustees to report that Loftus seemed to think he had acquired the right to the sculptures already found for the benefit of the Fund; but that Rawlinson would not hesitate to reoccupy from Loftus any sites wanted by the Museum. Loftus, he said, "will find the old cock sparrow a troublesome customer".[57]

Silence fell after this, so perhaps the quarrel was largely a product of the hot weather. It is equally reasonable to suppose, though, that it was a symptom of the growing financial difficulties of the Fund. That body had entered into some highly obscure negotiations with the King of Prussia which appear to have contemplated a donation by him of a sum (varying according to the account) of something between £500 and £2,000 in exchange for a satisfactory collection of Assyrian sculptures. It is a fair guess that Loftus knew his own income depended upon the successful acquisition of some finds for the King. Boutcher's salary was already in arrear.[58]

During the summer the Treasury suddenly relented and put a further grant of £1,500 at the disposal of the Museum Trustees. With a significant eagerness the Fund hastened to suggest that Loftus and Boutcher be transferred to Rawlinson's orders, on the footing that the Trustees should pay one half of their salaries. The Trustees were also to get the balance of the donations to the Fund (which turned out in practice to be negligible). After some bickering about who was to be entitled to surplus sculptures, which the Fund seems to have won, the transfer was agreed to for the period up to the end of March 1855. The news reached Rawlinson in the middle of September 1854.[59]

By this time Rawlinson and Loftus had made it up again. The provision of the new grant by the Treasury had enabled Rawlinson about July to send Christian Rassam to excavate on the same mound as Loftus, a certain recipe one would suppose for a lively dispute. It certainly produced one, which

[57] BM Corr.
[58] BM Corr and Gadd P. 110.
[59] BM Corr.

charmingly illustrates the random qualities of Victorian archaeology. On 31st August Rassam wrote to Rawlinson and after uttering some general complaints about Loftus reported that he had put six gangs along the walls of the North Palace to prevent Loftus digging under it, for Loftus had found a sculptured wall outside the Palace, about 15 feet below it. This villainy on the part of Loftus turned out, however, to have arisen merely from the fact that he was digging on the ground floor while Rassam was still on the first floor. Rassam was told to dig deeper.[60]

One may suspect that the news of Loftus's transfer to his command must have come as a relief to Rawlinson, for he could now dispense with Christian Rassam. Rawlinson opened the subject to Loftus with much tact. If Loftus were prepared to agree to the proposal, he said, the workmen at Mosul would be put under Loftus's orders from 1st October and Loftus was to account to him from that date. He would lay down a general plan of operation "leaving all detail of execution to your own judgement and convenience" and was desirous that his general direction "be as little irksome as possible to those employed under my orders". If Loftus agreed, he and Boutcher were to continue at the North Palace at Kuyunjik and to dig also at the South East Palace at Nimrud during the winter. Loftus's acceptance was prompt. He intended, he said, to use twelve gangs and to put the excavated slabs in a hut. This method was desirable as "Mr. Boutcher will thus be able to apply the Photograph which is impossible to use in the trenches" — such were the technical difficulties then to be overcome.[61]

So from October 1854 to March 1855 Loftus and Boutcher laboured at Kuyunjik and Nimrud, partly in excavation, partly in packing the slabs and other finds, including an important collection of ivories, to go down river to Basrah.

It is not my purpose to describe Loftus's results in detail. Gadd's *Stones of Assyria* and Dr. Barnett's *Catalogue of the Nimrud Ivories in the British Museum* do this as completely as the records permit and it is an expert's task. There are two things which can be said, though. The first is that what was

[60] BM Corr.   [61] BM Corr.

found represented a very substantial contribution to available Assyrian sculpture. (It was during this period that the four bas-reliefs which for about 100 years decorated (or overhung, depending on one's point of view) the stairs of the Literary and Philosophical Society of Newcastle upon Tyne were extracted and packed.) The second is that Loftus used his customary ingenuity and energy in the course of the excavations. Some of the slabs had been split by fire so he had them coated with bitumen to hold the pieces together.[62] The ivories, discovered early in February 1855, also presented problems. They lay, blackened by fire, among wood ash at the bottom of a chamber. Many had been broken up, probably to secure inlaid jewels or gold. "I have got up a horseload of objects, and am fitting them together as fast as possible, preparatory to boiling them in Gelatine," he reported to the Fund's Treasurer, "The whole room is not yet explored, as the earth must first be removed from above. I propose going down tomorrow."[63]

And while I say that Loftus laboured, suggesting a rather unremitting and dreary task, there was some variety. A correspondent from *The Daily News* paid a visit about November. Later on Loftus despatched some acorns to Kew and reported that but for a severe sun-stroke he had, thanks to a good constitution, got well through the summer.[64] He never mentions the Crimean War, which had begun before he left Baghdad for Mosul in the previous May, but not far to the North the Russians and the Turks were preparing for battle around Erzerum, and Col. Williams and Churchill, once of the Boundary Commission, were trying to organize the Turkish resistance.

Rawlinson formally terminated Loftus's engagement at the end of March 1855. During April Loftus was collecting flowers in the desert between Mosul and Iskenderun which rather suggests that he took ship from there to start home.[65] When he reached England I do not know, but he was certainly back by July.

The Assyrian Excavation Fund was by then no more. Its

[62] Athenaeum No. 1455 p. 791
[63] Athenaeum No. 1430 p. 351
[64] Kew Corr.
[65] Kew Corr.

second and final Report had appeared in February and consisted of complaints that its finances were exhausted, extracts from a number of letters from Loftus, some reproductions of Boutcher's drawings, and the admission, made as something of an afterthought but with considerable polish, that at some unstated date the services of their men in Assyria had been transferred to the British Museum.[66] Loftus was therefore without employment but with his usual thoroughness set to work to make as much use as possible of the materials to hand. He revised a report on the geology of the Turko-Persian frontier, which had already been read to the Geological Society, for publication in its Journal.[67] He wrote in September to the Literary and Philosophical Society, offering bas-reliefs from Nimrud on payment by the Society of the cost of carriage. He prepared a paper on the Susa excavations for the Royal Society of Literature, which was read to them in November. He got permission from the Museum Trustees to communicate to the Royal Geographical Society the Report written six years before on his journey from Baghdad to Basrah. (The Society enquired of Col. Rawlinson whether it was worthy of publication and that gentleman, being then in a good temper, declared that it was.[68]) In March, 1856 he read another paper to the Royal Society of Literature, this time on Warka.

In this description I have passed by the furious quarrel with Rawlinson, which occupied the pages of *The Athenaeum* during February 1856. It began with a lecture given by Rawlinson to the Royal Asiatic Society where he discussed an inscription from Nimrud which "he had recently met with". A fortnight later *The Athenaeum* carried a letter from James Radford (ably performing his duties as guardian, though I suspect that Loftus was the true author) pointing out that in the report of the lecture, "Mr. Loftus's name is, I observe omitted as the discoverer of the interesting inscription therein alluded to. This gentleman is well known to the readers of your columns as an indefatigable explorer . . ." There was more of the same, and, immediately below, a

[66] Fund II.
[67] GS Proc.
[68] RGS Corr.

violent reply by Rawlinson from which it is difficult to select the most offensive passages. Loftus, he said, was not an independent explorer. "When this inscription was found Mr. Loftus was *in my employ* (for the Museum) as a subordinate agent, paid by me, receiving all his instructions from me . . ." Loftus should have sent him the inscription at Baghdad. "Considering the inscription, however, to be of no use (at least, I presume such to have been the reason, for otherwise the concealment was dishonest) he kept it to himself for a whole year". Again there was more, a great deal more, of the same.[69]

As on the occasion of their earlier dispute, however, the disagreement was soon over. The next week Rawlinson was writing, praising Loftus's work, and saying that his previous letter "contained expressions, which, since receiving Mr. Loftus's explanations, I feel to have been undeserved, and which I regret, therefore, to have made use of".[70] His retreat however was observed elsewhere. Hormuzd Rassam evidently felt that this was the moment when his work too should be recognized, and by April the Colonel had to write again to enlarge on the help that he had also had from Rassam.[71]

In June 1856 the sculptures which Loftus had packed over a year previously arrived at Havre in the *Manuel* after a circuitous voyage via Bombay and the Cape. The British Museum cases were not easily identifiable so on Rawlinson's advice Loftus was called in to help. He replied grandly "I shall be happy to run over to Havre and point out the sculptures", and was there two days later. His journey through Paris enabled him to visit Major-General Williams, the newly-promoted Hero of Kars, who had been captured by the Russians in the previous November and had just been repatriated. Three days later Loftus reported the completion of the discharge of the cases and the drowning of a docker submerged beneath a barrow. (The Trustees very properly made a donation to the widow.)[72] He came back to report to the Lit and Phil that their slabs had been left behind at

[69] Athenaeum No. 1478.
[70] Athenaeum No. 1479 p. 265.
[71] Athenaeum No. 1485 p. 461.
[72] BM Corr and Min.

Basrah and then to await the birth of his fifth child in September, which, he complained, prevented his going to a meeting of the British Association.[73]

It is impossible to imagine him really idle. No doubt the summer was spent at work on his book, *Travels in Chaldaea and Susiana*, but as the year went on it must have become imperative that he should take up some employment. He cannot have been receiving any regular salary for over twelve months. The possibility of any other learned society accepting a paper from him was remote. His book was in proof by November. It is fairly evident that the inheritance from his grandfather was no longer producing much income, certainly not enough to support a learned gentleman of leisure with a wife and a family of five. At this rather awkward moment there appeared a chance of exercising his ability as a geologist in the sort of out-of-the-way area which undoubtedly attracted him.

In July 1856, Professor Oldham, the Superintendent of the Geological Survey in India, had been authorized to extend the scope of the Survey and to engage three or four assistants at a monthly salary of Rs. 200.[74] He seems to have asked Trenham Reeks, of the School of Mines, to recruit for him, and Reeks approached Loftus at the beginning of September. Loftus accepted promptly, claiming that he was "not entirely a novus homo in Oriental campaigning" and expressed the intention of taking his wife with him and leaving his children behind.[75]

Some frantic activity followed. He had some troublesome negotiations with the Royal Botanic Gardens with a view to selling them the specimens he had brought back from Assyria. He pointed out that as "I take part of my family with me I am obliged to husband my resources" so that he could not present the specimens to Kew. They were apparently "stowed away in a huge chest" in Newcastle but he was anxious that Kew should have them. Too much of his collection was at the British Museum and "you know the difficulty of recovering anything that falls into those voracious jaws".

[73] Kew Corr.
[74] IPP.
[75] IGS Corr.

Despite these considerations Dr. Hooker does not seem to have viewed Loftus's price of 10/- a hundred (for 1,700 specimens) with great enthusiasm though he did in the end acquire them at an unstated price apparently for the Calcutta Museum.[76]

At the same time Loftus was in brisk correspondence with the Royal Geographical Society about the printing of the maps to go with a paper on the River Eulaeus, and was writing the introduction to his book. He left England for the last time about 12th December 1856.[77]

He seems to have been told that the Survey was at work in the foothills of the Himalayas but he was never to work there. The date on which he took up his appointment at Calcutta, 3rd February 1857, was only three weeks before the mutiny of the 19th Native Infantry at Berhampur, the forerunner of the Mutiny itself. Three months later, after the outbreak at Meerut, the British lost control of events in Northern India for the rest of 1857.

Loftus was in Calcutta in June. Writing to Dr. Shaw of the Royal Geographical Society on the 20th of the month he reported that he had joined the Volunteer Defence Corps, which (in his view) the civilians had forced on the Government, a week previously, and had been on patrol duty from 1 a.m. to 4 a.m. "Things" he said, "are settling down", a remark which would have been ill received by the Europeans of Cawnpore who were massacred a week after the date of his letter. Loftus went on, "I much regret having joined this Survey. I find myself associated with boys who have just left apron strings! Is there any expedition afloat where I can be of use?"[78] There was evidently no answer to this *cri de coeur* and he was to spend most of his time in India either in the Raj Mahal hills some 200 miles North West of Calcutta or else in charge of the offices of the Survey at Calcutta itself.

One reason for his limited movement apart from the effects of the Mutiny was that he was a sick man. His obituary refers to sunstroke (or a *coup de soleil*, as it is there more elegantly expressed) but his illness was more deep-seated. The cause of his death was given as an abscess of the

[76] Kew Corr.
[77] RGS Corr.
[78] RGS Corr.

liver which is, I believe, consistent with his having suffered from amoebic dysentery. In October 1858 he was given leave to proceed to Port Blair in the Andaman Islands by the Company's steamer *Sydney*, in the vain hope one supposes that he might recuperate there. In November he obtained a medical certificate recommending that he be given leave of absence for eighteen months. Government granted leave for twelve months on 24th November and he sailed two days later from Calcutta for England on the S.S. *Tyburnia*.[79] He died at sea on the following day, 27 November, three days before his thirty-eighth birthday.

There is not much more to record. The news reached Newcastle only in March of the following year. Its arrival, ironically enough, coincided with the last stages of the erection of the Assyrian slabs on the Lit and Phil staircase.[80] In the same month Charlotte applied to the East India Company for a pension and was refused.[81] By 1st April the executors appointed by Loftus had renounced probate of his will and Charlotte, now living in Hoxton, herself took out letters of administration. The causes are obscure, but I would suppose that the estate, which was sworn as less than £5,000, was insufficient to support the rather ambitious designs of the will. A little later General Williams wrote a memorial letter of praise. After that there is nothing, save for the sad record in the Probate Registry for 1865 of the death of Charlotte and the appointments as administrators, and guardians of the infant children, of Edward Mather and John Gray, the original executors. In the result the vigorous inquisitive life of the man ceased with such abruptness as wrenched it out of general memory. Loftus will never be one of the heroes of Newcastle, but he deserves more recognition than he has had.

One reason for this lack is undoubtedly the inadequacy of the record he left behind him. While we have both his book,

[79] IPP.
[80] *Newcastle Courant* 11th March 1859. The reliefs remained in position until 1960 when they were sold. They are thought now (1971) to be in Los Angeles.
[81] IPP.

Travels in Chaldaea and Susiana, and a long paper on the geology of the Turco-Persian frontier, neither document is very satisfactory. Of the paper it is sufficient to note that it was rightly admitted by the editor of the Journal of the Geological Society of London to require a revision which it never got. The book covers a limited period only, primarily from 1849 to 1852 with some information on the early part of 1854, and does not for instance give any account of what was done at Kuyunjik. The narrative is somewhat confused, and though its plans and drawings demonstrate a due care for fact, it bears no resemblance at all to a modern excavation report. While his descriptions of the Arabs and their eccentricities throw some light on the attitude of the Englishman of that day towards the inferior Oriental there is nothing in them of any great distinction. One has the irritating feeling that there was in him a book of more lasting value, but that, due to inability to handle his materials effectively, it was never written.

He was also guilty of some quaint notions. A good example is his theory that outside the three principal ruins at Warka that whole enormous site was "filled with the bones and sepulchres of the dead" and that for 2,500 years Warka had been a sacred burial place to which the ancient people of Babylonia had transported their dead.[82] This theory was based on his observation of contemporary burial custom, coupled with his discovery of a large number of Parthian glazed sarcophagi, which must in fact have come from a very limited area as later excavators have found no such abundance of them.[83] The removal of one to the river forms the subject of the dramatic frontispiece to his book, where the workmen are depicted carrying a coffin on their shoulders, encouraged from behind by what is evidently Loftus himself on a horse, and thrusting their way through a band of apparently hostile natives, brandishing spears. These last were in fact the off-duty members of the work force engaged in jollifications. One suspects that this was intended to rival the equally dramatic representation of Layard moving the great winged bull from Nimrud, which appeared as the

[82] *Travels* p. 199.   [83] North p. 241.

frontispiece to *Nineveh and Babylon*. The comparison is on the whole slightly ridiculous and I have half wondered whether it was intended as an elaborate joke.

But that said, one is bound to admire the breadth of his interest and the uninhibited confidence with which he would move from collecting plants to digging up ivories, from drawing geological sections to administering rough justice among his Arab workers. No doubt the specialist of today would find the results below standard, but how many results were obtained! For instance, Julius Jordan, the first director of the German excavation at Warka wrote in 1928, "in . . . Loftus we possess already an outstanding presentation of the first ample excavation in Warka . . . the observations gathered by Sir William (sic) are of such versatility and so brilliantly presented that we felt solid ground under our feet from the very beginning of our work."[84] It is necessary to recollect the difficulties of transport, of health and of food and the danger of attack by local tribesmen which were the lot of anyone working in the disordered Iraq of that day to see what Loftus achieved in its proper perspective.

Of course the full promise of his life was unfulfilled. The Crimean War and then his breakdown in health occurred just when the extent of his talents had become apparent. He was, I think, in the true tradition of Victorian explorers and the essence of his spirit resides in that appeal from Calcutta — "Is there any expedition afloat where I can be of use?" Let us remember him by that.

ACKNOWLEDGEMENTS

I am very grateful to Dr. Richard Barnett, Keeper of the Department of Western Asiatic Antiquities in the British Museum, for access to extracts made by him and the late Dr. Gadd from the records of the British Museum Trustees. Without this help I could not have written this memoir.

I have also to thank for their patience, and help in providing me with information, the Librarians of the India Office

---

[84] North p. 190. The presence of solid ground beneath Dr. Jordan's feet is an interesting phenomenon in itself, but arises I suspect from the extraordinarily stilted English of Mr. North.

Library, of the Institute of Geological Sciences, of the Royal Botanic Gardens and of the Royal Geographical Society; the late George Fearon of Rye; Dr. N. McCord and Miss R. B. Harbottle.

REFERENCES

BM Corr	Original Papers of the British Museum Trustees.
BM Min	Minutes of Standing Committee Meetings of the British Museum Trustees.
FO Corr	Foreign Office Records at Public Record Office. FO 78:762 and 811. FO 248:139.
Fund I ⎱ Fund II ⎰	Reports of the Assyrian Excavation Fund dated respectively 28th April 1854 and 20th February 1855.
Gadd	C. J. Gadd *The Stones of Assyria* London 1937.
GC Proc	Geological Society of London Quarterly Journal 1854 Vol.XI.
IGS Corr	Correspondence of the Institute of Geological Sciences.
IPP	Indian Public Proceedings.
Kew Corr	Correspondence of the Royal Botanic Gardens: English Letters — Vols. xxxiii and xxxvi. E. Indian Letters Vol. iv.
NHS Min	Northumberland Durham and Newcastle Natural History Society Minutes.
North	Robert North *Status of the Warka Excavation* Orientalia Vol. 26 New Series pp. 185 ff.
Rassam	Hormuzd Rassam *Asshur and the Land of Nimrod* New York 1897.
RGS Corr	Correspondence of the Royal Geographical Society.
Travels	W. K. Loftus *Travels and Researches in Chaldaea and Susiana* London 1857.
Venn	John Venn *Biographical History of Gonville and Caius College* Vol. II 1898.
Ward	S. G. P. Ward *Faithful, the Story of the DLI* London 1963.
Waterfield	Gordon Waterfield *Layard of Nineveh* London 1963.
Welford	Richard Welford *Men of Mark 'twixt Tyne and Tweed* 1895.

Marmaduke Tunstall

George Allan

APPENDIX ONE

The Sebroke Crozier and the Nineteenth-Century *Newcastle Museum**

John Philipson

Abbreviations
Lit & Phil   Literary and Philosophical Society of Newcastle upon Tyne
NHS   Natural History Society of Northumberland Durham and Newcastle upon Tyne

When recently a question arose about how the Society† came to acquire the Sebroke Crozier, a difficulty was at once encountered in that its acquisition is not recorded in our Accessions Book, nor was subsequent search successful in revealing any minute of our Council which threw any light on how it came into our possession. On a metal collar on the staff is engraved: *This Crozier was found Anno 1741 in the Coffin of Thos. Seabrook chosen Abbot of Gloucester in 1450. He died in 1457. It was given to the Abby of Old Windsor by Dr. Milles[1] Dean of Exeter in 1764.* Helpful though this legend is, it leaves a sizeable gap between Old Windsor in 1764 and the Keep in Newcastle in our own time. Moreover no Abbey of Old Windsor appears to be known to history.

The thought that it may have come to the Society with the ivory crozier, latterly referred to as the "Allan" crozier,[2] prompted consultation of Fox's *Synopsis of the Newcastle Museum* (1827). It at once became apparent that the Sebroke crozier, like the ivory crozier, came to Newcastle, and later to our Society, through the purchase in 1822 by the Newcastle Literary & Philosophical Society of the collection to which at that time reference was mostly made as the Wycliffe Museum.

*Reprinted from *Archaeologia Aeliana* 5th Series, Vol. IX.
†Reference to the Society and to 'us' and 'our' in this paper should be understood as referring to the Society of Antiquaries of Newcastle upon Tyne.

THE WYCLIFFE MUSEUM

A history of this collection, and some account of the two men who founded and developed it, may be found in Fox's introduction to his *Synopsis*, but a summary must be given here. Marmaduke Tunstall, born 1743, educated at Douai, and as that implies a Roman Catholic, spent some years in London as a young man, forming the nucleus of his collection. He was elected FSA in 1764 and FRS in 1777. On his marriage in 1776, he left London and settled on a family estate at Wycliffe on the Tees. After preparing a suitable room in his house, he removed his collections there about 1780 or 1781. A contemporary visitor alludes[3] to the "invaluable collections of manuscripts, books, prints, coins, and gems, besides a spacious museum stored with rare birds, and many other curiosities relating to natural history."

Tunstall's interests, as became a country gentleman of his time, were wide rather than deep, but if there is an area in which he could claim a more than ordinary qualification it is in the field of ornithology. He kept exotic birds and when they died he had them stuffed. By this means and by purchase, he built up a considerable collection of stuffed birds. He corresponded with the great Linnaeus, and had privately printed an essay at a systematic list of British Birds in Latin, French and English.[4] In his last years he invited Thomas Bewick, whose engraving of the Chillingham Bull he had commissioned, to visit his collection. There was some slight delay in Bewick's acceptance and it was not till after Tunstall's death in 1790 that Bewick stayed for a period at Wycliffe and a number of the birds in Tunstall's museum became the originals of illustrations in Bewick's *British Birds*.

After Tunstall's death his museum was bought in 1791 for less than £700 by George Allan and removed to his house at Blackwell Grange, near Darlington. A great deal is known about George Allan as he left vast quantities of paper, and indeed, some valuable collections of manuscripts passed through his hands; his family, too, remained in the area and in their piety preserved much of his paper for posterity. So addicted was he to documentation that, besides spending untold days in transcribing manuscripts, he installed a private press, equipped with a wide range of Caslon Old Face type, and multiplied copies of selected documents as well as printing odds and ends of ephemera. Allan was a Fellow of the Society of Antiquaries of London, corresponded with notable antiquaries of his day such as Richard Gough, and collaborated closely with Hutchinson in the production of his *History of Durham*.

From the surviving Visitors Book, dated 1795, it seems that the museum was exhibited in Darlington from 1792 to 1794 before being established at Blackwell Grange. Allan added to the collections and from Fox's account, substantiated by some surviving evidence, did much work listing and labelling. He in turn died in 1800 and the museum languished and decayed till it was sold in 1822, for £400 and through the agency of G. T. Fox, to the Literary and Philosophical Society of Newcastle upon Tyne. Fox had the collections conveyed by wagon to Newcastle. As the Lit & Phil building was uncompleted, they were taken into storage at the works of Doubleday and Easterby, and remained there for two years. A long room on the second floor of the new Lit & Phil building in Westgate Street was prepared as a museum room. Meanwhile the birds had been found to be in a state of some decay and a Mr. Wingate was employed to rehabilitate them.

THE NEWCASTLE MUSEUM

The Lit & Phil was founded in 1793 and had the widest interests. Lectures, discussions, meteorological observations, formation of a library, the holding of stock of scientific apparatus and its loan to members, correspondence with savants overseas, almost nothing seemed irrelevant to their enquiring minds. Not unnaturally then they began to attract the gift of scientific collections, some of these of abiding significance. But these random collections took on a different scale when in 1822 they were persuaded to buy the Wycliffe Museum. There were critics of the decision at that time (Mackenzie, 485), mainly at that stage on the ground of the dilapidated condition of the considerable collection of stuffed birds.[5] When they did move the material the room provided proved too small.[6] Nevertheless some progress was made. In 1826 the material was moved in and some regulations for the museum agreed. In 1827 Fox produced his *Synopsis of the Newcastle Museum*. This catalogue is a rich source of information for the history and content of the museum, listing, not merely the Tunstall/Allan collections, but the direct acquisitions of the Lit & Phil both before and after the purchase date. One a little suspects that Fox persuaded the Lit & Phil to buy the Wycliffe Museum to enable him to produce this catalogue. It is a satisfying monument for any man to leave as presently he fades from the scene (retiring to Durham) leaving the Lit & Phil struggling like a Laocoon with too much material, a limited space, limited funds, and a measure of disagreement among themselves whether the struggle was one in which they ought to be involved at all.

In desperation in 1829 the Lit & Phil appointed a Museum Committee, but already another solution was emerging. The difficulties were that the revenues of the Lit & Phil were inadequate to cover the running of a museum in addition to their other activities, and that their large membership with diffused interests made it difficult to channel voluntary activity into the care of a museum. The solution was the formation of a Natural History Society, with its own membership and its own subscription income, primarily directed to running the museum. On 19th August 1829 a meeting was held in the Lit & Phil building and the Natural History Society established. We are not here concerned with the history of the NHS, which has been told elsewhere, but it may be said that over the following years the NHS was able to command the labours of many distinguished scientists making valuable contributions not merely to the museum but to the greater body of science.

The situation was complicated at once by a resolution of the annual general meeting of members of the Lit & Phil in 1829 rejecting, rather decidedly, a request of the NHS to purchase the museum material. Later that year however the Lit & Phil committee agreed to allow the NHS to undertake "superintendence and arrangement" of the museum, but expressed the wish that it be a "mutual understanding of the two committees that the museums be not separated." Thus early is ambiguity introduced into the situation. The Lit & Phil was inhibited from unequivocally handing over its collections, and for some years continued to reappoint its Museum Committee, and funds of that committee (by then £5 1s 9d) were not absorbed into the general fund until 1834. Meanwhile obviously the NHS was at work. In January 1831 they rented Mr. Anderson's showroom in an adjoining property and in February the Lit & Phil gave leave for part of the collection (the foreign birds) to be removed there, and these were insured for £600 in the names of the Lit & Phil, the NHS, and Mr. Hutton.

Already in 1831 the NHS had formulated a project to secure a "gallery" to be placed on a site adjoining to and communicating with the Lit & Phil, which notes in its 38th Report (1831) a proposal "to combine its funds with those of the Antiquarian and NH Societies to secure the accommodation, under one roof, of our various collections." In 1833 plans and a request for a site were submitted to the Lit & Phil. The latter in April further defined the proposal:

> The NHS to take charge of the Museum of this Society arranging the specimens in it along with their own . . . This Museum to be called the Newcastle Museum, and to be the property of the two Societies; the specimens and the furniture belonging to each being all carefully marked.

For the plot of ground behind the Lit & Phil together with the right of access along Library Place, the NHS was to pay the Lit & Phil £400. The entrance from the Library Place was to be for the public, but a door communicating directly from the Library of the Lit & Phil would give the members of the latter Society free access to the Museum. In return the Lit & Phil was to pay the NHS £40 a year. In 1834 the building was finished, Mr. Wingate was appointed Keeper in June and at a Special General Meeting of the NHS on 3rd December the museum was formally opened. To make clear the light in which the transaction was viewed by the NHS it is necessary, at the cost of some slight repetition, to quote from the report read at this meeting which recalled that "Lit & Phil had for some years been possessed of an extensive Museum, containing many objects of great value and scientific interest, and as they declined a proposal of selling their collection, it was deemed advisable . . . to consolidate the collections, by the formation of a joint Museum. It was with pleasure that the Committee found this proposal met by the Lit & Phil Society in the readiest and most liberal manner."

Meanwhile our Society had for some years been occupying two rooms on the ground floor of the Lit & Phil building. We also had a problem: the weight and bulk of the Roman incribed and sculptured stones with which competing donors generously presented us. In 1829 John Hodgson and John Adamson wrote to the Lit & Phil seeking permission to erect a wooden shed against the wall that divided the property of the Lit & Phil from that of Mr. Anderson, the cabinet-maker. This lean-to was for the accommodation of our Roman stones and the permission was given.

Then on 4th June 1834 the NHS wrote to our Secretaries as follows:

> Gentlemen: By the direction of the Committee of the NHS, I beg leave, through you, to make the following proposals to the Antiquarian Society, viz. that they may rent a piazza and the two meeting rooms at the end of it in the new Building for the sum of £25 a year, this sum to include lighting heating and the attendance and services of the keeper of the Museum who will be constantly on the spot. The members of your Society to have free access for themselves and their Friends to the collections of Natural History dayly from 12 o'clock and the Committee of the NHS would beg to suggest that the rooms and piazza should be accessible to vistors during the time the Museum is open. The NHS further propose to deposit with your Society all specimens and remains of Antiquity whatever which may come into their possession with the old collection, these specimens being marked and a Catalogue of them kept.

The letter goes on to make some reservations about use of the rooms for meetings and concludes with details about dates for occupation and about accrual of rent.

I have been unable to trace in the records of the Lit & Phil or the NHS any specific authority sought or given for such a transfer of property to the care of a third party. To understand how such a loose arrangement should have been acceptable, was indeed part of the whole conception, we have to remember two things. First that the active members of all three societies were often the same people, the town's intellectual elite, revolving like a stage army in support of all three societies. Secondly that they had all accepted the principle of a Newcastle Museum, the name which Fox had proposed for the Lit & Phil museum in 1827, which was now to have a wider context as a joint museum to be run in a building communicating with the Lit & Phil, and of which our Society was to occupy the ground floor. At this stage, and for some years, the museum was seen as a co-operative effort. It was not till 1836 that the Lit & Phil called to mind that the agreement with the NHS had not been formally executed by the trustees of the two Societies. Prompted on this point, the committee of the NHS, still evidently in honeymoon mood, considered that it was "highly unlikely any wish should exist in either Society for the dissolution of a union, advantageous to both," and authorized their trustees to sign.

This clearly remained the prevailing view for many years to come. There are evidences however from time to time that there were those in the Lit & Phil who had some degree of misgiving about the loss of control of their property. For example in 1847 Law LXXII of the Lit & Phil provided that *specimens, belonging to this Society, which have been placed in the Museum of the NHS shall remain deposited with, and entrusted to the care and management of that Society.* Then, in 1848, its Librarian was instructed to examine the various articles belonging to the Lit & Phil lately arranged with the antiquities in the Museum, checking them with the list, and that the same be retained in the Museum of the NHS.

In view of the date of this agitation it may have been prompted by the prospect of the removal of our Society to the Keep. No evidence was found that any action was taken and a possible interpretation of these gestures is that they were in part cosmetic, designed to placate some legalistic agitator on the Lit & Phil committee or in the membership. Certainly our own Society did not conceal its possession of these antiquities. Our first catalogue was printed and published in 1839. It openly lists fifty articles, including the Sebroke crozier, which are acknowledged, perhaps a little disingenuously, to the "Allan Museum," rather then explicitly to the Lit & Phil. Some further sixteen articles may, some with certainty others with a high degree of probability, be ascribed to the same source.[7]

In 1822 and for some years after it was most common to refer to the material purchased from the Allan family as the Wycliffe Museum. In his *Synopsis* (1829) Fox advocates the adoption of the title the *Newcastle Museum*, but he emphasizes the contribution made by Allan in adding to Tunstall's collections. More significantly, he adopted *Allan Museum* as the running headline to that section of his volume covering the 1822 acquisition. For the accessions from this source our 1839 catalogue relied heavily on Fox and it is probable that it was this headline that led the copyist to attribute these articles to the "Allan Museum".

The text accompanying Oliver's 1844 edition of his map of Newcastle begins by saying that the collections of the three societies, arranged under the general name of the Newcastle Museum, were open, without fee from 12 to 4 each weekday. He proceeds to give so precise a description of the rooms with exact internal measurements that, with the aid of a site-plan in the archive of the NHS, it has been possible to make a conjectural reconstruction of the ground and first floor plans of the museum, which has been drawn by Mr. Tristram Spence.[8]

The most vivid account of the building housing the joint museum from 1834 is that of R. O. Heslop in the centenary volume of *AA*. "The older and newer buildings formed three sides of a four-square gravelled court, in the centre of which stood a rain gauge. On two sides the NHS's walls, unpierced by windows, rose high above, while below they were supported in piers, leaving a gallery open to the quadrangle. The claustral effect of the sub-structure impressed itself upon contemporaries, one of whom describes it as the "collonade" (sic) and another as the "piazza in which are deposited the Society's valuable collection of Roman altars."

APPENDIX ONE: THE *NEWCASTLE MUSEUM* 205

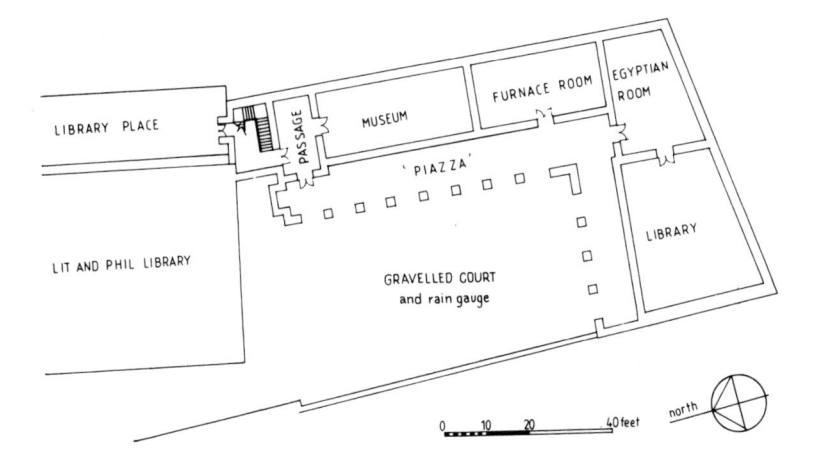

Fig. 1. Newcastle Museum *c.* 1844, ground floor

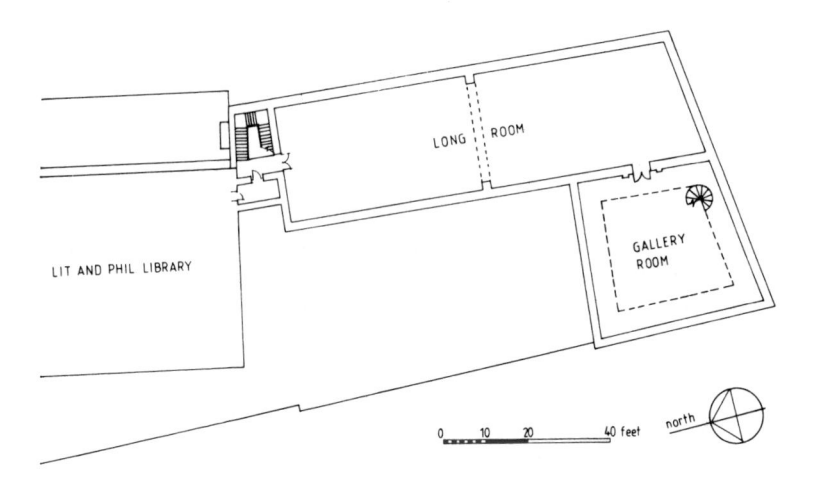

Fig. 2. Newcastle Museum *c.* 1844, first floor

It will be remembered that our Society secured the lease of the Keep from 1848. Some renovations were carried out and all our museum objects must have been transferred there by 1849 when our tenancy in the old museum ended. By 1850 tenancy of the ground floor we formerly occupied had been taken over by the Fine Arts Society. The piazza was glazed and heated and used by the students of the Government School of Design under William Bell Scott. This school of Design was the forerunner of the later School of Art in the University, now the Department of Fine Art.

Meanwhile the space available to the NHS was, with the growth of their collections, gradually becoming less and less adequate. Some photographs from late in their time in the old building show the museum as being richly overcrowded. Also with the growing standing and independence of their Society, the naturalists increasingly found it irksome to be seen as a junior society down a side-alley of the Lit & Phil. This feeling of unrest was expressed eloquently in a report by Albany Hancock in 1864. The report is far from being an objective assessment of what the NHS owed to the Lit & Phil, but there is no denying the need for a move to larger premises. Nevertheless it was not until 1884 that the NHS was able to move its museum to their present building.

When their move finally did come, the ambiguity about who owned what was happily resolved by payment by the NHS to the Lit & Phil of a nominal consideration of £100 for such specimens, the property of the Lit & Phil, as they wished to remove to their new Museum. A signed schedule thereof was supposed to be handed to the Trustees of the Lit & Phil. The money was paid, but no copy of the schedule has been traced. Knowing how unwelcome the preparation of schedules is to those who have to do the work, the possibility must be accepted that no schedule was ever prepared, and that the Trustees of the Lit & Phil may have failed to make themselves sufficiently disagreeable to secure one. The NHS sold the site and building of the old museum to the North Eastern Railway for £12,830, thus making a helpful capital gain.

Apart from the Egyptian antiquities and the more

ethnographical material, most of the antiquities from the Newcastle Museum remained with our Society, and many still remain. The tacit assumption behind the break-up of the *Newcastle Museum* was surely that exhibits are best in the care of those within whose field of specialism they lie. Of the three Societies it was in our hands that medieval antiquities should most naturally have come to rest, and among them, the Sebroke Crozier, with which our present study began.

It would not be unreasonable to argue that Fox was mistaken in advocating the purchase of the Tunstall/Allan collections. By modern standards it was altogether too miscellaneous an assemblage, and its major element the stuffed birds was one peculiarly susceptible to decay. Nevertheless 1822 was a fateful year for museums in Newcastle. The modest and rather random collections of the Lit & Phil, important as some of their elements have proved to be, and the nucleus of our own collection of Roman inscribed and sculptured stones, were not on a scale to present serious problems. But the introduction of the Tunstall/Allan collections raised the combined operation to a scale too large for the Lit & Phil to keep it as a minor side-issue. Hence the NHS and hence for half-a-century *The Newcastle Museum*. At the mid-century our own Society opted out of the joint museum taking with us many objects which only gradually did we learn to value. From the continuing Newcastle Museum in due time emerged the splendid Hancock Museum.

THE SEBROKE CROZIER

The history of the crozier from its emergence as part of the Wycliffe Museum is now sufficiently clear. It remains to trace its earlier history and to consider the implications of the inscription cited in our opening paragraph. The crozier itself is discussed in the appendix below.

The Benedictine house of St. Peter at Gloucester was founded in 681, and Thomas Sebroke was elected Abbot in 1450. He began the building of the "exceeding fair and square tower in the middest of the church" (Camden) and, after his death in 1457 the work was continued under the direction of Robert Tully, one of the monks. Sebroke was buried in a chapel at the south-west end of the choir. When in 1741 Bishop Benson repaved the choir, Sebroke's coffin, and a number of others were opened. No contemporary account of the opening of the coffin has been traced, but Dugdale's editors in 1817 add a footnote: *In the Hon. Mr. Bateman's catalogue of furniture removed after his death from Old Windsor, and sold in May 1774, in London, No. 73 was this article "An ancient Greek crozier in ivory; and the crozier of Seabrook, Abbat of Gloucester 1457, taken out of his coffin."* (Dugdale, 536n) Cowen (AA^4 xlv, 204) has shown that this sale took place at Christies, and consulting their copy of the catalogue, found that Lot 73 brought £1 17s 0d. Cowen surmises that the purchaser was Tunstall who, as stated above, spent these years in London making the purchases that formed the nucleus of his collections. Though from Fox *(Synopsis,* 179) it is evident that Allan did buy antiquities from other collections, it is probable that, were there evidence then surviving that in this case he had done so, it would have been cited by Fox, as he does for example with the material purchased from Boulter.

For the attribution to Sebroke and to Gloucester we are primarily dependent on the authenticity of the inscription on the collar. The entry in the sale catalogue has no independent authority, but derives from the inscription, as the footnote in the *Monasticon,* in its turn, derives from the sale catalogue. The text of the engraved legend is circumstantial and refers to events and people independently attested. We know from other sources that Bishop Benson had the choir of Gloucester Cathedral repaved in 1741 and that Abbot Sebroke's coffin was then opened. Moreover we know a great deal about Dr. Milles.[9] Though Coleridge in another context, probably uncharitably, said of Milles, *though only a dean, he was in dulness and malignity, most episcopally eminent*, what is pertinent to our enquiry is that he was interested in antiquities, indeed pre-eminently so, being President of the Society of Antiquaries of London. So that it is inherently probable that a medieval crozier might pass through his hands. Even if Coleridge were wholly right about Milles'

APPENDIX ONE: THE *NEWCASTLE MUSEUM* 209

dullness, the crozier falls within an area in which Milles was best qualified to hold an informed view. Many of the papers he wrote for *Archaeologia* relate to the medieval period, and in his influential church circle (his father-in-law was Archbishop of Canterbury) he had the opportunity to be fully informed about events such as the opening of Sebroke's coffin. For Milles this was a contemporary event, indeed he was elected a Fellow of the London Society in the same year. No record of his acquisition of the crozier has yet been traced, but it must have been Milles as donor who told the recipient in 1764 about its source, which he was in a good position to know.

At first sight the alleged recipient, the "Abby of Old Windsor", defies all augury. There is no such abbey in Dugdale, nor in *VCH Berkshire*. The answer lies in the whimsies of a delightful character who flourished from about 1705 to 1773.

The Hon. Richard Bateman[10] was a man of means, and taste, and fashion, moving in the highest Society of Hanoverian England. Henry Fox and he were rival claimants for the hand of Isabella, grand-daughter of the Great Duke of Malborough. A poem entitled *Isabella* by a contemporary wit begins:

> The monkey, lapdog, parrot and her Grace,
> Had each retired from breakfast to their place,
> When hark, a knock! "See Betty, see who's there!"
> 'Tis Mr. Bateman, ma'am, in his new chair!'
> 'Dicky's new chair, the charming'st thing in town,
> Whose poles are lackered and whose lining's brown.'

So it goes on. Disappointed in the Duchess, Dicky remained a bachelor, able unhampered to indulge his lightest whim.

About 1730 Bateman fell in love with a house on the Thames at Old Windsor, of which, with much surrounding property, he became lessee and which he proceeded to embellish, first in a Chinese taste, with pagodas, bridges, and temples. Horace Walpole claimed the credit of Bateman's switch from about 1746 to a gothic taste. "Every pagoda," it was said, "took the veil." By 1760 the house was a mock-monastery with cloisters, refectory, and stained glass, a faithful echo of Strawberry Hill.

Bateman chose as the fictitious founder of his monastery Caducanus,[11] Bishop of Bangor from 1215 to 1236. Not far from the refectory, he had erected a mausoleum which was the actual tomb of Caducanus, removed from the Abbey of Dore in Herefordshire, and re-erected at Grove House. Upon the altar in this mausoleum with other relics we are told there lay a crozier. We cannot know that this is Sebroke's crozier, but it does provide a motive for Bateman coupling the broken staff together, and of the two croziers, the ivory one without a staff and this with, it is the more suitable for the purpose.

It may be thought strange that a clergyman should give a crozier for a purpose of such levity, but we should recall that they saw things more objectively in the eighteenth century, the social differences too were much more significant then, and that Mr. Bateman was a man of the highest fashion whom a clergyman even of Milles' standing would be glad to oblige.[12] It is certain therefore that Bateman is the author of the inscription. Anyone else would describe the gift as to Mr. Bateman rather than to the "Abby". It was all part of the show.

Bateman died 1st March 1773. His heir incontinently sold everything in a six-day sale at Christies.[13] Horace Walpole wrote on the second day of the sale: "Strawberry Hill is almost the last monastery left, at least in England. Poor Mr Bateman's is despoiled. Lord Bateman has stripped and plundered it . . ." As we already know, Sebroke's crozier was among the relics sold and it is probable that it was the buyer who brought the crozier to the north of England.

For 284 years the Sebroke crozier may be supposed to have lain with the remains of the proud and masterful abbot.[14] Then for 93 years it changed hands with some frequency and was probably viewed by visitors as various as Horace Walpole, John Wesley, Thomas Bewick and Edward Pease. Finally after 147 years in our possession, for part of that time a mute witness of a significant development in the cultural history of Newcastle, it has been refurbished, something has been learnt of its story, and bringing our regard to bear upon the thing itself we can observe an object of intricacy and interest, a fitting subject for further comparative study. Stylistic study, for which the writer is not equipped, is called for to confirm or deny the origin of the crozier in 1457 the date of Sebroke's death.

For access to the records of the Literary & Philosophical Society and for assistance in many ways I am indebted to Charles Parish, librarian of that Society, as also to his assistant Mr. N. Baumfield. I had the same ungrudging help from Mrs. Grace Hickling, honorary secretary of the Natural History Society, and valued help, too, from Dr. Ian Doyle, Durham University Library, Mr. J. Hopkins, librarian of the Society of Antiquaries of London, Mrs. Copeland, Darlington Branch Library, Mr. Alistair Elliot, Newcastle University Library, and the Bodleian Library. I am grateful to Mr. Tristram Spence R.I.B.A. for drawing the conjectural plans of the old Newcastle Museum as it was in 1844. My discussion of the croizer itself would have been even more inexpert without the guidance of Miss L. Allason-Jones, to whom my best thanks.

SUMMARY

Thomas Sebroke, Abbot of Gloucester, died in 1457 and was buried in a chapel in the Abbey. His coffin was opened in 1741 and this crozier is said to have been removed. The crozier was acquired by Dr. Milles, Dean of Exeter, and in 1764 given by him to Hon. Mr. R. Bateman of Old Windsor. After his death it was sold at Christies in 1774 and bought perhaps by Marmaduke Tunstall. In 1791 the contents of Tunstall's museum were bought by George Allan of Blackwell Grange, Darlington. Long after the latter's death his successors in 1822 sold the collections to the Literary & Philosophical Society of Newcastle upon Tyne. By 1827 they had been added to the collections of that Society, and the crozier is listed in their catalogue. An attempt is made to trace the evolution, development, and dissolution of the Newcastle Museum, including the period of involvement in it of our own society. The crozier probably passed to our Society in 1834 and has remained in our possession since.

APPENDIX

Description of the Sebroke Crozier

The staff is apparently of oak. Between the embellishments which ring the staff the wood has been worked down to a square section with chamfered corners. The ornamental rings are integral with the staff; their surface is alternately ribbed and diapered, or in sartorial terms, puffed, slashed and quilted. A ring of cabling divides the embellishment from the plain sections of the staff.

The crozier-head is carved out of a wood of closer grain and has been gilded. Its outer curved surface is adorned with oak-leaves carved in low relief and enriched at intervals with projecting wooden acorns. One of the latter is missing and it may be seen from the hole it should occupy that the acorns were plugged in like rivets. As like the oak-leaves themselves they might more naturally have been carved out of the solid wood, Miss Allason-Jones suggests that their form as separate studs was traditional, derived from a type of crozier which required metal studs to affix the leaf-ornament — gold leaves, perhaps, to a silver crozier-head — and that the original form had been retained, though no longer appropriate to the new material.

Fox failed to indentify the figures on the crozier-head. The dedication of the abbey from 1239 was to St. Peter and St. Paul, and the attributes of the two seated figures are those of these two apostles. Both were commonly shown in tunic and toga as these figures are. St. Peter should have, and has, a round bullet head, broad rustic features, a short beard, tonsured head, and a book in one hand. There is a hole piercing his right hand which would have taken the ring from which his keys, perhaps in a precious metal, depended. St. Paul should have, and has, a longer beard, a receding hairline, one hand on his breast, and should hold a sword in his right hand. The sword is missing, but his right hand too is pierced to accept some metal object. These indentifications, which mark the crozier-head as associated with a house dedicated to St. Peter and St. Paul, by themselves go far to confim the claim engraved on the collar that the crozier comes from Gloucester Abbey.

When they came into Fox's hands, head and staff were separate. He joined them together, found they fitted exactly, and concluded they were designed to be one. That the wood is different is readily explained if it is considered that oak was chosen to give the staff strength and a closer-grained wood was chosen for the intricate work on the crozier-head. The correspondence of the ribbed and diapered ornament on the head with those on the staff confirm Fox's judgement.

It is impossible not to be struck by the shortness of the staff. Sebroke may of course have been a very short man, but it is more probable that the explanation lies concealed by the metal collar which Fox called a clasp. As a hand-grip it is in quite the wrong place. A staff with its weight preponderantly in the head would be grasped near the top. That the collar does conceal a break in the staff is shown by an observation made by Mr. J. Atkinson, conservation officer of the North of England Museum Service, that the planed oak surfaces entering the collar at either end are out of alignment, as are the ribbings and diapering on the carved ornamental rings either side of the collar. That the staff should have been broken will surprise no reader who will consult a communication in *Archaeologia* ix (1787) describing the disorderly opening at Gloucester a generation later of the tomb of an earlier abbot, John Wigmore. His crozier was also of wood, and is described as neatly adorned with silver, which has been gilt and burnished. When the writer (J. Cooke) first saw it, "it was intire", but a few days later a verger showed him the remains of the head, while the master of the workmen had the greater part of the staff. So that staff, too, was broken; evidence of the slight value placed upon such remains in the Age of Reason.

If we suppose that this central section of the staff had originally a length medial between those of the other two sections, it is estimated that the overall length of the crozier would have been just short of six feet, a more probable length.

The inscription on the collar has been discussed above, but it remains to add that the style of engraved lettering is consistent with a late eighteenth-century date. A small round label bearing the letters LS attached to an upper surface of the staff must date to the 1830s and refer to the "Literary Society" or Lit & Phil.

BIBLIOGRAPHY

Manuscript sources: The fullest source for the *Newcastle Museum* is the series of minute books of the Literary & Philosophical Society. Clearer, because more exclusively concerned with the Museum, are those of the Natural History Society, together with their annual reports and some correspondence. These include a site-plan of the Old Museum, and there are two interior photographs of the further gallery. The records of our own Society yield very little.

About George Allan there is abundant material, Most of the deposit at the Darlington Branch Library relates to his private press, but they hold the Visitors Book dated 1795 for the museum while it was in Allan's possession. Much of the manuscript material that passed through Allan's hands is deposited with the Durham Cathedral Library. More valuable for our purpose is Volume I (Land Birds) of Allan's manuscript catalogue which was given to the Durham University Library (Add. M.S. 598.2 A6) by Dr. A. N. L. Munby who found it in a Cambridge bookshop. The location of Volumes II and III, if they survive, is not known to the writer. There are also some papers of Allan's at the Record Office at Northallerton.

PRINTED SOURCES

Period before 1822

Anon., *Windsor, and its Environs,* London, 1768.

Tunstall, M. C., *Ornithologia Britannica Catalogus,* London, 1771.

Gough, R., *Sepulchral Monuments,* London, 1796.

Dugdale, W., *Monasticon Anglicanum,* ed. Ellis *et al.,* 1817.

Ed. Allan, R. H., *Life of the late George Allan,* Sunderland, 1829.

Harwood, T. E., *Windsor Old and New*[15], London, 1929.

Cowen, J. D., "The Allan Crosier", *AA*[4] ix, 246 *et seq.* Newcastle, 1932.

Cowen, J. D., "The Allan Crosier Again", *AA*[4] xlv, 203 *et seq.* Newcastle, 1967.

APPENDIX ONE: THE *NEWCASTLE MUSEUM*

For both Tunstall and Allan there is much material in *The Gentleman's Magazine* and in John Nichols' *Literary Anecdotes* Vol. VIII (London 1814), but most of this has been used by Fox in his *Synopsis* (below). See also AA[4] xliv, 61 *et seq.*

Period since 1822

Fox, G. T., *Synopsis of the Newcastle Museum*, Newcastle, 1827.

Mackenzie, E., *History of Newcastle upon Tyne*, Newcastle, 1827.

S.A.N., *A Catalogue of the manuscripts books Roman and other Antiquities belonging to the Society of Antiquaries of Newcastle upon Tyne*, Newcastle, 1839.

Scott, W. B., *Antiquarian Gleanings in the North*, London, 1851.

Watson, R.S., *History of the Literary and Philosophical Society of Newcastle upon Tyne*, London, 1897.

Heslop, R. O., "The Society's Museum", *AA*[3]x, 17-18 Newcastle, 1913.

Goddard, T. R., *History of the Natural History Society of Northumberland, Durham and Newcastle upon Tyne* Newcastle, 1929.

NOTES

1. Incorrectly transcribed by Fox as 'Miller' and so followed by the Society's catalogue in 1839.
2. The epithet 'Allan' seems first to have been given to this ivory crozier by J. D. Cowen.
3. *Archaeologia*, ix (1789), 286.
4. The copy of this rare work now in the library of the Literary and Philosophical Society was presented in 1825 by John Trotter Brockett, who had moved the resolution to purchase the Wycliffe museum.
5 But see Fox's *Synopsis*, 41.
6. *The Newcastle Magazine* (1826), 454.
7. Of aid in these identifications is the Lit & Phil copy of our 1839 catalogue annotated by J. D. Cowen.
8. The size and lay out of the rooms is fairly certain. The disposition of the stair-case and the means of access from the library are more conjectural.†
9. Milles, Jeremiah (1714–1784), ed: Eton and Corpus Christi, Oxford; pluralist and antiquary; Dean of Exeter from 1762, FSA 1741, FRS 1742, President of the Society of Antiquaries of London 1768 to 1784; fortunate or prudent in choice of relatives as an uncle bequeathed him a fortune, and his father-in-law, an archbishop, secured him comfortable preferments; involvement in the Chatterton affair added nothing

†It is now known the staircase should spiral in the reverse direction.

to the lustre of his name as a scholar, but he is notable as having attracted adverse comment from critics as distinguished as Coleridge and Horace Walpole, to which may be added the crowning glory of being caricatured by Rowlandson.

10. The whole account of Bateman and Grove House (later Old Windsor Priory) is derived from the 14th chapter of Harwood's *Windsor Old and New*. This reference I owe to Mr. J. Hopkins, librarian of the Society of Antiquaries of London. A contemporary description of the contents of the house may found in *Windsor, and its Environs*, 79-86.

11. In the vernacular, Cadwgan; also called Martin. In 1236 Cadwgan was given permission to retire as a simple monk at Dore where he died in 1241 (DNB).

12. For a light-hearted implication of venality in the officers of the Society of Antiquaries of London, see *The Nabob* by Samuel Foote, first performed in 1772, at a time when Milles was President. The author of a comedy, it need hardly be said, is not upon oath.

13. There was certainly a copy, though imperfect, of the sale catalogue in the British Library (Dugdale 1817 cites MSS Cole Vol. xxxv, p.9) as late as Harwood 1929, but Cowen (*AA*xlv, 204 (1969)), states "the Sale Catalogue is not in the British Museum Library and the only copy in this country is that still in the possession of Messrs. Christie Manson and Woods!"

14. Sebroke's motto, *Fiat voluntas domini*, argues humility, but his name, motto, and arms *(Ermine a cinquefoil sable)* were stamped on the bricks paving the choir, his effigy in alabaster and full pontificals lies upon his tomb in a chantry chapel built by himself to receive it. The inscription on the arch at Gloucester (Gough 182—3) conveys that his was the driving personality behind the building of the tower.

15. Bateman himself mounted on a grey may be seen on a plate facing page 306 and that facing p. 320 shows Grove House (the "Abby" of the inscription) in 1760. Both plates are from drawings by Paul Sandby in the Royal collections at Windsor.

APPENDIX TWO

Officers of the Society from 1897

Year of appointment
Year of death or resignation

PRESIDENTS

1860	William George Armstrong, 1st Baron	1900
1901	Robert Spence Watson	1911
1911	Sir Joseph Wilson Swan	1914
1914	Richard Oliver Heslop	1916
1916	Sir Charles A. Parsons	1931
1931	G. M. Trevelyan	1939
1940	C. H. Hunter Blair	1960
1961	T. M. Harbottle	1961
1962	A. D. S. Rogers	1966
1967	P. L. Robinson	1968
1969	J. Philipson	1978
1979	S. T. L. Harbottle	1986
1987	D. T. Turnbull	

VICE-PRESIDENTS

1878	D. Embleton	1900
1881	Sir Joseph Wilson Swan	1911
1891	Thomas Hodgkin	1913
1893	Robert Spence Watson	1900
1901	J. H. Merivale	1916
1901	John Pattinson	1912
1911	Richard Oliver Heslop	1913
1911	Sir William Henry Hadow	1920
1911	F. W. Dendy	1940
1912	Sir Charles A. Parsons	1916
1913	J. T. Merz	1922
1914	J. T. Dunn	1939
1916	C. H. Eastwood	1924
1916	N. Temperley	1923
1920	W. S. Corder	1933

Year of appointment / Year of death or resignation

VICE-PRESIDENTS (continued)

Year of appointment	Name	Year of death or resignation
1922	A. Hamilton Thompson	1922
1923	C. H. Hunter Blair	1939
1923	Miss D. F. P. Hiley	1934
1924	Laurence Richardson	1953
1933	A. H. Dickinson	1946
1935	J. B. Gaunt	1949
1939	J. M. Baily	1949
1940	W. Deans Foster	1941
1941	W. L. Renwick	1945
1941	J. Wight Duff	1944
1945	W. Walton	1950
1946	Miss H. M. Gurney	1954
1946	W. G. Kinghorn	1959
1949	P. L. Robinson	1966
1949	A. Watt	1957
1950	E. R. Thomas	1975
1953	G. R. Goldsbrough	1963
1954	A. D. Minton-Senhouse	1960
1958	T. M. Harbottle	1961
1958	J. E. Butt	1959
1960	J. Philipson	1968
1961	F. C. D. Thomson	1973
1961	C. H. Hunter Blair	1962
1963	G. B. A. Fletcher	
1964	B. W. Abrahart	1965
1965	H. Boag	1965
1966	C. E. Kellett	1975
1967	P. Ure	1969
1969	S. T. L. Harbottle	1978
1970	A. W. Willis	1987
1973	D. T. Turnbull	1986
1976	S. Chaplin	1985
1976	D. W. Elliott	
1979	Mrs. E. Williams	
1986	Mrs. G. Hickling	1986
1987	R. B. Thompson	

APPENDIX TWO: OFFICERS OF THE SOCIETY

Year of appointment — Year of death or resignation

VICE-PRESIDENTS (continued)

1987	N. McCord	
1988	P. M. Watson	

HONORARY TREASURERS

1889	C. J. Spence	1905
1905	T. Edward Hodgkin	1921
1921	W. Deans Forster	1938
1939	A. D. S. Rogers	1961
1962	G. W. Duncan	1962
1963	H. J. H. Sisson	

HONORARY SECRETARIES

1893	Alfred Holmes	1933
1895	Frederick Emley	1925
1925	A. H. Dickinson	1933
1933	T. M. Harbottle	1957
1933	E. R. Thomas	1934
1935	R. H. Fallaw	1957
1957	W. G. Kinghorn	1959
1957	S. T. L. Harbottle	1968
1959	A. H. Meikle	1980
1969	N. T. Garbutt	1975
1975	P. M. Watson	1980
1980	K. A. Carlisle	
1981	J. F. Waldie	1989
1989	J. E. C. Potts	

LIBRARIANS

1892	Henry Richardson	1925
1925	E. Austin Hinton	1932
1932	M. C. Pottinger	1946
1946	Frank Rutherford	1963
1963	Charles Parish	1987
1987	Miss M. Norwell	

SUB-LIBRARIANS

1922	F. Wolff	1923
1924	E. Austin Hinton	1925

Year of appointment / Year of death or resignation

SUB-LIBRARIANS (continued)

1925	T. H. Marr	1930
1930	M. C. Pottinger	1932
1932	J. D. Reynolds	1934
1934	S. J. Marks	1936
1936	W. Middleton Martin	1939
1945	Miss G. Brown	1964
1978	S. Goldwater	1979
1979	Mrs. A. Gunning (acting)	1981
1986	Miss M. Norwell	1987
1987	Mrs. E. A. Pescod	

MUSIC LIBRARIAN

1987   Mrs. M. Oates

Index

Allan, George, 198-9
Armstrong, William George, *1st Baron*, 17,21,24,46,72-3
Armstrong College, 2,27,32,61
  see also College of Physical Science; King's College; University of Newcastle upon Tyne
Arts Subjects Panel, 43
Assyrian reliefs, 43 and n, 46-7
  see also Loftus, William Kennett
Backworth Classical Novel Reading Union, 63
Banks, *Sir* Joseph, 121-136 *passim*, 137-163 *passim*
Barber, Joseph, 35
Barlow, David, 32
Basement Book Store, 47
Bell, Gertrude Margaret Lowthian, 26n.
Bell, *Sir* Isaac Lowthian, 25-6
Bell, John, *the elder*, 35
Bewick, Thomas, 28, 138, 147-9, 198
Binding and conservation, 44, 47-9, 54
Birmingham Library, 8, 44
Blair, C. H. Hunter, 41, 44
Blair, Robert, 33
Bolbec Hall, 42, 46, 56-60
Bolbec Room, 46-7, 59
British Library, 39, 48-9, 51
Broome, Noel, 32
Brown, *Miss* G., 41
Bulmer, William, 137-163
Bunting, Basil: Poetry Competition, 52
Cambridge University Extension Lectures *see* University Extension Courses
Carnegie United Kingdom Trust, 39-40
Catalogues, 1796-1903, 10-14, 17-19, 21-3, 26
Central Library for Students, 39
  see also National Central Library; British Library
Charitable status, 44
Charnley, William, 35
Children's books, 29
Chirnside, R. C., 73n.
College of Physical Science, 2, 4, 18, 50, 61
  see also Armstrong College; King's College; University of Newcastle upon Tyne
Concerts *see* Music: lectures and recitals
Conservation *see* Binding and conservation
Co-operation, 38-40, 44, 49, 51
Crawford, C. P., 54
Crawhall, Joseph, *the elder*, 28
Crawhall, Joseph, *the younger*, 28
Crawhall, *Miss* M. E., 28
Davies, *Sir* Henry Walford, 31
Dendy, Frederick Walter, 25n., 62n., 74n.
Development Appeal, 44, 53-4
Dewey, Melvil, 21-2
Dewey Decimal Classification, 18-19
Dixon, George, 121-136 *passim*
Dobson, John, 46
Dolmetsch, Arnold, 31, 72
Durham Local Collection, 22
Dyer, Ernest: Memorial Lectures, 77
Early printed books, 23
Economic Society, 21
  see also Newcastle Economic Circle
Edwards and Partners, 47, 60
Ellerington, T. E., 51

Embleton, Dennis, 24-5
Emley, Frederick, 19, 40
English Heritage, 60
Fallaw, R. H., 41
Fiction, 13, 19, 20, 29
Films, 77
Fine Arts Society, 206
Fox, G. T., 199
Fraser, *Mrs.* Kennedy, 31
Gaskell, Elizabeth Cleghorn, 106-120 *passim*
Government School of Design, 206
Gramophone records, 31
Grierson, John, 77
Hadow, *Sir* Henry, 29, 31
Harbottle, S. T. L., 46
Harbottle, T. M., 41, 44
Harris, Keith, 50
Heslop, Richard Oliver, 56 and n., 57, 61 and n., 204
Hickling, Mrs. Grace, 54
Hinton, E. Austin, 34, 37-40
Hodgkin, Thomas, 61 and n., 73, 74 and n.
Hodgson, Thomas, 14
Holmes, Alfred, 41, 62
Honorary members 121 and n.
Kilburn, N., 76
King's College, 31, 64
  see also College of Physical Science; University of Newcastle upon Tyne.
Ladies' Room, 24
Lecture theatre, 24, 44, 46-7
Lectures, 24, 25, 42, 46, 54, 72-103
Lectures in French, German and Italian, 77
Lee, Ernest Markham, 30-31
Lit. and Phil. — centenary, 20-21
  — 150th anniversary, 77, 99 and n.
Local History Group, 45-6
Loftus, William Kennett, 47, 164-195
Loftus Room, 47

Lunchtime concerts see Music: lectures and recitals
Lyall, William, 35
Manchester Literary and Philosophical Society, 9
Marks, S. J., 40
Marr, T. H., 22, 40
Marshall, John, 35
Martin, W. Middleton, 40
Members' Room — *see* Loftus Room
Membership, 15-17, 21, 24-5, 28, 33, 38, 41, 43, 53
Middlebrook, Sydney, 2
Milner, Arthur, 32
Mining Institute, 4, 17-18, 51, 56-7
Moises, *Rev.* Edward, 7-8
Morden Tower Collection, 52
Mortgage Redemption Fund, 60
Moulton, Richard Green, 62-3, 76-7
Mudie's Lending Library, 16-17
Murray, Gilbert, 3
Music Group, 45
Music: lectures and recitals, 31-2
Music Library, 29-31
National Central Library, 39
Natural History Society of Northumbria, 4, 35 and n., 196-216 *passim*
Newcastle Chronicle Poetry Competition, 52
  see also Bunting, Basil: Poetry Competition
Newcastle Economic Circle, 21, 78
Newcastle Festival, 32
Newcastle Libraries Joint Working Party, 50
Newcastle Museum, 4, 196-216 *passim*
Newcastle Polytechnic, 49, 50
Newcastle Public Library, 2, 49, 50
Newcastle University
  see University of Newcastle upon Tyne
Noble, *Sir* Humphrey, *Bt.*, 47
North East Coast Engineering Employers' Association, 58

INDEX

North East Coast Institution of Engineers and Shipbuilders, 58
North Eastern Railway Company, 18, 58
North of England Institute of Mining and Mechanical Engineers *see* Mining Institute
Northern Arts Manuscript Collection, 52
Northern Regional Library System 39-40, 59
Northumberland Local Collection, 22
Norwell, *Miss* Margaret, 51
Offices, Shops and Railway Premises Act, 60
Page, B.S., 41
Parish, Charles, 44
Parsons, *Sir* Charles, 41
Pattinson, Hugh Lee, 25
Pattinson, John, 73n.
Peddie, R. A., 22-3
Philipson, John, 51
Photographic Survey, 33
Play Reading Group, 45
Poetry competitions, 44, 52-3
Portlock, Nathaniel, 121-136 *passim*
Pottinger, M. C., 40
Priestley, Joseph, 8
Proprietary Libraries, 8-9
Quarterly Bulletin 38
Radio Discussion Groups *see* Wireless Discussion Groups
Rating and Valuation Act, 1961, 43
Reading Room *see* Sir James Knott Room
Record Room, 59
Refreshment Service, 44-5
Reynolds, J. D., 40
Rich, F. W., 58
Richardson, Henry, 19, 23-5, 33-4, 37
Rogers, A. D. S., 44
Rosner, R., 51
Royal Society, 9, 123, 137-163 *passim*

Rutherford, Frank, 41-2, 44
Sale of books, 42-3, 60n.
Science Revision Panel, 42-3
Scientific Societies Act, 44
Scott, William Bell, 206
Sectional Societies, 21, 44
Self-Organising Groups, 44-6
Sharp, Cecil, 31
Sir James Knott Room, 18, 24
Skipsey, Joseph, 35-7
Society of Antiquaries of Newcastle upon Tyne, 4, 33, 196-216 *passim*
Special collections, 44, 51-2
Special lectures, 76-7
Spence, Robert, 35
Staff training, 38-9
Stephenson, Robert, 16n.
Stroud, H., 72-3
Swan, *Sir* Joseph Wilson, 73 and n.
Temperley, Nicholas, 64
Terry, *Sir* Richard Runciman, 30
Thompson, Alexander Hamilton, 63-4
Thornhill, John, 35
Tracts Collection, 23 and n.
Trevelyan, G. M., 41
Tunstall, Marmaduke, 198
Turner, *Rev.* William, 9-10
— and his family, 106-120 *passim*
Tyneside Film Society, 77
University Extension Courses, 4, 22, 28, 31-2, 42, 61-71
University of Newcastle upon Tyne, 50, 64
— Adult Education Dept., 46
— Centenary, 2, 50
Wailes, George, 35
Watson, Joseph, 1
Watson, Robert Spence, 1-5, 25, 61 and n.
Welford, Richard, 23, 61 and n.
Whittaker, W. G., 29-31
Willis, A. W. 51-2, 54
Wireless Discussion Groups, 21, 77-8
Wolff, F., 34
Wood, Christopher, 32
Wycliffe Museum, 28, 196-216 *passim*